P9-CQB-652

Springer Series on Family Violence
Albert R. Roberts, PhD, Series Editor

Thomas Underwood, PhD is the Executive Director of the Joint Center on Violence and Victim Studies, an interdisciplinary affiliation between Washburn University and California State University at Fresno. As Executive Director, he coordinates the development of professional training programs, promotes academic education programs, oversees research initiatives, and advocates for public policy initiatives. Dr. Underwood serves as faculty for the Department of Human Services at Washburn University and for the Department of Criminology at CSUF. Some of his research includes a study of the professionalization of victim assistance and community assessment of victim services.

Christine Edmunds is a Victim Rights and Services Consultant and serves on the Executive Committee of the Joint Center on Violence and Victim Studies. She was instrumental through her work with the National Organization for Victim Assistance (NOVA) and with the National Crime Victim Center in developing public policy initiatives and training programs on the federal and state levels. As a consultant to the Office of Victims of Crime, she served as the primary author and editor of *New Directions from the Field: Victim's Rights and Services for the 21st Century*. She cofounded the National Victim Assistance Academy (NVAA) in 1995 and has served as senior faculty since that time. She is an adjunct professor for the California State University at Fresno and for Washburn University.

Victim Assistance

Exploring Individual Practice,
Organizational Policy,
and Societal Responses

Thomas L. Underwood, PhD
Christine Edmunds
Editors

Springer Series on Family Violence

Springer Publishing Company, Inc.
536 Broadway
New York, NY 10012-3955

Acquisitions Editor: Sheri W. Sussman
Production Editor: Sara Yoo
Cover design by Joanne Honigman

03 04 05 06 07 / 5 4 3 2 1

Library of Congress Cataloging-in-Publication Data

Victim assistance : exploring individual practice, organizational policy, and societal responses / Thomas L. Underwood, Christine Edmunds, editors.
        p. cm. — (Springer series on family violence)
    Includes bibliographical references and index.
    ISBN 0-8261-4751-8
    1. Victims of crimes—Services for. 2. Victims—Services for. I. Underwood, Thomas L. II. Edmunds, Christine. III. Series.

HV6250.25 .V48 2003
362.88—dc21

2002075892

Printed in the United States of America by Sheridan Books.

Contents

105827

Contributors

Richard Ellis, PhD, is an Assistant Professor and the Department Chair of the Human Services Department at Washburn University and serves on the Advisory Council for the Joint Center on Violence and Victim Studies. His research, professional writing, and teaching addresses a variety of issues, including drug and alcohol use and victimization, hate crimes, culturally competent practices, community development, and social advocacy. In addition to his work with the Joint Center on Violence and Victim Studies, Dr. Ellis has served as faculty member for the National Victim Assistance Academy.

Kristine J. Hart is the AmeriCorps VISTA Community Service Coordinator in the Human Services Department at Washburn University. She serves on the Advisory Council of the Joint Center on Violence and Victim Studies and is a board member-at-large for the Rape Victim Advocacy Program in Iowa City, Iowa. In addition, Kristine is a consultant in the victim services field with a focus in the areas of domestic violence, the elderly, drunk driving and persons with disabilities. She has contributed to research and education projects of the Joint Center on Violence and Victim Studies on the topics of violence against women and crime victims with disabilities. She has also been a faculty member and faculty assistant coordinator for the National Victim Assistance Academy.

Nancie Palmer, PhD is a Professor of Social Work at Washburn University and serves on the Advisory Council of the Joint Center on Violence and Victim Studies. Her professional work experience has focused on victims of trauma, particularly child abuse and neglect. Much of her research, professional writing, and teaching focuses on issues regarding sexual trauma and resiliency. In addition to her work with the Joint Center on Violence and Victim Studies, Dr. Palmer has served as faculty for the National Victim Assistance Academy.

Dan Petersen, PhD is the Associate Dean of the School of Applied Studies and faculty in the Department of Human Services at Washburn University.

He also serves on the Executive Committee of the Joint Center on Violence and Victim Studies. In addition to his work with the Joint Center on Violence and Victim Studies, he served on the National Victim Assistance Standards Consortium and has been the academic coordinator for the National Victim Assistance Academy. His research, professional writing, and teaching has addressed many areas, some of which include crime victimization and persons with disabilities, community assessment of victim services, privileged communication, and antecedents to violent behavior.

Steven Walker, PhD is a Professor at California State University at Fresno where he teaches and administers the Victim Services Certificate Program. He was instrumental in the development of the Fresno program, the nation's first victimology degree. He serves on the Executive Committee of the Joint Center on Violence and Victim Studies. He served on the National Victim Assistance Standards Consortium and has been academic coordinator and program coordinator for the National Victim Assistance Academy. Some of Dr. Walker's research, professional writing, and teaching has addressed the historical context of the victim movement, rural crime victimization, and the use of substances and crime victimization.

Acknowledgments

This book has been made possible through the efforts of a host of people, especially the contributing authors. The faculty at Washburn University and California State University at Fresno have committed a tremendous amount of time and energy out of a commitment to the cause—not out of any hope of fame and fortune. Friends and colleagues external to the universities have been very supportive and have served as authors, instructors, advisors, and marketers as the Joint Center on Violence and Victim Studies coordinated the writing of the book as an instrument for the course, *Advanced Institute on Victim Studies: Critical Analysis of Victim Assistance.*

Thanks to Susan Engelhardt for her painstaking copy review. Her gentle corrections have hopefully made this more readable.

Finally, there have been those, particularly B and Jim Horne, who have been with the program since the beginning and continue to humble us with their gracious sharing of their victimization experiences.

Introduction

This book is based on the instructional content of the highly acclaimed professional education and certificate program, *Advanced Institute on Victim Studies: Critical Analysis of Victim Assistance*, offered by the Joint Center on Violence and Victim Studies of Washburn University and California State University at Fresno. The goal of this book, as a reflection of the program, is to serve as a vehicle that promotes professional skills, understanding, and critical reflection in order to enhance services to victims at the individual, organizational, and societal levels. This is accomplished through a design that embraces theoretical constructs with an applied emphasis that is focused on the practitioner.

Recognizing the multiple disciplines and systems that constitute victim assistance, this book does not favor a certain system area, victim type, or discipline. The contributing authors represent a balance of university faculty from a variety of applied academic areas, as well as experts from the professional community. This combination provides a balance that lends itself to an integration of theory to practice.

This book identifies core content areas essential for any practitioner working with crime victims. The first several chapters provide a foundation of concepts and theory for the diverse array of learners. "Concepts of Victim Assistance" starts the book with an exploration of the concept of victim through discussion perceptions, characteristics of crime victims, theoretical explanations, and an overview of the comprehensive continuum of victim services. The ripple effect of crime victimization, as applied to cases of victimization, is described in the "Ecological Perspective of Victimization." The chapter "Exploring Attitudes Toward Violence and Victimization" challenges the readers to explore their own victim-blaming attitudes and practices with a foundation of theoretical explanation.

The next several chapters focus on concepts for direct application. "Barriers to Services" addresses the obstacles often faced by victims who bring unique challenges to service providers regardless of the type of crime victimization experienced. The "Impact of Stress" provides comprehensive exploration of the physical, emotional, and behavioral responses often experienced by crime victims. This chapter serves as a foundation to "Trauma Response," which addresses the skills and strategies of effective crisis intervention.

The "Justice System and Victims" provides an in-depth exploration of the component roles and relationships of the primary system in which most crime victims interact. Exploration of contributing factors, characteristics, and intervention strategies of specific types of crimes are fully addressed in the chapters that address sexual assault, criminal death, violence within the context of the family environment, and hate and bias crimes.

A broader approach concludes the book with the last two chapters. "Victim Advocacy and Public Policy" presents discussion on the role of advocacy and the process of policy change. This is highlighted with discussion of some of the critical events that reflect the legislative, judicial, and executive aspects of victim services. "Issues for the Profession" explores the attributes required for victim assistance to continue its emergence as a professional occupation.

Concepts of Victim Assistance

Thomas L. Underwood

Victim is a concept that is subject to personal and social definition. Practitioners, educators, researchers, and policy makers have certain conceptualizations about crime victims that are influenced by a host of factors, such as their current work environment, educational background, life circumstances and experiences, and perhaps more subtly, the social mood of the times. Conceptualizations are also influenced by the reports of crime prevalence and the theories that attempt to explain the problem. These conceptualizations affect policy and practice throughout the continuum of victim services.

This chapter introduces the reader to a variety of concepts considered critical as a foundation for understanding the issues surrounding crime victimization. The reader is challenged to develop an individual working definition about the concept of *victim* as the characteristics of crime victimization and general theoretical explanations of crime victimization are explored.

EXPLORING CONCEPTS OF VICTIM

Most people have a general image of the concept of victim. Like other socially defined groups, such as poor or professional, this image is often a perception of an idea based on personal experience and common social messages. But when asked to articulate a comprehensive definition or to consider variations of the concept, many people are less than consistent. As a concept, victim is an enigma that is difficult to comprehend and explain. To paraphrase Supreme Court Justice Stewart Potter's response about defining another social concept, victim may be something that is difficult to define, but you know it when you see it.

1

It is a concept that may be considered in a very broad and inclusive context or, to the other extreme, it may be narrowly defined with conditions that limit its applicability. In the daily language of the public, the term has a common meaning as referring to those individuals who suffer from "some form of hardship as a result of more worldly causes" (Kennedy & Sacco, 1998, p. 4); who "experience injuries, losses, or hardships due to any causes" (Karmen, 1996, p. 2). These definitions reflect a general use of the term and, while the focus of this text is victims of crime, these broader views of the concept include victims of natural disasters, fires, poverty, war, disease, corporate negligence, discrimination, political aggression, and so on.

There are benefits to this broad conceptualization. Most everyone, at some point in their lives, has experienced a loss or hardship due to some outside cause: their car was damaged from the limb that was blown down in the storm; they or a loved one has been afflicted with an illness; they have been treated inappropriately in a social situation because of their skin color or gender; or their mailbox was vandalized in the middle of the night by a group of teenagers. While most people do not consciously label themselves as such, practically everyone can identify with being a victim. Considering this realization, "becoming a victim may actually make us part of the 'norm.' Perhaps with this realization, we will avoid the erroneous view that victims are an aberrant form of humanity" (Sank & Sank, 1991, p. 9). This recognition fosters empathy, at least to a degree, with the turmoil that victims of more serious events may experience. For example, while thankfully not everyone really knows what it is like to lose a loved one to homicide, most everyone can identify with the untimely loss of a loved one, even if it was due to natural causes.

The negative aspect of these broad definitions is that, by considering victimization in the normative sense, it may trivialize the trauma of more serious events. There is a risk of desensitization and thereby not attending to the unique needs of victims. Furthermore, if everyone is a victim, then there is no need for social concern, intervention, or resources.

Another approach to defining the concept is offered by Bayley (1991), who formalizes it with conditions:

People are victims if and only if

- They have suffered a loss or some significant decrease in well-being unfairly or undeservedly and in such a manner that they are helpless to prevent the loss;
- The loss has an identifiable cause; and
- The legal or moral context of the loss entitles the sufferers of the loss to social concern.

The first condition includes several characteristics to consider. First, there must be a loss. While this may seem straightforward enough, *loss* is a concept with which insurance companies and courts regularly grapple. How is loss measured? A study of the costs of crime victimization (Miller, Cohen, & Wiersema, 1996) identified losses to victims typically to include tangible costs such as health care bills, property loss and damage, and reduced productivity. Further, there is also the intangible aspect of lost quality of life. How relevant are the intangibles of fear, pain, suffering, inconvenience, loss of innocence, or loss of social status? Can society really put a price on the intangible aspects of loss? Using various methods of analysis, the authors assert that intangible costs "are clearly the largest cost component for crimes of violence" (p. 15).

The first condition also suggests that the loss cannot be due to any fault, contribution or negligence by the individual and could not be prevented. For example, a person who knowingly builds a house on a flood plane and then loses the house from flooding was negligent and could have prevented the loss. While this person may warrant social concern and sympathy, the status of victim and the commensurate services, such as government compensation, is not obligated. Similarly, this position would argue that those who do not take necessary precautions to protect themselves against crime would not meet the criteria of victims. For example, leaving a portable stereo in an unlocked car parked in the school parking lot is negligent, theft of the stereo being in this case preventable. Bayley (1991) notes that, contrary to natural disasters, the state does have an obligation to deter crime and "when it fails in its obligation restitution is appropriate" (p. 56).

The second condition is that the loss must be from an identifiable cause. Someone who is sick from food poisoning caused by improper food handling is a victim; someone suffering from a common cold is not. A child whose lunch money is taken out of his/her book bag is a victim; a child whose lunch money is misplaced is not. Bad luck does not make a victim. Of course, luck is also a construct influenced by perception.

Accidents on the highway or in the workplace are commonly referred to as a matter of bad luck. Upon closer inspection, however, it is often found that there is indeed an identifiable cause that could have been prevented. Auto crash injuries from drunk driving used to be considered bad luck until organizations such as Mothers Against Drunk Driving (MADD) influenced public understanding that drunk driving crashes are criminal, not accidental.

Violence and victimization in school and work environments have often been considered normal aspects of those environments and that the status of student or employee involves an acceptable level of risk. Traditionally, the child who is emotionally and physically antagonized by the schoolyard bully, the employee who works in an atmosphere where sexual innuendos are pervasive, or the store clerk who is threatened by a disgruntled customer have not been considered as victims of criminal behavior. Rather, the inappropriate behaviors described were considered risks associated with that territory, and students or employees subjected to those behaviors were said to have simply had bad luck. Increasingly it is recognized that these behaviors are being defined as more than inappropriate, they are being defined as criminal; and the persons subjected to these behaviors are increasingly being defined as victims, not just persons who are unlucky in hostile environments.

Finally, the loss entitles social concern. The loss of money from the stock market may draw sympathy, but sympathy is not socially expected. In other words, there are no social sanctions against those who do not express concern for a person who lost money in this situation. The entitlement of social concern can also apply crime victims. Do those who are injured during the commission of an illegal activity warrant social concern? Do prisoners who are assaulted in institutions warrant social concern?

Though the concept of victim is typically considered in an individual context, groups and organizations can also be victims, such as in the crime of embezzlement, shoplifting, or property vandalism. Even when individuals are victimized, organizations are often the target in large scale crimes. The federal government in general as well as all the agencies, governmental and non-governmental, housed in the Alfred P. Murrah Federal Building in Oklahoma City were direct victims of the 1995 bombing. The motive in this tragedy was to attack the building that symbolized the federal government. While this does not diminish the victimization of each of the 169 individuals killed or the 500 individuals wounded, these individuals were considered by the perpetrators merely as casualties. The same can be said for other terrorist or mass killing tragedies, such as the World Trade Center attack and Columbine High School shooting. Further discussion of groups and organizations and the impact of crime victimization can be found in chapter 2.

The focus of this book is on victims of crime. However, many of the concepts discussed have general application to victims of acts of nature. Regardless of the nature of the victimization, individuals may experience the emotional responses of anger, fear, frustration, and guilt as well as physiological responses of shock, exhaustion, and somatic complaints. Further, there may be secondary victimization, or negative experiences, inflicted by the systems intended to provide victim services, such as the criminal justice system, insurance system, or health care system. Professional insensitivity, lack of information, and unnecessary delays are all examples of actions that may further insult the injury of victimization; these examples are prevalent in all systems that serve victims, regardless of whether they are victims of crime or victims of nature.

There are, however, some distinguishing characteristics that make crime victims unique (Bard & Sangrey, 1986):

- *Human Agency vs. Act of God.* Central in the victim's perception is that another person was responsible for the harm caused. "The criminal act of violation compromises the victims' sense of trust" (p. 14) of society. Future interactions with other humans may be significantly impaired.

- *Chaotic vs. Intact Environment.* A victim's immediate world becomes totally disoriented while the outside world remains intact. This contrast creates dissonance whereas for victims of natural disasters, such as a hurricane, the internal disorder is congruent with the external disorder. The external environment is as chaotic and strewn about as the internal, thus no dissonance.
- *Isolation vs. Togetherness.* Most crime occurs outside the view of others. People usually do not know if the person who lives down the street, or the person in the elevator, or the person in the grocery store has been a crime victim. In most natural disasters, such as a flood, everyone is a victim or intimately knows others who are victims. Thus, the victim does not experience such a sense of isolation, rather, victims feel a sense of mutual support.
- *Stigma vs. Acceptance.* In an effort to understand crime, society looks for reasons for the tragedy and often blames victims for their victimization. The individual is not usually blamed, though, when a tornado destroys a home or when a person dies from illness.

Thus, the similarities between victims of crime and victims of nature allow for general application of the concepts discussed in this book. It also allows the person who has not experienced criminal victimization to have a degree of personal understanding and empathy. However, there are differences, and these differences may profoundly affect recovery.

THE LANGUAGE OF VICTIM ASSISTANCE: VICTIM vs. SURVIVOR

Language is very powerful. It can shape perceptions and may reflect an ideology that can affect interaction with other professionals as well as with persons who have been victimized. Language can also be mundane. Frequency and duration of use may cause certain words or terms to evolve as mere aspects of commonality void of any philosophical bias or intent.

Crime victimization is a multidimensional occurrence and the services and interventions draw from a wide array of disciplines and service systems. As such, the various disciplines and systems use jargon that describes the clientele of that area. The term victim and the term survivor are both utilized in this multidisciplined/multisystem field. Though both are commonly used by the general public, each reflect values and systems preferences.

Historically, the definition of victim was one who was sacrificed to appease some supernatural or higher power for the benefit of the community. Common usage of the term victim often conjures up a perception of one who is weak and was overcome or manipulated by an external source, possibly due to his/her own negligence or helplessness. This suggests an individual powerlessness over internal resources and a dependence on others to rectify the situation (Andrews, 1992). The term is commonly used in the criminal justice system where legalistic definitions of victim and *offender* are an important aspect of the system's functions.

The term *survivor* has traditionally meant the surviving family members of a homicide victim. It has also been used to describe those who have recovered—physically and emotionally—from the victimization, thus suggesting an internal strength and an empowerment to cope with life's crises. This implication of positive growth reflects the values of community-based service organizations such as domestic violence shelters and rape crisis programs.

Figley (1985) describes the process of recovering from traumatic events as the

> transformation from being a victim to being a survivor. The victim is immobilized and discouraged by the event, the survivor has overcome the traumatic memories and becomes mobile. The survivor draws on the experiences of coping with the catastrophe as a source of strength. . . . What separates victims from survivors is a conception about life, an attitude about the safety, joy, and mastery of being a human being. Being a survivor, then, is making peace with the catastrophe and its wake (p. 399).

In the context provided, these terms can be viewed from different perspectives. Victim is a sociological concept, a status given to a member of society who has experienced an act or event. Survivor, on the other hand, is more of a psychological concept that refers to an individual who has experienced growth in relation to the victimization.

It is important that service providers consider the preferences and needs of the individual in their use and conveyance of meaning for these terms. While being a victim is not a status that one strives to obtain, it is a status that becomes a part of that individual and further defines that person. Similarly, to become a survivor may be critically important to an individual in his or her conceptualization of recovery. The ideological biases that service providers may attribute to a term may influence the perceptions of the individual client, at which point recovery is at risk of not being a person-centered process, but rather a service provider-centered process.

While there may be individual and systems preferences, the terms are often used interchangeably by various agents. The underlying conceptualization of the two terms should be recognized and integrated into the professional and policy language as appropriate. It is important, though, that practitioners who serve individuals who have been victimized not get caught in a semantics quagmire that may prove to be divisive among professionals and counter to crime victim needs. Furthermore, it should be recognized that the term victim is probably used by professionals and the public alike to a greater extent than survivor and that its common usage describes a whole host of people who have experienced traumatic events.

THE SOCIAL MOVEMENT OF VICTIM ASSISTANCE

The history of victim is as old as society itself. Throughout this book, historical references will be made as appropriate. It is generally recognized, though, that a victims' movement started in the United States only a few decades ago. What was happening in the United States during the 1960s and 1970s that made it possible for a movement to begin? There were four other movements that preceded the victims' movement and opened the door for its grassroots advocates.

The civil rights movement was the first grassroots movement in modern American history to use civil disobedience and "street" politics. Its focus was on the lack of political and economic power for American minorities. The inequities of the criminal justice system were seen for the first time by many Americans who watched on national television. This movement stated that the Declaration of Independence should apply to all Americans and that unjust laws must be disobeyed by just citizens.

The antiwar movement derived its methods of nonviolent resistance from the civil rights movement, but it was not as hopeful that the U.S. Constitution would be applied to all citizens without a complete overhaul of the present leadership. This movement proved again that the powerless in a society, in this case the youth, could make changes. It questioned all authority and leadership and demanded that the paper promises in the Bill of Rights become a reality in American socioeconomic life. Because of these questions, America no longer views its leaders and heroes in the same way.

The most influential movement has been the women's movement. The earliest victim advocates, setting up shelters and counseling centers, came directly from this movement. Its focus was on the belief that the other half of the American public deserved equal political and economic opportunities. It soon focused on the biases and chauvinism of the criminal justice and mental health systems. As more and more surveys and studies indicated that women and children were the predominant victims in American society, social activism became political. This movement is responsible for many of the major legal changes in victims rights over the last 25 years. What was once a man's domain now could become a safe place for women and children also.

The final movement that came late to the victims' movement was the law and order movement. Initially it provided little support because any group that asked for financial assistance and governmental involvement was suspect to the law and order movement. Its focus was on retribution for victims through increased punishment for criminals. By the early 1980s, this movement had shifted its focus to increasing victims' rights, instead of just decreasing criminal rights. Once this shift took place, the legislative efforts of victim advocates expanded dramatically. This began with Congress passing the Victim and Witness Protection Act of 1982, followed by the enactment of the Victims of Crime Act in 1984. Public policy reform efforts continue today with the current push for a federal victims' rights constitutional amendment.

The victims' movement would not have started in the 1970s without the impetus of the civil rights movement and the antiwar movement. On the other hand, the at times uneasy marriage between the passionate morality of the women's movement and the political savvy of the law and order movement has been very productive for victims in American society.

CRIME VICTIMIZATION:
EXTENT AND EXPLANATION

Like the related concept of victim, *crime* is a social construct. Formal definitions vary according to the passage of laws and ordinances that, in theory, derive from public sentiment or are passed for the public good. What is considered criminal behavior is not stagnant; it is ever evolving according to the social values and pressures of the time. For example, rape was traditionally defined as "carnal knowledge by a male of a female, who is not his wife, forcibly and against her will" (Doerner & Lab, 1998, p. 98). Though a significant variance exists across jurisdictions, laws have changed over the years to eliminate the gender bias and to recognize that males can be victims and females can be offenders; to include sexual assault between marriage partners; to include acts beyond penile penetration; and to reflect degrees of assault depending on extent of injury, use of weapons, and so forth.

There may be jurisdictional variations as to the definition of crime. What is considered a crime in one jurisdiction may not be so in another; or possibly the classification of that crime may vary so that in one jurisdiction the crime is a felony while in another it is a misdemeanor.

Definitions of crime are also influenced by the culture. There are crimes that typically are not considered criminal, and possibly are even considered acceptable, by at least segments of the general public. For example, it is not uncommon for teenagers to knowingly and enthusiastically exceed the speed limit. For some, to not speed may be considered abnormal. This concept also applies to other levels of crime. There are subcultures where crime and violence are omnipresent and are even the accepted and expected mode of interaction and problem solving (Moore & Toney, 1998; Hawkins, 1995; Wolfgang, 1978). Though these interactions may not be accepted by the larger social structure, they are normative within certain environments and thus are not considered deviant.

Crime victimization, according to public opinion polls, is ranked among the most serious problems in America (Saad, 2000). Even though statistics have consistently shown that crime has decreased, public opinion about the existence of crime is varied. According to the Gallup Poll, the majority of people believe that crime is higher in the United States in a given year than it was in the previous year. However, 1998 was the first year in which people reported the belief that crime was down in their area.

Along with these perceptions about the prevalence of crime is the notion of fear. Ferraro (1995) defines fear of crime as "an emotional response of dread or anxiety to crime or symbols that a person associates with crime" (p. 8). This response is evoked from one's perception of risk that is based on data sources available. One source of data is one's own personal experiences. Having been personally victimized in the past, or knowing others who have been victimized, enhances awareness and perception of risk, especially in regards to property crimes (Ferraro, 1995). By not having a personal experience with crime victimization, people tend to distance themselves from crime. That is, the persons and places related to crime are someone or somewhere else.

Perceptions may also be influenced by secondary sources, such as stories related by acquaintances or the media. Regardless of the source, perception of prevalence and fear of crime is driven by awareness. The immediacy and extent of crime reporting through the various and plentiful media outlets allows a passive public to become fully aware of local as well as national events—often as they are taking place. Daily accounts of victim misery and related indifference of the criminal justice system and other systems are presented as well. A review of the research literature by Heath and Glibert (1996) found that there tends to be a correlation between television news viewing and newspaper news reading and fear of crime. However, the relationship is not simple because there are a myriad of factors that influence perception. Some of these factors include the "level of sensationalism, randomness, and location of the crime" (p. 383).

Generally it has been shown that fear of crime is relatively congruent with the reality of risk. That is, the level of fear reported is relative to overall risk. For example, contrary to conventional wisdom, the elderly "are not prisoners of fear of crime. Indeed, they are generally less likely than younger people to be afraid of crime" (Ferraro, 1995, p. 80). This is consistent with the victimization rates for the elderly who generally experience the lowest levels of victimization as compared to other age groups. On the other hand, women in general are more fearful of crime than men even though men generally are more likely to be victimized. This holds true for all offenses except rape. It is possible that this fear is based on the association of all crime as having the potential for also being a sexual crime (Ferraro, 1996) or due to physical vulnerability should a violent crime occur (Rountree, 1998).

What is the response to this fear of crime? Even with the drop in crime, potential victims are increasingly protecting themselves through means such as security systems and devices for the home, car, and self. Spending on electronic security products and services is growing at an estimated 8.7% per year and approximately 17.5% of the households in the United States are protected by professionally installed and monitored electronic burglar alarm systems (National Burglar and Fire Alarm Association, 2001). According to one survey, more than 62% of security alarm owners expressed concern about crime in their communities as compared to less than 40% of nonowners. (Perlik, 2001) This suggests that regardless if there is statistical evidence of a crime problem, those persons more concerned about crime are more likely to protect themselves through home security systems.

THEORETICAL EXPLANATIONS OF CRIMINAL VICTIMIZATION

Data regarding criminal victimization reveals that certain groups of people tend to be more at risk than others. Critical analysis of the data is fostered by having a general understanding of theoretical explanations of victimization. This analysis and understanding is the nature of victimology.

Opportunity Theories

The event of a criminal victimization requires not only an offender but an opportunity to act. Crime can be understood, in part, by viewing the opportunities to victimize that are available to potential offenders. There are two related theories under the category of Opportunity Theories.

Routine Activities Theory. Routine Activities Theory (Cohen & Felson, 1979; Cohen, Kluegel, & Land, 1981) assumes that the variables of crime are a motivated offender, suitable targets, and capable guardians of persons or property. In other words, the likelihood of criminal victimization increases when there is a person or persons motivated to commit a crime, there is someone or something available, and there is an absence of guardians, either persons or structures, to deter the criminal activity. This theory notes that there has been a shift of the routines in modern society that has resulted in the decrease of guardianship of self and property. Resident, employment, education, and leisure structures and activities have changed over the decades so that individuals and families are increasingly away from their homes. Whereas it used to be families, often extended families, engaged in daily life activities within the context of the family unit and the neighborhood, modern society is characterized by individualism and mobility. Thus, criminal opportunity is increased when there is a potential victim and/or property who is not well protected either by being in the company of others or by being physically secured.

While it may seem that this theory applies only to stranger offenses where there is a potential offender calculating the cost-benefit of engaging in a criminal act, the theory is also applicable to victimizations where people know each other and there is no apparent economic gain. For example, the routine activities of modern society have tended to loosen the social ties of extended family and social institutions that may deter unacceptable behaviors. This social isolation may enhance the opportunity to engage in behavior defined as criminal.

Lifestyle-Exposure Theory.   Related to Routine Activities Theory, this theory considers the relationship between victim lifestyle and risk of criminal victimization . Lifestyles differ to the extent in which people are in places or circumstances where victimization is more likely to occur. Lifestyles characterized by time spent in public places, time spent with nonfamily members, and time spent interacting with others who share similar lifestyle are some of the factors associated with victimization (Hindelang, Gottfredson, & Garofalo, 1978). A common example is the contrast of lifestyles between young males, a high-risk group, and elderly females, a low-risk group. Young males are at a higher risk for victimization than elderly females in part because they associate with others more likely to offend and they frequent places where offending tends to occur.

Victim-Offender Interaction Theories

Victim-offender theories recognize that criminal victimization is an event that does not occur in isolation. Rather, it is a social event that involves exchanges between the victim and the offender. These theories look at how the individual victim may have contributed to, or precipitated, the victimization. For example, assaults and homicides may result from a series of exchanges that are started by the victim through words or actions and then evolve as a matter of "saving face" (Luckenbill, 1977; Wolfgang, 1958). These exchanges suggest that violence may be a process during which the parties involved may make choices regarding their involvement. The status of victim, then, may be bestowed on the individual who happens to have been the weaker of the two parties.

While there is value in understanding the dynamics of interactions, there is danger in the potential implications of victim blaming. That is, to what extent is criminal behavior justified due to an assessment of victim precipitation? Yet this very assessment occurs regularly by agents of the justice system, including those who assess the merits of victim compensation.

A criticism of victimological theories is the interpretation that such study shifts the focus of responsibility away from the offender and onto the victim. From this criticism, there is often a negative perception about the term victimology as equated with victim blaming. "A superficial understanding of these theories might create the impression that, in a peculiar way, victims cause crime" (Kennedy & Sacco, 1998). Such is not the intent, however, in the study of crime victimization and the realization that certain characteristics tend to be correlated with risk.

MEASURING CRIME VICTIMIZATION

The study of crime victimization can be very complex and the findings of different studies may seem contradictory. This may be due, in part, to methodological approaches to a study. The operational definition of crime victimization is one of the methodological challenges. As noted earlier in this chapter, is it best to use a legal or cultural definition? Since most studies occur postvictimization, can the interpretation of the event by the victim be considered accurate considering the obvious bias? Crime victimization often involves multiple actions. Therefore, is each action considered a separate victimization or is the victimization as one event measured?

There are two main sources of measurement used by the Department of Justice: the *Uniform Crime Report* and the *National Crime Victimization Survey*. While these two measurements should not be considered the only sources of information and, as will be discussed, both have weaknesses, these sources are recognized official measures.

Uniform Crime Report

The *Uniform Crime Report* (UCR) is a yearly report disseminated by the Federal Bureau of Investigation. The UCR collects information from the nation's law enforcement agencies regarding committed offenses known to police. The UCR is divided into two categories, Part I: Index Crimes, and Part II: Crimes. Index crimes are those considered the most serious and, therefore, most likely to be reported. These crimes include homicide, forcible rape, robbery, aggravated assault, burglary, larceny-theft, motor vehicle theft, and arson. Information on age, race, and gender of the suspects is also collected on the Index Crimes. Arrests are reported for additional crime categories.

A limitation of the UCR is that it only reports crimes known to police, therefore, it is limited by what is reported. Only about 40% of all crime is reported, but this may vary according to the type of crime. For example, while violent crime is generally reported more frequently than property crimes, there are exceptions. Reporting rates for rape and sexual assault vary from 16% to 30%, while auto theft is reported close to 80% of the time (Bureau of Justice Statistics, 2000). Also, since the UCR relies on the voluntary reporting by law enforcement agencies, there is the possibility of bias either due to agency methodology of counting or political reasons (Wallace, 1998). Finally, though it was never intended to serve this function, the UCR does not provide information about victims. The UCR is currently being converted to a more comprehensive system called the National Incident-Based Reporting System (NIBRS), which will report detailed information about each criminal incident and arrest within 22 categories.

National Crime Victimization Survey

The National Crime Victimization Survey (NCVS) was started in 1973 by the Bureau of Justice Statistics. The NCVS explores in detail crime incidents, victims, and trends. Information is gathered via survey of a nationally representative sample of the general population. Information is collected on crimes suffered by individuals and households regardless of whether the incidents were reported to law enforcement. Detailed characteristics about the victim, the offender (including relationship with the victim), and the incident are gathered. Also, questions are asked regarding the reporting, victim experiences with the criminal justice system, self-protective measures, and possible substance abuse by the offender. The NCVS does not gather information on crimes against children under the age of twelve. Also, it does not gather information about the crimes of homicide, arson, or commercial crimes. As with any survey that draws from a sample, the NCVS is subject to a margin of error.

CHARACTERISTICS OF CRIME VICTIMIZATION

The UCR and NCVS provide the most comprehensive information on crime and victimization. Exhaustive detail regarding types of crimes and certain demographic characteristics is beyond the scope of this book, but can be obtained through reports issued by the Bureau of Justice Statistics of the U.S. Department of Justice. The intent here is to provide general information regarding crime rates, patterns, trends, and victim profiles by description of the what, who, where, when and how of crime victimization.

What

Much of the response to crime—by the public, media, policy makers, and criminal justice system—is in reference to violent crime. When compared to nonviolent crime, violent crime has much more of an impact on the individual as well as on the social psyche. In the overall perspective, however, violence is relatively rare. About 85% of all crime is property crime (Rennison, 2000). The likelihood of being a victim of homicide is about 7 in 100,000 as compared to the odds of being a victim of heart disease, which is about 258 per 100,000 (Minino & Smith, 2001).

Who

Gender.   Overall, males are one third more likely to be victims of violent crime than females. Males account for three fourths of all murder victims and are about twice as likely as females to be victims of aggravated assault or robbery. However, females are victims of sexual assault over seven times more often than males (Rennison, 2000).

Recognizing that males are more likely victimized than females, it is also important to consider that males are more often the perpetrators of crime. Males comprise about 78% of all arrests: close to 84% of violent index crime arrests and 71% of property index crime arrests (Bureau of Justice Statistics, 2000).

The relationship between males as primary offenders and males as primary victims is significant. Males tend to be more aggressive than females and tend to display that aggression against other males. Is this a reflection of the saving face phenomenon? What other factors contribute to this? Whether male aggression is due to socialization or biological differences is beyond the scope of this discussion. It should be noted, however, that arrest rates for females, especially juveniles, have risen at a higher rate than those of males over the past decade.

Age.   Young people face the greatest risk of being crime victims. According to the NCVS, the violent crime victimization rate for the 12 to 24 years age group is more than twice that of the next highest risk age group of 25 to 34 and it is about 8 times that of persons over the age of 50 (Rennison, 2000). Homicide is the second leading cause of death for youth age 15 to 24 (Anderson, 2001). Those in the age group 16 to19 years had the highest rates of sexual assault of any age group.

As with gender, young people are also more likely to be offenders. Serious violent crime by juveniles saw a dramatic increase in the early part of the 1990s, though since that time it has leveled off at or below early 1980s levels. On the average, juveniles are involved in about one fourth of serious violent victimizations (Snyder & Sickmund, 1999).

The lifestyle common to young people, such as being more active at places away from the home and interacting in places where drugs and alcohol may be present, offer a reasonable explanation as to why they are at higher risk for victimization than adults.

Race.   African Americans have significantly higher victimization rates for all types of crimes as compared to Caucasian and people of other races (Rennison, 2000). African Americans are six times more likely to be murdered than Caucasians; they are also seven times more likely than Caucasians to commit homicides (Fox & Zawitz, 2000). Most crimes are intraracial.

These figures should not be interpreted to mean that race is in any way a predisposition to commit crime. Race in the United States, as it relates to crime victimization, is closely related to age, income and residence.

Income.   Generally, crime rates increase as household income decreases. Over 57 out of 1,000 criminal incidents occurred in households with annual income less than $7,500, whereas for households with income greater than $75,000, the rate is about 23 per 1,000 (Rennison, 2000).

For household property crime victimization, however, the relationship between income and victimization is more curvilinear with both the lowest income level and the highest income level at approximately the same high rate. This may be explained in part due to what types of crimes are included in the category of household property crime. The crime of motor vehicle theft is more significant for all the income ranges above the lowest level of income. However, generally, auto theft appears to be relatively congruent among the income categories. There is a fairly consistent relationship between the crime of theft and income—the higher the income, the lower the rate of theft. This makes sense when the definition of theft as used by the NCVS (Bureau of Justice Statistics, 2000) is considered. Theft is defined as a loss of property by a person who has a legal right to be in the household, such as a housekeeper or a delivery person. On the other hand, the crime of burglary, defined as theft by a person who has no legal right to be in the dwelling, is correlated with the lowest income level being victimized almost three times that of the highest (Rennison, 2000).

Marital Status.   Persons never married and persons divorced are significantly more likely to be victims of violent crime than married and widowed persons (Rennison, 2000). Marital status tends to be related to age and lifestyle. Never married persons tend to be younger whereas widowed persons tend to be older. Single persons tend to engage in social activities away from home that may have a higher risk of criminal activity. Married and widowed persons, on the other hand, may be more inclined to spend free time within the confines of the home with family and friends.

Victim-Offender Relationship.   Data regarding the relationship between the victim and the offender are separated into nonstranger, which includes intimate, other relative and friend/acquaintance, and stranger. Relationships are relatively easy to determine for violent crimes since face-to-face contact is required. However, even in these cases, the "victim-offender relationship may not be known or may be reported inaccurately" (Laub, 1997, p. 17).

More than half of homicides are committed by nonstrangers, 14% by strangers, and about a third is unknown (Fox & Zawitz, 2000). The high percentage of unknowns is, of course, due to the fact that there is not a victim available to identify whether the offender was known or not. This is not the case in other violent crimes where the unknown percentage is inconsequential. For sexual assault, 69% are committed by nonstrangers, 30% by strangers; for robbery, 34% nonstrangers and 64% strangers; and for aggravated assault, 49% nonstrangers and 48% strangers (Rennison, 2000). These rates may vary considerably when considering gender differences. For example, sexual assault against females is committed by nonstrangers 72% of the time while nonstrangers sexually assault male victims 45% of the time. Similarly, aggravated assault against females is committed by nonstrangers 59% of the time, whereas nonstrangers commit aggravated assault against males 43% of the time, a 16% difference (Bureau of Justice Statistics, 2000). Thus, women are more likely than men to be victims of violent crime committed by someone they know.

This also applies to victimization between intimates. According to a report by the National Institute of Justice and the Center of Disease Control (Tjarden & Thoennes, 2000), women were more likely to be victims of rape, physical assault, and stalking when the offense was committed by an intimate as defined as "current and former spouses, same-sex and opposite-sex cohabiting partners, and dates" (p. 7). Specifically, considering all of these types of victimizations, over a fourth of women have been victimized by an intimate in their lifetime as compared to less than 8% of men. This study also found that persons who at some point lived in a same-sex cohabitation "reported significantly more intimate partner violence than did opposite-sex cohabitants" (p. 30). This suggests that persons in same-sex relationships are victimized by intimates more so than those in opposite-sex relationships, but the authors clarify that males are significantly more likely to be perpetrators of the violence. Thus, regardless of the current or past living situation, persons are more likely to be victimized by males than females.

When

According to the NCVS (Bureau of Justice Statistics, 2001), over half of the violent crimes occur between 6 a.m. and 6 p.m. and almost 36% occur at night; time is unknown or not available for over 12% of the incidents. Time analysis differs on whether the offenses are committed by adults or juveniles. In general, the number of violent crimes committed by adults increases hourly from 6 a.m. through the afternoon and evening hours, peaks at 11 p.m., and then drops hourly to a low point at 6 a.m. In stark contrast, violent crimes by juveniles peak in the afternoon between 3 p.m. and 4 p.m. (Snyder & Sickmund, 1999, p. 64).

Where

Generally, victimization rates are highest in urban areas, followed by suburban areas with rural areas having the lowest victimization rates. Differences between levels of urbanization with regard to sexual assault are relatively nominal (Bureau of Justice Statistics, 2001).

The western region of the United States generally has higher victimization rates than other regions. Rates of murder, especially those involving guns, are higher in southern regions, that is the South Atlantic, East South Central, and, especially, the West South Central, regions of the United States (Fox & Zawitz, 2000).

How

A significant portion of violent crime involves weapons. In addition to guns, weapons can include knives, rocks, sticks, and about anything else besides the human body. Firearms are used in about 70% of homicides (Fox & Zawitz, 2000). Weapons are used in 47% of robberies; about half of these being firearms; 14% are knives. For assault, weapons are used 23% of the time; 6% are firearms and 7% are knives.

COMPREHENSIVE CONTINUUM OF SERVICES

In the context of research and measurement, crime victimization is often considered as just an incident, but "victimization is a dynamic process that occurs over time, involving one or more individuals in an environmental context" (Andrews, 1992, p. 14). That is, victimization occurs in stages that range from previctimization on through to recovery. Service providers function within these various stages, often without interaction during the other stages. While the functions of a service provider may be limited to a specific area of intervention, an understanding and appreciation of the entire process is essential for effective victim services.

The following is a brief description of the comprehensive continuum of services for crime victims as identified by Andrews (1992). These include: prevention, early intervention and risk reduction, crisis and initial intervention, recovery assistance, collaboration, and advocacy. Most of these components are addressed more fully in other sections of this book.

PREVENTION

The goal of prevention is to "reduce the likelihood that individuals will develop the propensity to be perpetrators or victims and that situations in the social and physical environment will create opportunities for victimization" (Andrews, 1992, p. 139). Prevention efforts strive to enhance well-being of all people through competence building and empowerment of individuals and groups. These often intangible goals make it difficult to assess the impact of such efforts on the complex social problem of crime victimization. The myriad of contributing factors challenges clear identification of activities and initiatives that can be shown, with any significant confidence and in a timely manner, to be effective.

Regardless of this challenge, prevention is a proactive, socially valid response to social problems. By enhancing individual, family, community and society competence, vulnerability to dysfunction and, hence, risk of victimization should be reduced.

Individual prevention activities include promotion of basic life skills such as communication, problem solving, stress management and physical health enhancement. Preventative measures targeted to the family include child care resources, family life education, and social supports such as self-help groups and religious organizations. Community prevention includes: enhanced neighborhood support, such as churches and recreation centers; physical enhancements such as graffiti and trash removal; neighborhood crime prevention programs; supportive school environments that promote tolerance and use cooperative learning activities; and, supportive work environments that provide wellness programs and on-site child care. Finally, prevention measures targeted to the general society include economic development and a prosocial media.

EARLY INTERVENTION AND RISK REDUCTION

Also known as secondary prevention, early intervention and risk reduction strategies target at-risk populations and places which are identified through early warning signs or after mild forms of victimization have already occurred.

While prevention programs are intended for anyone wishing to participate, maximum impact of prevention can be achieved by targeting those at the greatest risk. Hawkins and Catalano (1995) identified an array of community, family, school, and individual/peer risk factors that research shows contribute to adolescent health and behavior problems. For example, some of the community factors include the availability of drugs and firearms; one of the family factors is the existence of family conflict; one of the school factors is early academic failure; and some of the individual/peer factors include friends who engage in problem behaviors or depression of an individual. Thus, behavior problems in children such as aggression may be a manifestation of several factors, including community values, family violence, academic failure, and depression. Early intervention involves an assessment of these various risk factors and implementation of strategies to enhance protective factors.

Risk reduction involves strategies that limit criminal opportunity through environmental design and behavior changes. Lighting, locks, surveillance cameras, alarms, fences, and open building designs are examples of changing the physical environment to deter crime. Individual and public behaviors include an array of personal safety strategies regularly communicated by law enforcement, such as locking valuables in the trunk when shopping, walking with companions, and keeping car doors and windows locked.

CRISIS AND INITIAL INTERVENTION

Crisis and initial intervention is focused on the well-being and safety of a victim immediately following victimization. Well-being includes addressing the immediate physical injuries through emergency medical care and the psychological turmoil through support and coping assistance. Safety is insured through assistance in contacting family or friends, finding alternative places to stay, and, if necessary, assistance in obtaining security.

Crisis and initial intervention is fully addressed in chapter 6.

RECOVERY ASSISTANCE

Recovery assistance involves a whole array of services intended to help the victim adapt and heal. Depending on the needs of the victim, this level of service may include the systems of health care, mental health, social services, and criminal justice.

Health care assistance may involve a variety of services necessary for physical recovery, such as hospitalization, dental care, physical therapy, and speech and hearing therapy. Mental health assistance may involve counseling for the individual and family or even psychiatric hospitalization for severe debilitation. Social services assistance may include case management, referral services, respite care, transportation assistance, home and food assistance, and assistance for those with special needs, such as people with disabilities and non-English speaking persons. Finally, criminal justice assistance may be the most comprehensive, ranging from law enforcement through corrections. It may include information regarding the police investigation, notification of court hearings, witness preparation, and assistance with restitution and compensation claims.

COLLABORATION

The system of victim assistance, as previously suggested, is comprised of an array of services, most of which are characterized by a very specialized focus. In those areas where services are readily available, gaps in services may exist due to the limitations of organizations as determined by legislative, policy, or mission parameters. In some areas, services may be nonexistent or, if they do exist, be inaccessible due to limited resources. The challenge of victim services as a system is to provide the comprehensive level of services required for the dynamic and unique needs of crime victims. In order to do this, collaborative efforts are required.

Examples of collaboration include interagency assessment and referral, interagency treatment planning and service provision, interagency purchase agreements, joint staff training, colocation of offices, and joint fundraising. Examples of community collaborations are identified throughout the Office for Victims of Crime initiated report, *New Directions from the Field: Victims' Rights and Services for the 21st Century* (1998).

ADVOCACY

Advocacy involves efforts to promote social attitudes and behaviors, policy, and resources that are victim-oriented. Advocacy activities include raising public awareness of problems and services, soliciting resources, and promoting pro-victim policies and legislation through lobbying efforts directed at policy makers. Examples of specific advocacy practices can be found in *New Directions from the Field: Victims' Rights and Services for the 21st Century* (1998) which lists 25 recommendations specific to the advancement of victims' rights.

Advocacy is fully addressed in chapter 12.

SUMMARY

Victim is a concept that is subject to imprecision of definition; it is a social movement of a relatively recent history; it is a word that may be symbolic of conflicting ideologies; it is a source of fear; it is a subject of theory; it is an event to measure; it is the focus of services. This chapter has provided an overview of victim from these different considerations in order to lay a foundation for the remainder of this book.

Ecological Perspective of Victimization

2

Thomas L. Underwood and Nancie D. Palmer

An ecological perspective is a model of understanding the dynamics of victimization on the individual and beyond. It is a perspective of victimization that is holistic and considers the complex relationship between the individual and the extended environment. With the victim at the center, crime is like a pebble in a pond; it ripples, extending its impact outward. The individual and the broader social environments of the family, the small group, the organization, the community, and society are all affected by a criminal act.

Characteristics of the individual and the environments in which they function can enhance coping for the victim. On the other hand, these very supports can also be impediments to recovery. "Social reaction is generally unkind to crime victims" (Young, 1991, p. 37). Victims often feel isolated, blamed, and ignored. The environments are in constant dynamic interaction with each other and with the individual. The ecological perspective focuses on the relative strengths and mutual supports of the individual and the broader environments. These complex interrelationships are essential in understanding the impact of a criminal act and the process of recovery.

"How we interact at any specific time arises from a synthesis of what is happening in the world within us (the individual), what is happening in the world around us, and how we interpret events" (Miley, O'Melia, & DuBois, 1998, pp. 35–36). The individual's internal world is in itself another complex interactive system of physiology and psychosocial forces. For example, internal forces may include but not be limited to: perceptions, feelings and emotions, beliefs, values, physical heartiness, and the experience of pain. Yet all of these internal experiences are influenced by external contextual influences. For example, external contexts may include: family, culture, ethnicity, socioeconomic status, gender, sexual orientation, race, and age.

21

Internal and external forces are interactive, that is, they are influenced by each other. Threaded within these constant interactions is the tendency to homeostasis. This important ecological concept postulates that all living things strive in maintaining a steady state within "preferred and familiar ranges" (Goldenberg & Goldenberg, 2000, p. 67). This striving is characteristic then of individuals, families, groups, organizations, and societal institutions.

The ecological perspective of victimization is explored through the context of the following case scenarios of victimizations:

Margaret

Margaret, age 72, lives alone in a house located in a moderate to low socioeconomic neighborhood. The house was purchased by Margaret and her husband, Bill, over 40 years ago when two of their eventual five children were still very young. The house was close to the church they attended, of which Margaret was an active member, and close to Bill's work at the industrial shop. Bill died 10 years ago from cancer. Three of the five children live in or near the same city; the other two live in different states.

The neighborhood has been in a decline over the past several years. With increased building of new homes on the outskirts of the city, properties in the neighborhood have not kept their value. Though there are still many properties that have been well maintained by long-term residents, more and more of the houses are ill-kept rentals with a more transient residency.

One day after coming home from the store, Margaret entered her house to find that her house has been ransacked. The house was in shambles; dishes and mementos from her china cabinet and shelves were broken on the floor, her jewelry box was totally emptied, her mattress was overturned, dresser drawers were dumped out, and so forth. Gripped with fear, she ran from the house in hysterics to a neighbor. The police discovered that the intruders had entered the house by cutting a window screen to an open window.

Jimmy

Jimmy, age 11, is the oldest of four of Ron and Nancy. The other children include 9 year old twins Timmy and Tammy, and 18 month old Melissa. Ron works as a computer operator. His hours sometime vary; the job often requires that he work into the evening. Also, he often works overtime when there is the opportunity. However, he makes time to be involved with the children through oversight of their studies and extra activities, such as helping out with Jimmy's scouting. A strict disciplinarian, Ron has high expectations of the children. Though a caring father, he does not hesitate to spank the children if he deems it necessary.

Despite Ron's reluctance, Nancy recently went back to work part-time at a discount store. Ron wanted Nancy to be at home with the children, but finances were such that additional income was needed. With a toddler at home, though, Nancy could not afford to work too much due to the cost of child care and there was no extended family close enough to watch the children for her. So on occasion, when both Ron and Nancy's schedules overlap, the children were left at home alone with Jimmy in charge of his siblings.

One day Ron came home from work to find that Nancy had unexpectedly gone to work. The house was cluttered, the television was blaring, and someone had spilled soda on the carpet. Further, on the counter was Jimmy's report card which showed several subjects with lower grades than the last grading period. Ron exploded at Jimmy—he yanked Jimmy by the arm causing him to experience tremendous pain in his shoulder. He then proceeded to spank Jimmy with a belt on his bare bottom. Jimmy was required to clean the entire house and then to go to his room to work on studies. The other children were made to sit quietly on the sofa the entire evening. A few hours later when Nancy returned home, Ron yelled at her for being an unfit mother.

The next day at school Jimmy was unable to write due to his sore shoulder. His teacher sent him to the school nurse who suspected that the shoulder may have been dislocated. She had him remove his shirt to view the shoulder better and saw the belt welts on his back. Law enforcement and social services were called to the school and Jimmy was placed in emergency foster care.

John

Helen, a 53 year old divorced mother of three grown children living in a large community, was exiting a community event with approximately 30,000 other people. As she entered the parking lot, she was shot and killed by gunfire exchanged when two gangs came across one another. A teenage boy was also a homicide victim of the cross fire.

John, her eldest child, lives in a community several hours away with his wife and young child. He is a manager for a large corporation. The other siblings, Beth, a graduate student at a small university several states away, and Doug, a graphic designer and fledgling artist who lives in a community about 30 miles from John, are both unmarried. John was contacted in the middle of the night by an uncle who lived in the same city as his mother. John immediately drove to the city where his mother had resided.

INDIVIDUAL

The individual is at the center of the model. Each individual "is a complex organic system, demonstrating unique physical, cognitive, social, emotional, and behavioral characteristics" (Andrews, 1992, p. 11) influenced by nature and nurture. Because of the uniqueness of each individual, responses to individual events—to trauma—are also unique. No two individuals will respond to criminal victimization in exactly the same way. Tragedies where more than one individual is victimized provide a good illustration of the uniqueness of individual response.

It is essential for the victim assistance practitioner to recognize the complex nature of individuals and uniqueness of each person in his or her response. Many practitioners have been trained to focus on primarily one area of the person: physical, psychological, social, spiritual, educational, and so forth. By not considering all of these mentioned areas, the whole being is not addressed and important aspects of intervention may be missed.

The range of emotions that may be experienced by a victim may impede one from being his or her typical self. The outgoing person may be reclusive, the friendly person surly, the controlled person may feel helpless. It is impossible for people to truly be themselves or to be completely rational while all of the emotions and thoughts are running. Thus, the victim may not interact with service providers in a 'normal' sense. Because each individual views the world differently, a communication barrier may exist between the victim and professionals.

The systems that serve crime victims are characterized by processes that typically are very prolonged. Most victims, of course, have no idea of the time frame and find their exposure to these processes to be very difficult and hindering to their own emotional healing. Victims wants to be in control yet they are involved in a complex area that they know nothing about. Service providers, such as law enforcement and district attorneys, may sense anger and frustration in victims.

Margaret

Everything that Margaret held dear to her had been violated: the home in which she and Bill had raised a family; the jewelry, though mostly inexpensive, was invaluable as most of it had been given as gifts by her husband and children; the china had been her mother's. She was fearful for her own well-being. How easy is was for someone to come into her home; what was to stop someone from coming back and maybe causing her harm? She became immobilized, almost catatonic, by fear.

Grief over the loss of things held precious and fear of future intrusion prompted a variance of emotions and behaviors ranging from extreme sadness, marked by uncontrollable sobbing, to hyper-vigilance and security, marked by a startled response to noises and isolationism from the world. Margaret had a security company conduct a service check of the house and, though she could not afford an electronic system, she did have additional locks put on all doors and windows and exterior motion lighting installed. She started keeping the interior lights on all the time, even when she was in bed. She slept sporadically, getting up every few hours to check the doors and windows. All these actions underscored another fear—the loss of independence; she did not want to have to leave her home. The stress of the event took its toll on Margaret physically. She lost weight and started suffering from various ailments. Fearful to leave her home, she was reluctant even to see her physician.

Jimmy

All Jimmy wanted was for his shoulder not to hurt so he could do better in school. He did not want to talk any more to the school nurse, the police officer and the social service worker. He told them that he hurt his shoulder by accident and that he got the whipping because he was bad.

The overwhelming emotion he felt was fear. He was afraid of law enforcement and social services; that his parents might get in trouble, that his siblings might be put in a strange house like he was, that they might never let him go home. He was afraid of his family—that his parents might not want him home, that his siblings might get hurt if he was not home, that his father would be even angrier then before and he might be hurt worse next time. Mixed with fear was the emotion of relief; at least his father would not hurt him tonight.

John

John felt a range and intensity of emotions never previously felt. The anxiety of the event heightened his sense of mission to find out what happened to the extent that he seemed to operate on auto-pilot. He did not recall the three hour drive to the city where his mother had lived; he did not recall buying the morning newspaper; he did not recall asking directions to the police station. The more he found out about the details from both the police and the newspaper, the more reality he accepted and the wave of his emotions of mourning surfaced. Also, the emotion of fear surfaced—fear of a lack of control. John had confidence that there were not any previous issues in his life that he could not somehow correct or easily adapt to. But this was something totally beyond any control he could exercise. The fear came from knowing that he was powerless. If something like this happened once why couldn't it happen again?

With mourning came a rush of questions and regret. Why did this happen to his mother? Why wasn't he there to prevent it? How could God have let this happen? How could he have been a better son?

John had a great deal of anxious energy and turned it toward his mother's case. He began his own investigation into the events surrounding her death by talking with the detectives collecting evidence and the district attorney's office.

All too quickly Helen was buried and John was faced with getting back to the responsibilities of life, all within the course of just over a week. His emotions were still pretty intense—anger, sadness, fear, anxiety. In addition, he did not know if they were normal. He had bad dreams on a regular basis and suffered from panic attacks. For years he would avoid public events similar to the one his mother attended. He began to doubt that he would get through this; that he would be able to cope.

FAMILY

For most individuals, the family is the primary source of support. While most families have some characteristics of dysfunction, they also have strengths and supports that are essential for individual recovery. The family is an indirect victim of a crime perpetrated on an individual. The family's life as it once was is irreputably changed. The roles of protector, nurturer, or lover may be compromised. The family may also be the primary victim, such as in a house burglary.

The family is most often considered as the primary influential ecological and external force in an individual's life (Lamanna & Riedman, 1997; Goldenberg & Goldenberg, 2000; Devore & Schlesinger, E., 1999, Burt & Burt, 1996). Given this prevailing perception, it is important to note, however, that there is a basic contrast between the "values and assumptions of the client and those of the service culture" (Devore & Schlesinger, 1999, p. 132). The concept of what defines a family is one such example that illustrates the ecology or interrelatedness of systems.

Until the recent decade, the term family had been narrowly defined according to both tradition and law. Historically, the family has been defined as consisting of people related by blood, marriage or adoption (Lamanna & Riedman, 1997; Goldenberg & Goldenburg, 2000). Yet the composition and the social recognition of existing variations of family is changing in terms of racial/ethnic distribution, persons living alone, the prevalence of unmarried couple households, same sex couples, and young adults who live with their parents beyond what was considered the norm. Further, half of all children of divorce under age 8 live with one parent and re-marriage (stepfamilies) make up an increasingly large portion of all marriages. The rate of births to unmarried mothers remains very high and more than three million children live in the homes of their grandparents, a 40% increase from 1980–1990, 80% due to parental drug abuse of their parents (Lamanna & Reidman, 1997, Burt & Burt, 1996).

Yet social and legal institutions have been reluctant to recognize these variations in family life. For example, it was not until 1967, in *Loving v. Virginia*, that the U.S. Supreme Court declared that interracial marriages must be considered legally valid in all states. Grandparents are still striving for appropriate legal opportunities and recognition. Marriage between same-sex couples is not allowed in any of the United States and in fact many states have passed legislation denying recognition of any such unions in other states should they be legalized. As families have become less traditional, a term often used to convey the perception of the nuclear first-marriage family as the 'gold standard' (Burt & Burt, 1996, p. 20), social and legal institutions have been pressed to respond. Judge Vito J. Titone of the New York Court of Appeals (1989) in his summation stated that the definition of the family, "should not rest on fictitious legal distinctions or genetic history, but instead should find its foundation in the reality of family life" (Lamanna & Riedman, 1997, p. 6) Judge Titone's definition then recognizes great variation of family constellations. Examples include the following:

- Black or African Americans incorporating a wide informal network of kin and community;
- Italian Americans including godfathers and old friends in decision making;
- Chinese Americans who include all of their ancestors and descendants in family membership;
- Native Americans who include multiple households and non-kin as family members;
- Hispanic Americans who reflect deep pride in family membership with the man using both his father's and mother's name in his given name;
- Same-sex families who are increasingly adopting or having children through insemination.

It is important to emphasize that within diversity is greater diversity. Thus, the list of aforementioned examples is extremely limited and is presented to reflect some examples illustrating the presence of great variation among and within families.

UNDERSTANDING FAMILY DYNAMICS AND INFLUENCE

There are innumerable ways to examine the inner workings and influences of the family system as an ecological unit in its own right. For purposes of understanding victims in the familial context, it is most useful to think of a family under stress or in crisis. How an individual or family interacts at any specific time arises from a synthesis of internal and external influences or forces. The concepts of coping and adaptation are useful in understanding how a person or family responds to stress and crisis. A stressor may be normative, or expected, such as the birth of a child or move to improve career opportunities or non-normative, sudden. Stressors may be brief or prolonged, and external to the individual or family or internal (within the system). Internal stressors tend to depress or demoralize the individual or family because of the tendency to externalize or 'blame' someone (Lamanna & Riedman, 1997). Additional information should include the duration and stability of the stressor. For example, the death of a loved one may produce a sudden crisis of loss and prolonged secondary losses while grief may lessen over time.

Crucial to the family is the larger community and social contexts in which it resides. One must consider whether there are timely and appropriate social supports and resources, to what extent there is a fit between family needs and resources, whether the individual or family values are reflected in the nature of social and institutional response, and whether the persons and agencies who serve or respond are culturally competent.

Families have ecological factors which may help their members and the unit cope more effectively with stress and crisis. Factors that help a family cope and adapt include a prevailing belief in its own efficacy (ability to navigate the situation), high self esteem, the presence of a spiritual approach to life (higher power), open supportive communication between its members, informal social supports, and help-seeking behavior that enhances its ability to secure needed resources.

The absence of these supportive and facilitating factors may not only impede an individual's or family's recovery, it may result in less than effective response to service providers. The overlay of organizational and social values will also impact the manner in which these entities perceive and respond to victims of crime.

FACILITATING THE FAMILY ASSESSMENT

Family assessment of existing internal and external resources may be most rapidly accomplished through use of the Four-R Model of Family Dynamics. This model looks at family interactions through four domains: rules, roles, relationships, and rituals. Rules refer to those norms that govern behavior, structuring, and permission granting. Roles provide status differential, gender behaviors, and division of labor. Relationships reflect the configuration of connectedness, communication dynamics, and power orientation. Rituals are those highly valued activities that are most often habitual and consistent over time.

The domains of rules, roles, relationships, and rituals are not only developed within a family both from intergenerational forces and influences, but they are also influenced by culture and social institutions. In addition, these family domains influence help-seeking behavior and/or response to community, social, and service systems which serve victims. Crisis occurs when an event is experienced and perceived as threatening and the individual's or family's capacities and resources are exceeded.

The impact of a crime on a family can be tremendous. "A dramatic event requires major alterations in the way family members think, feel, and act" (Lamanna & Reidman, 1997, p. 436). This is true for every type of crime victimization but may be even more pronounced in a homicide, as in the example of John's response to his mother's homicide, for "unlike most losses in which there is time to mentally prepare and say good bye to one's loved one, the sudden and violent nature of murder leaves surviving families with an immense burden, a burden weighted by the survivor's 'unfinished business' with the victim" (Cummock, 1996, p. 5). Families, following the application of their ecological context, then, also experience the influence of their own interactions with the larger communities and social systems. Assessment of these systems is

crucial to the provision of strategic and appropriate responses and resources
that can enhance individual and family recovery.

As the reader follows the case scenarios, it is useful to think about the
following questions:

- What rules did individuals and the families have to follow in
  responding to the victimization? In what way might the rules affect
  perception of the event, individually and family? What way did
  family rules contribute or impede help seeking behavior?
- What were some of the roles of the family members? Do the roles
  reflect cultural norms?
- How did the family (and members) relate to community and service
  providers? How did community and service providers relate to them?
- How would the existence of non-traditional characteristics, such as
  blended family, same-sex couple, or other dynamics effect the rules,
  roles, relationships, and rituals? In what way would service providers
  and social responses be different?

The amount of time required to reach a reasonable point of well being
is severely impacted by the family's strength and its ability to cope. In the
end, it is not just an individual issue, it is a family issue. Recovery depends
on how a family can deal with the trauma together, not just individually.

Margaret

*Margaret did not want to tell her children what had happened. Though she
remained close to her children she had noticed that since the death of her husband they, especially her oldest daughter Kate, had become a bit over-protective.
They had urged her to move out of the house either into a retirement community or to live with one of them. Margaret did not want to leave her home, though,
and she feared that telling her children what had happened would only force the
issue further.*

*Kate and the other siblings noticed that their mother became increasingly moody
and reclusive. They also noticed that her normal frequent contact with them and
her grandchildren had lessened. When they would inquire about Margaret's
well-being, she would become very emotional, usually irritable.*

*Kate stopped by one afternoon and noticed Margaret's declining health.
Margaret became quite agitated at Kate's inquiries, told her that she was just fine,
and did not need to see a doctor. Kate talked with her siblings about her concerns
and discussed the possibility of contacting an attorney regarding guardianship
over Margaret.*

Jimmy

*Ron was outraged when he was contacted by law enforcement about the alle-
gations of abuse toward Jimmy and by his placement in emergency foster care.*

Ron considered himself a good father; he worked hard to be a good provider and set high standards for the children. He was committed to making sure that his children did not turn out like so many others; underachievers with discipline problems.

Nancy was confused. Surely the police were exaggerating the injuries. She was certain that Ron would never cause real harm to the children. Yes, he was a very strict disciplinarian and she thought he spanked too often and too hard, but he was a good person who wanted only the best for her and the children. Besides, even if he did get a bit heavy handed, she felt like she was really at fault. She had picked up a few extra hours at work without checking with Ron and without making sure the house was in good order. She should not have expected Jimmy to handle it all.

Nancy felt a range of emotions when she saw Jimmy at court the next day. She was relieved to see him; she was angered when she saw the welts and read the reports; she was fearful to realize that such force could be meted out by her husband, especially when she thought about his temper and the potential to not only hurt Jimmy again, but the other children as well; she was sad as she loved her husband and did not want to choose between her children and him.

The twins, old enough to understand at least some of what was happening, were frightened. Jimmy had always been there for them. He was the cushion between them and the tirades of their father. The children started to spend a lot more time in their room when Ron was home.

John

Although his mother's death affected John significantly, it also affected his wife, Karen, as well. She experienced some of the same emotions as John, although to a lesser degree. At the same time, however, she was faced with helping John through the most difficult period of his life. The array of emotions previously described continued to be very intense for John and his reactions to situations were impacted by his state of healing. It became more and more difficult as time went by for Karen to understand that John's anger was not related to her, but was still part of the emotional healing process. Fortunately the marriage was very strong, characterized by trust and acceptance, though getting through the ordeal was still extremely difficult for both. Faced with trying to handle everyday life responsibilities while also trying to heal, the couple had to develop their own coping mechanisms. John had to clearly understand and accept the impact of his mother's death, while Karen had to ignore emotional outbursts and help him identify their source. Both had to communicate often and openly.

John's siblings, Beth and Doug, looked to John to manage the situation, including contact with the criminal justice system. It was difficult for Beth, as a student, to devote the time and energy to be involved in the related affairs. Doug, though he would become involved when asked, grew relatively detached from both the process and the family and instead threw himself into his work and his art. He was considering taking a job in a large city in another state.

SMALL GROUP

A group is defined by its membership and purpose. Groups may be educational, supportive, enhance social connections, or therapeutic. Groups, therefore, may enhance personal or family well-being (therapeutic or self-help), skill development such as coping responses (psychoeducational), or effect environmental change (social action). Groups offer "resource generating alliances" (Miley et al., 1998, p. 332). Like families, organizations, and other ecological systems, groups may have facilitating or impeding characteristics.

A significant amount of a person's time is spent in formal and informal small groups, such as classes, work teams, recreational sports teams, college dormitory halls, and other friendship networks. Like the family, these groups are critical supports for the individual and are themselves impacted by the criminal victimization of one of their own.

The residents of a college sorority, for example, may provide significant social support for a rape victim through words and actions of encouragement and understanding. The other women in the sorority are also, albeit indirectly, victims of the crime. Their thoughts, feelings and behaviors will be forever influenced through their association with the victim. Not a stranger you read about in the newspaper, but one of their own has been assaulted. Formerly held thoughts and beliefs about trust and innocence may be shattered; feelings of anxiety may surface; and behaviors associated with normal daily functions may be altered. However, groups also reflect the attitudes and norms of their members and communities. For example, if the victim of a rape was a homosexual or transgendered, would the college sorority or fraternity be as responsive? "Evidence of homophobia is seen in the fraternity membership selection process. Rushees who are suspected or perceived to be homosexuals are frequently summarily rejected from consideration and if it is learned that a pledge is gay, he is likely to be "depledged . . . Fearing that other members might question their sexual orientation if they defend the prospective member, gay and gay-tolerant brothers usually remain silent . . . thereby reinforcing the homophobia of the group" (Windmeyer & Freeman, 1998, pp. xxiii–xxiv).

Since the small group is the primary means of interpersonal communication outside of the family, an understanding of its impact on the individual is important for effective intervention. The value of the small group as a support is evidenced by the effective use of support groups and therapy groups.

Margaret

Margaret was a member of the sewing circle at her church, played bridge once a week at the local senior center, and on occasion would go on short trips with a couple of long-time friends. Her next-door neighbors of thirty years, Harvey and Mildred, were among her circle of friends who were involved in some of these activities. These were the same neighbors to whom she had gone when the crime occurred.

After the crime it was rare for Margaret to participate with her small groups as she had before, and then it was only when Harvey and Mildred would badger her to the point that she would finally go with them. Through Harvey and Mildred, her other friends in these groups became aware of the crime. Her friends talked about how terrible it all was, how it was a shame that the community had deteriorated so, how the intruders were probably teenagers on drugs, how Margaret's crime was a good example as to why one cannot be too careful and must always secure windows and doors, and how fortunate Margaret was to be all right. They did not understand why Margaret did not want to participate in the activities. With Margaret's continued absence, friends eventually stopped calling.

Harvey and Mildred continued to watch out for Margaret, but even that was becoming taxing as she continued to isolate herself and exhibit her anxieties. Recognizing the impact that the crime had on Margaret, their frustration in her decline in spirit and health, and the demise of the neighborhood, Harvey and Mildred discussed the possibility of moving to a retirement community on the other side of town.

Jimmy

The overlapping members of the neighborhood children, classmates, and the scout pack were Jimmy's small groups. Everyone in school knew before the end of the day that something had happened to Jimmy at home and by that evening all the parents also knew. By being taken out of the home and placed in foster care, Jimmy was essentially removed from his small group supports.

The children in the neighborhood and the boys in the scout troop knew that Ron was strict on Jimmy. They had seen him spank Jimmy and the other children, but never actually hit them. Parents questioned their children about the event. Their thinking vacillated from the belief that Ron must have really have lost control this time, to the assumption that Jimmy must have really done something bad to deserve such a severe punishment, to questioning whether the school and law enforcement (and Jimmy) were making a big deal over a parent's right to discipline. Regardless, parents started to question whether this was a family they wanted their child to associate with.

John

Initially, there was a great deal of support from those people who knew John and his wife in small group settings. There were many cards and letters; they read each one and derived strength form the sentiments expressed. After the funeral the amount of communication decreased significantly. Though the family still had a long way to go to heal, to many of the people they knew the event was over. Some of the friends and associates distanced themselves from John and his wife, *seemingly in order to maintain the thought that there is something different about them and the tragedy that befell him and his family could never happen to them. When this happened, the family felt alone and abandoned. Some of their friends and associates felt victimized themselves in that they felt less secure about their own world.*

John's direct supervisor and office peer group was an example of one of his small groups. After a couple of weeks, the office expectations were that John should have gotten over the tragedy and would be as productive as before. John quickly noticed, however, that his ability to handle stress in his high-pressure administrative job was not the same as it had been. His motivation was lower due to questions he had about life's purpose and length; he was more easily angered; and he struggled with bouts of depression.

The court process also caused a strain with his employee small group. John wanted and needed to be actively involved in the process. Court cases were continued and meetings were rescheduled. While his boss was flexible, the result of John's conflict in focus was his having to choose between spending more time on his professional responsibilities or attending the trial for his mother's murder.

ORGANIZATION

Organization may be conceptualized as a body that "provides a specific range of social services for members of a population group that has (been) or is vulnerable to a specific social problem. The agency or organization may be funded by combinations of philanthropic contributions and privately solicited donations, by governments, by fees paid by those served, or by third party payments" (Garvin & Seabury, 1997, pp. 253). Inherent in any organization is the reflection of the values and norms of those who develop and control it. Organizational features include hiring practices, policies that guide operations, defining who is eligible for services (Miley et al., 1998; Hopps et al., 1995).

Organizations are the societal institutions in which the individual is involved, though not necessarily because of their victimization. The institutions of work, church, and school are examples of organizations. As larger extensions of small groups, organizations affect and are affected by an individual's victimization. For example, inadequate safety protocols and environmental designs, such as poor security coverage and lighting, at a work site may enhance the chances of employee victimization for those who get off work late at night. The organization of employer can be viewed as contributors to the risk of victimization. Poor employer response to victimization after it occurs, such as refusal to allow time off work, impedes recovery and further victimizes the individual. Likewise, the victimization event may also affect the organization. Fellow employees, fearful that they themselves may become victims of crime, may become anxious at the workplace and, consequently, productivity may be impaired. On the other hand, the workplace organization may respond positively to the victimization. A positive response may be to an individual victimization, such as review and modification of leave policies, as well as to the employee base as a whole, such as providing prevention information to employees and implementing security structures.

Other organizations are those in which the individual is involved because of his or her victimization. These may range from small, grassroots agencies to large national or international associations. Organizations differ in their focus: they may have an intervention focus, such as a rape crisis hotline; a medical focus, such as a hospital emergency room; a treatment focus, such as a mental health center; a spiritual or religious focus, such as a church; or a legal focus, such as a law clinic or a police department. The response of these organizations can have a significant impact on the recovery of the victim.

Secondary victimization occurs when the very organizations that exist to assist the victim actually cause harm. Organizations may impede or even create secondary victimization through their personnel, practices, and policies. For example:

- Can persons with disabilities (consider those with difficulties hearing, walking, seeing, language, intellectual or emotional challenges) access the agency readily?
- Is the organization's physical environment culturally open and inviting?
- Is the organization child friendly (providing books, games, furniture, materials reflecting cultural diversity?
- Is material and information multilingual?
- Does organization material/information reflect varying family constellations? (use of concepts such as partner, kin, godparent, extended family)
- Does organization staff reflect diversity?
- Are services available in a timely manner?
- Does the organization use an advisory committee that reflects the population served?
- How does the organization view its users: deviant, client, recipient, etc? (Miley et al., 1998, Hopps et al., 1995, Garvon & Seabury, 1997)

"Culturally relevant services lead to policies that strengthen the health of the ethnic community, [sic individual and family], reinforce action, self-esteem, pride, self-assertion, and mastery among its members" (Hopps et al., 1995, p. 131). Recall that these are the same elements that were identified as facilitating characteristics to help individuals and families cope more successfully and adapt to changing situations and circumstances.

In order to cope and adapt, people must not only have or attain certain attributes, the environment (ecological systems) must provide correspondingly favorable conditions to facilitate adaptation, including changing the environment (Lee, 1994).

Secondary victimization can occur through a host of bureaucratic policies and procedures that are intended to assist the organization's operation, such as paperwork processing, layout of the physical environment, or hours of operation. For example, a victim whose house has been vandalized is asked irrelevant personal information, such as height, weight, hair color and eye color as a part of the police report; a rape victim is required to wait in the hospital public waiting room pending examination; a burglary victim goes to the courthouse to provide required paperwork for restitution only to find out the office is closed for lunch.

Margaret

Police interaction with Margaret was minimal. They investigated the break-in and took a report. The officers were pleasant and offered suggestions regarding enhanced security that Margaret should implement. She was told that the report would be filed and was given a case number. A few days late she contacted the police department to check on the progress of the case and left her name, case number and phone number with the property crimes department. Having not heard anything she called again the following week. She talked with someone (she could not hear what he said his name was when he answered the phone) who told her, pleasantly enough, that police would contact her if something happens in the case. Margaret continued to ask questions of the person regarding the case, her safety, and so forth. She was told that this kind of thing happens all the time and the best she can do is try to not let it happen again.

Margaret's daughter, Kate, finally convinced her to go to the doctor due to her significant weight loss and nausea. Margaret still had not told Kate about her victimization and did not volunteer the information to the physician. The doctor expressed some concern over Margaret's declining health but did not assume it to be anything more than a serious case of influenza. He urged to drink plenty of fluids, get some rest, and call back in a few days if things did not improve.

Jimmy

Jimmy was placed in an environment and a situation very foreign to him. All he was told was that he had to go to a court hearing (he did not know what a court hearing was). The social service worker, different from the one who met with him at school, who picked him up to take him to the court hearing asked him about how he was getting along in the foster care home and if he liked it there. At the court house (there was a metal detector they had to walk through and there were police at the front door), a person (who must have been very important because she was all dressed up) who identified herself as a guardian ad litem asked Jimmy about abuse (another term he did not know). Then he was led into another room with a large table. His parents were sitting on one side of the table—Nancy jumped up and gave Jimmy a hug; Ron looked down at the table. The judge walked into the room (odd that a man would wear a dress) and everybody came to attention. It was decided that Jimmy could return home pending further court action as long as Ron was not alone with Jimmy.

When Jimmy returned to school, the counselor met with him and offered to meet with him if he ever wanted to talk. The counselor also spent some time with Jimmy's teacher to advise her of some of the emotional, cognitive and behavioral manifestations often seen with abused children.

John
Due to his emotional struggles, John chose to seek professional mental health assistance shortly after his mother's murder. He started seeing a psychiatrist on a regular basis who prescribed some antianxiety pills. The pills did not help much and John felt that the weekly sessions with him did not help much as he was not offered much feedback. He still thought that he was abnormal and that he should be functioning better. He then switched to a psychologist who gave John materials about trauma and victimization to read. The psychologist also engaged in much more discussion about the event and his recovery. Here he found relief in understanding that his symptoms, although individually different, were normal under the circumstances.

John joined a local support group for homicide survivors. He found the group helpful in that it legitimized the feelings he was having. He found comfort in knowing that he was not crazy and that others had experienced similar feelings.

COMMUNITY

Typically, a community is viewed as a "set of people who share either a locality, identity, history, or other social status and who perceive this commonality as a basis for significant interdependence" (Garvin & Seabury, 1997 p. 274). It is a social unit of interactions that promote a collective identity that may involve space or activities. Perceived membership is a feature of community. For example, there are 'insiders' and 'outsiders,' or membership defined along cultural, ethnic, or other lines such as sexual orientation. The geographic community of the neighborhood is a prime example.

Communities may serve as crucial supporters and resource suppliers to individuals, families, or groups. Neighborhoods that are active in neighborhood watch programs, for example, can provide a sense of safety. Especially for individuals who are distant from their family, neighbors may serve as a significant personal support.

Communities, likewise, reflect certain norms and values that may invite or impede service response. Overwhelmed clients who are victims of crime and violence may also live in communities that are likewise 'violent and unsafe' (Hopps et al., p. 30) and such communities may be further avoided or less provided for by helping service providers. "In poor neighborhoods, with poor housing and always at prey and vulnerable to violence, it is small wonder that residents' self-esteem, competence, and self-sufficiency are nourished at all" (Hopps et al., p. 41). Community risk factors for criminal victimization include the availability of drugs, the availability of firearms, community laws and norms, media portrayals of violence, transitions and mobility, low neighborhood attachment and community disorganization, and extreme economic deprivation (Hawkins et al., 1995). The ecological component of community once again illustrates the essential features needed for effective coping and adaptation.

The neighborhood also suffers when an individual is victimized, especially if the crime was close to the individual's home. The vandalism of a mailbox, a robbery, or a sexual assault of the women down the street heightens the sense of vulnerability to victimization and affects the thoughts, emotions, and behaviors of the entire neighborhood.

Margaret

Margaret's neighbors, Harvey and Mildred, were very aware of the impact that the crime had on Margaret and they were increasingly sensitive to the decline of the neighborhood. They had to make a decision about their future. They were torn between wanting to stay in the neighborhood that had been home for so long or to move to a retirement community. They had heard about neighborhood watch and community clean-up programs. They attended a Neighborhood Improvement Association meeting and discussed their concerns. Shortly afterward a representative from the police department came to the meeting to discuss Neighborhood Watch Program and general safety issues. Though Margaret continued to struggle, Harvey and Mildred had hope that maybe things would get better in the community. Within 6 months, however, there were four burglaries, a raid on a suspected drug house, and a rape in their area. Harvey and Mildred moved to the retirement community. The young couple who purchased their house were there less than 2 years before moving.

Jimmy

The school district and neighborhood were communities impacted by Jimmy's victimization. As awareness of the charges of abuse became more prevalent, regardless of whether people knew Jimmy and his family or not, there was reflection on the issues of child development, parenting, prevention, and system responses to allegations. One person in the area decided to put together a list of volunteer parents who might be willing to serve as a resource for children who had to be left alone for brief periods of time. The school addressed the issue of parent stress in a newsletter and decided that some aspect of parenting or child development would be included in future newsletters.

John

The city in which Helen resided, as a whole, was significantly affected by her murder. Since she was struck by a stray bullet at a public event, many felt that they themselves were no longer safe. There was a public call for action and prosecution. Local politicians quickly went to work defending safety in the community and indicating that this tragedy was a unique situation. Even though John did not live in that community, this political response angered him; he felt that they were quickly trying to bring the case to closure in order to divert public attention and he had information from local police contradicting certain statements being made.

SOCIETY

Society is the broadest level of the perspective. Public attitudes, public policy, and social institutions reflect the culture and mores of a society. Pollsters are constantly asking the public what they think and how they feel about something. Public opinion counts in the marketing of soft drinks and laundry detergents. It also counts in the election of political candidates. How do the constituents feel about taxes, foreign policy, and casino gambling? What kind of services should society undertake to prevent crime, intervene with offenders, and provide services to victims? Yet often the attitudes expressed by the public are inconsistent with each other and with its behaviors.

Society as a whole is most often not interested in sharing a victim's grief. Rather, society distances itself and offers reasons as to why tragedies occur. Most often, social understanding of victimization is obtained through the brevity of filtered media news and entertainment. Exposure to media coverage of victimization often has a surreal effect on members of society. Although the events are real they are not determined to be so real that they become personal.

Public attitudes affect public policy. For example, the get-tough-on-crime movement of the past couple of decades evolved, in part, from public disgust over violent crime. This has translated into the building of new prisons and longer sentences, with America being second in the world in incarceration rates (Mauer, 1995) and in many jurisdictions, the budgets for corrections exceed those for education (Allen & Simonsen, 1998). Yet the overwhelming majority of offenders are imprisoned not because of violent offenses, but because of drug or property offenses.

Finally, society is represented by social institutions; they are agents of culture. Educational, economic, and justice institutions perpetuate the social mores. Thus, as public attitudes impact public policy, these attitudes are manifested in these social institutions. This is not to say, of course, that this is an unidirectional process. Social institutions also influence policy, which in turn shapes public attitudes. Many would argue that these societal institutions are hegemonic in nature in that they perpetuate the mores and values of the dominant culture, maintaining a societal status quo over women, minorities, and other traditionally deprived groups (Karmen, 1996; Rubenson, 1989). "The larger community must recognize its responsibility for the well-being of all its members. Imperative is the need to understand and share the concept of common-weal and solidarity with others, including those who are different . . . It is only through this ethos and these values that the work can begin for revitalization of caring at a community level" (Hopps et al., 1995, p. 129). It is not enough to more adequately serve favored individuals or families, for the strength of even the favored or privileged rests within their inextricable presence in ecological environments far greater than itself.

Society has changed over the years in its response to crime victimization. Through the efforts of grass roots efforts as well as organizational initiatives, public attitudes, public policy, and social institutions have become more responsive to the problems of crime and the social group of victims. But the three case scenarios presented beg social analysis.

Margaret

How is it that a neighborhood can deteriorate so? What is the role of government to prevent or correct this blight? What are the social conditions of the residents that encourage crime? Are the economic, educational, and social opportunities such that criminal behavior is a rational choice?

Jimmy

What are the societal factors that influence an acceptance of corporal discipline? What is the balance between parental right to discipline and the government's right to intervene? What conditions have influenced that evolution? What are the economic and social impediments for parents to be able to stay at home with their children? Does the traditional agricultural foundation of the school day, which creates a situation where children are often left unattended, make sense in today's society?

John

What are the conditions of violence in society? To what extent, as evidenced by popular entertainment, is violence accepted or even encouraged? To what extent does public policy prevent violence? To what extent does public policy offer effective responses to violence? What are the social conditions that foster the existence of gangs?

SUMMARY

The use of case scenarios provides direct application for understanding. The ecological perspective challenges service providers to consider the effect of a single crime victimization. Is our understanding of victimization too confined to one realm? Are our intervention responses to victimization too narrow? What are the implications of an ecological perspective to policy and service delivery?

Focus exclusively on the individual is limiting and, probably, ineffective. Professional practice, organizational policies and societal responses must consider the impact on and the influence of victimization for the family, small groups, organizations, community, and the culture or society.

Exploring Attitudes Toward Violence and Victimization

3

Steven D. Walker and Thomas L. Underwood

Amerian society has long been conflicted in its attitudes towards both criminals and victims. With regard to criminals, since the 1970s there has been a shift from the rehabilitation model back to the punishment model. In this same time span, the view of the victim's plight has changed dramatically from victim blaming to victim support. However, on a day to day basis with even more violent crimes on the evening news, the American public often quickly shifts back into a blaming stance. Even practitioners, at times, blame certain types of victims for their misfortune. Why does this second victimization occur?

This chapter will survey past and present attitudes toward victims and will explore the social and psychological roots of these attitudes. The two opposing viewpoints of victim blaming and victim defending will be discussed in detail. Finally, the role of professionals in perpetuating victim blaming will be analyzed.

ATTITUDES TOWARD VIOLENCE

Is violence an acceptable part of American culture? The public is horrified by mass violence tragedies where children are shot in school yards or federal buildings are bombed. At the same time, the American public enjoys media and sport entertainment that is inherently violent; most generally endorse U.S. military action when the nation's vital interests are at risk (Saad, 2000); and 70% are in favor of capital punishment (Gillespie, 1999).

"As a society that professes the value of humanitarianism, Americans have a curiously flexible tolerance towards violence" (Muldray, 1982). In

41

other words, attitudes about violence are variable and situation specific. The circumstance and context of violence is considered relative to an assessment of right and wrong. Reactions to violence are based on the preconceptions about the justifiability of the act. For example, many voiced approval when Jack Ruby shot and killed Lee Harvey Oswald, the alleged killer of John F. Kennedy; when America engaged in military action against Iraq after that country invaded Kuwait; and when Timothy McVeigh was sentenced to death for bombing the federal building in Oklahoma City. These examples are all supported based on the perception that the violence is justified; that the recipient got what was deserved.

The mundane instances of violence, such as child abuse or rape, that occur every day elicit justifications too. For example, hitting a child may be justified on the grounds that the child "needed to learn a lesson"; rape may be justified on the grounds that "she led him on." Attitudes of justification affect individual practice, organizational policy, and societal responses toward crime victims.

ATTITUDES TOWARD VICTIMS

Three trends or viewpoints have historically developed in criminology. These were originally statements about criminals, their behavior and motivation. Since the 1950s, however, these trends have also been applied to the behavior and motivation of victims.

CONSERVATIVE TREND

The first of these trends is the conservative trend. This perspective focuses on street crime and crime control through retribution and punishment (Wallace, 1998). Although today this trend supports victims' rights and services, it originally did not because it was suspicious of any societal change that would increase taxes and the need for more government programs. This perspective proposes that individuals should be self-sufficient and take care of their own needs and problems. This includes the task of protecting oneself from society's criminal element. When a person is victimized, this trend analyzes what the victim did that was inappropriate, faulty, or not intelligent, and then concludes that the victim needed to have been much more careful. An assumption is that victims only want retribution and nothing else, therefore, stiffer penalties and more prisons are the prescription for a safer society. The conservative trend finds any discussion of restitution or compensation to be suspect and peripheral because they are costly and do not directly protect society as a whole.

LIBERAL TREND

The liberal trend has a somewhat broader focus in that it looks at street crime, corporate crime, and government crime. This viewpoint permeated the rhetoric of the founders of the victims' movement in the early 1970s (Karmen, 1996). It proposes a major shift away from criminal rights. Victims should have "equal protection" under the law. Whatever rights the criminal has, the victims deserve at least the same. At first, this trend pushed for rights to be taken away from defendants; today, the predominant position is that the rights should be better balanced and that this can be accomplished by increasing the laws that are supportive of victims, such as the Victims of Crime Act, the Violence Against Women Act, and so forth. This trend is based upon the philosophical assumption that society has two major responsibilities toward the victim: (1) to provide a societal safety net in times of tragedy and crisis, and (2) to "make the victim whole" in all aspects. A democratic society that allows a maximum level of freedom has a responsibility to protect its tax-paying citizens when criminal acts result from this open environment. Restitution and compensation are deemed as two major ways in which society accomplishes these important responsibilities.

RADICAL/CRITICAL TREND

The third trend, the radical/critical trend, only wants to look at the "big picture." Although it looks closely at government and corporate crime, any focus on particular crime is too limited (Karmen, 1996). The real issues are the larger issues of racism, sexism, governmental corruption, poverty, economic policy, and so forth. This trend views the other two trends as far too limited in their scope, and therefore, inadequate in their solutions to assist victims. American bureaucracy in foreign countries and on American streets is very violent and does little to diminish crime in our society. In fact, the entire criminal justice system is biased toward the rich and powerful and is a tool to maintain control and perpetuate the status of the lower class. The system will do just enough for victims to temporarily appease them; it will not use its resources to make the victim whole until radical changes occur; the entire system may need to be destroyed and replaced by one created and controlled by victims themselves. Restitution, compensation, and most current laws are limited and designed for failure.

THEORETICAL FOUNDATIONS OF ATTITUDES

Why does Western society have such a long history of blaming victims for their victimization? Some of the answer comes from our Judeo-Christian roots, which states that bad things only happen to bad people, (i.e., sinners). This theology has continued despite the fact that the Old Testament book of Job clearly states that plagues are visited on a righteous person. In times past, this might have been an adequate explanation, but many in our society would not intellectually accept this religious view today, yet victim blaming continues to be pervasive. There are two major theories in social psychology that address this issue: The theory of cognitive dissonance, and attribution theory (Myers, 1996).

THEORY OF COGNITIVE DISSONANCE

The theory of cognitive dissonance addresses the process by which a person's attitudes and beliefs change over time (Myers, 1996). Although human beings view themselves as logical, our attitudes are usually more *psycho*logical—they make more emotional sense than cognitive sense. We are often unaware of the inconsistencies in our beliefs or values, but when we *do* become aware that we are maintaining two inconsistent (dissonant) beliefs (or a belief and the opposite behavior), we become very anxious because we feel a great need to be consistent in our lives. This anxiety creates much discomfort and a desire to reduce it. The easiest method to reduce this anxiety is not to change our behavior, but to convert one of the inconsistent beliefs into a consistent one. When a good person is victimized, an ugly inconsistency raises its head, so the uncomfortable dissonance is reduced by changing our belief about the person's goodness. Again, this is much easier than altering our daily behavior and checking on the specifics of the crime, the victim's situation, the criminal's motivation, and the environment surrounding the incident. Therefore, one reason for victim blaming is that it is a simple, quick means of dealing with many of the inconsistencies created when a crime occurs. Figure 3.1 presents a graphic depiction of the cognitive dissonance process.

ATTRIBUTION THEORY

Attribution theory is a theory of causation; it discusses how we determine the causes of events in our environment. This pertains to both events in our lives and the lives of others (Myers, 1996). We make decisions about causation very quickly to decrease our stress and anxiety. This theory states that these quick decisions are made due to two basic human needs. The first, noted above, is the need for consistency in our lives and in our environment—or at least the appearance of consistency. For humans, this is a psychological and a perceptual need. We see Christmas trees and the human face as symmetrical; we prefer balanced pictures and remember them more readily. The second need is the need for control over our environment. We have a very strong need to be the master of our ship, and it is important for others to be in control also; if

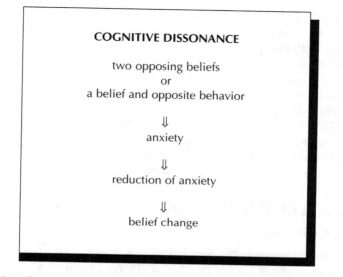

FIGURE 3.1   Process of cognitive dissonance.

others (victims) lack control, then it reflects poorly on us and potentially puts us at risk in the future.

These two very basic needs for consistency and control drive us to make two immediate decisions about events:

- Was this crime precipitated by internal or external causes?
- Was this crime due to a general or a specific cause?

Internal causes pertain to the psyche or the actions of the victim, that is, something they did to precipitate the crime. External causes have to do with issues outside of the victim in the environment; these are issues beyond their control. General causes are situations that are present much of the time, while specific causes pertain only to this crime and may only take place under certain specified conditions. Specific causes may often be easier to connect to the crime.

In making these two decisions quickly, attribution theory states that we often make a fundamental error and exhibit a self-serving bias. The fundamental error is that in judging the events in the lives of others, we always tend toward internal causation. In other words, whatever happens to others is caused by something they did. We more easily focus on them than their environment (external) because we are seldom aware of the precipitant environment or the resultant consequences. So it is a natural bias to blame others for what happens to them; this clearly pronounces that they are in control. On the other hand, we apply internal causation to ourselves only when we succeed; when we fail, we tend toward external causation ("The devil made me do it."). Therefore, we would blame ourselves less than others for being victimized. Figure 3.2 presents a graphic depiction of attribution theory.

In summary, in an attempt to make sense of senselessness (cognitive dissonance), people strive to find cause or reason (attribution). Cause may be attributed to some abnormality of the offender. Sense is restored if the insanity of a crime can be explained by an offender's insanity—illness or social depravity—thus setting the offender apart from the rest of society. Or cause may be attributed to society—declining moral values, declining educational standards, declining meaningful job opportunities. Or cause may be attributed to the victim.

VICTIM BLAMING VERSUS VICTIM DEFENDING

VICTIM BLAMING

The purpose of every bureaucratic institution in the criminal justice system is to place blame for the criminal incident. Criminologists in the first half of the twentieth century focused on the criminal, his or her background, biology, and environment. As the field of victimology began in the 1950s, Von Hentig, Mendlesohn, and Schafer began to focus on the victim's motivation. In the various crimes that they studied, they supposedly found numerous incidents of "shared responsibility" (Karmen, 1996). The early days of victimology were unfortunately noteworthy for blaming the victim for the criminal's behavior.

Karmen (1996) identified three types of shared responsibility: facilitation, precipitation, and provocation. With facilitation, the victim did something to increase the possibility of a crime, such as leaving their car unlocked or leaving a window open in their home. Precipitation meant that the victim did something to start the criminal process; a rape victim wore seductive clothing or verbally aroused the poor unsuspecting rapist. At other times, there was victim *provocation,* in which the wife or a drinking buddy said something or did something to make a situation instigated by the criminal worse. The result of all three types was that the victim was blamed for the crime, so no changes were demanded of basic American attitudes or of the criminal justice system.

Even though victim blaming has had a strong theological base in our culture that influenced the initial authors in victimology, its influence in American jurisprudence lasted just over 100 years. Prior to 1850, victims had control over many aspects of the criminal justice system. They often paid for the posse to catch the criminal and for the prosecutor to try the case when the circuit judge came to town. However, with the advent of elected district attorneys, victim rights diminished as an emphasis on public protection became preeminent. Between 1850 and 1970, victim blaming evolved from three assumptions and into three types of arguments.

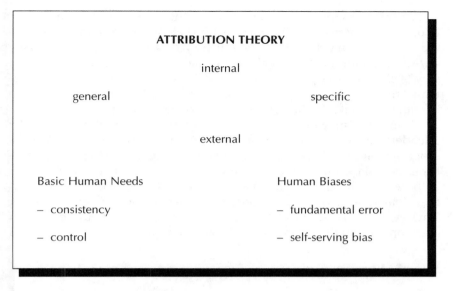

FIGURE 3.2   Process of attribution.

The victim-blaming perspective assumes that victims are different than nonvictims, just as criminology's basic assumption had always been that criminals differed from noncriminals. Various differences were discussed and researched—biological, psychological, and sociological. The second assumption was that whatever the difference was caused the problem, that is, the crime. Stupidity, naivete, inattention, hyperactivity, poor family, need for love, and so forth, caused the victim to place themselves in a bad situation—or worse yet, to precipitate the bad situation. These two assumptions accepted as truth led to the final conclusion that the victim must change whatever is wrong with them. Decreasing crime is in the hands of the victim—not the responsibility of the criminal (Karmen, 1996).

Four different groups espoused arguments that supported these victim blaming assumptions. First, the American conservative tradition supported a view of individualism that said that everyone has control over their lives and must be resourceful and self-sufficient. Victims must take full responsibility for altering their environment so they will not be victimized again.

Social science academics developed numerous theories, especially psychological theories, that focused on internal causation. The Freudian perspective saw victims as wanting to be punished or unconsciously searching for parental love. Most psychological perspectives placed the onus of change on the victim and often intimated that the victim was to blame. These theories were readily accepted by an American public that already tended towards victim blaming.

The third group to utilize and expand the victim blaming argument is offenders themselves. Besides using the concept of American individualism and much of the academic psychobabble, they utilize many self-serving arguments of their own: "she shouldn't have dressed that way," "she shouldn't have been so loose," "he acted like a country bumpkin," "they left their lights on and door unlocked," and so forth. Victim blaming fits well into the sociopathic reasoning of most offenders.

Victims, too, may blame themselves with the same arguments used by offenders. In an attempt to find a reason for the chaos—to explain the disorder in their world—victims question what they did that may have contributed to the crime. Under the influence of their own need to attribute, both victims and their loved ones are ripe to decide that the victim has been somehow unwittingly responsible for his or her own injury (Bard & Sangrey, 1986). These self-defeating would've-could've-should've type of questions add to the feelings of confusion and guilt.

VICTIM DEFENDING

Starting in the 1970s with the advent of the victims' movement, a new perspective began to permeate American society and the criminal justice system. Victim defending directly attacked the assumptions of victim blaming with the following major statements (Karmen, 1996):

- Victim facilitation occurs in very few crimes; victim blaming overstates the incidence of facilitation.
- Research indicates no differences between victims and non-victims. Biological, psychological, and sociological anomalies do not exist.
- Even if the first two victim blaming assumptions were true, victim change would be difficult. Many victims do not have the necessary psychological, social, or economic resources available to make major changes in their lives.

There is no shared responsibility for a criminal's actions. Almost all victim behavior is in reaction to this crisis event. Victim defending states that victims should never be blamed for their own victimization. However, as noted above, blame has to be placed somewhere. This need creates two types of victim defenders. The first type places the entire blame on the criminal with no exceptions. Despite his physical, psychological, or social problems, he must be held responsible for his actions. This type of victim defender might entertain subsequent punishment or punishment and treatment. The second type sees society as the problem; neither the victim nor the criminal are to blame. Society's socioeconomic structure needs to be changed, social programs need to be instituted to increase opportunities, and treatment needs to be provided to both the criminal and the victim.

Even though victim defending is predominant in society as seen in the increase in laws and state constitutional amendments supporting victim rights, victim blaming continues to persist in our values, beliefs, and social behavior.

THE ROLE OF PROFESSIONALS IN VICTIM BLAMING

LIMITS OF THE DISCIPLINE

Standard education and training for many professionals includes the use of statements that would suffice in most professional encounters but are inappropriate with victims in crisis situations. Until recently, most graduate education did not include in-depth information on trauma and crisis response. Even with this, little time is spent in these classes on the specific traumatic effects of violent crime. Therefore, when a professional is confronted with a crime victim for the first time in his or her career, there is often a basic insecurity that can lead to statements of trite and inadequate theories which create a second victimization. When these statements do not seem to work, the professional may withdraw and create an emotional distance, leaving the victim to believe, again, that something is wrong with him or her. These victims, who often do not return to this (inadequate) therapy, are then labeled as failures by the professional; this means that something is wrong with the client, and in the absence of direct feedback about their therapeutic responses, the professional will continue to respond in the same manner and blame more victims in the future.

Many of the basic theories in psychiatry and psychology have an abnormal focus, concentrating on explanations of aberrant behavior while inadequately surveying the range of normal reactions; therefore, the view of many professionals is limited to the unusual responses—often out of context or without being aware of the victim's context. These theories have often enhanced victim blaming as they have become more available to the American public through various types of media. Freudian theory states that victims are masochistic, self-destructive, wanting punishment, looking for father's/mother's love, and so forth. Humanism, while more positive overall, also espouses internal explanations: the victim was looking for love, self-actualization, or personal power or lacked assertion, self-esteem, or self-efficacy. The focus continues to be on how the victim needs to change—a basic assumption of victim blaming. Behaviorism has a broader focus which does include the environment (context), but its major prescription for change is new learning: assertion techniques, stress management techniques, self-defense, better decision-making, and so forth. Although there is no direct blaming of the victim, the implication is that the victim needs to change, not the criminal or the societal response. As can be noted in this discussion, the intent of these professional responses is usually not to blame and revictimize the victim, but the result of inadequate training, insecurity, faulty theoretical inferences, and overall societal biases leads to continued second victimization by many professionals.

PROFESSIONAL SURVIVAL

Most practitioners who work with victims entered the field, in part, because they wanted to make a difference. But it may often seem that a difference is not being made. A continuous flow of cases representing the darkest side of humanity is confronted daily. Professionals face their own sense of vulnerability—and dissonance—if they find they are like the people they serve. Professionals are used to being in control—to be a victim is not to be in control. Thus, professionals may blame victims out of a sense of professional survival.

PRESERVATION OF THE SOCIAL SYSTEM

An even more jaded view of victim blaming by professionals comes from the radical/critical trend. From this perspective, professionals are invested in victim blaming in order to maintain the status quo. Without a "sick" group of individuals, there is no need for treatment, no money to be made, and, therefore, no status. By maintaining a focus on victims and criminals, professionals assist the rich and powerful in avoiding the light of exposure. The real crimes in society are racism, sexism, poverty, and inadequate opportunities; professionals help the elite of our society divert the middle and lower classes from these real problems. Victim blaming has a great secondary gain for themselves and the rich. It is not inadvertent; it is very purposive.

Possibly a less conflictual view, professionals are employed in systems that may, through policy and resources, further victimize individuals and contribute to further problems for the victim. But the organization is where the professional spends a significant amount of time; it is a place of professional identity. What kind of dissonance is created if a significant social system is attacked as inadequate or unresponsive? By ignoring the victim blaming aspects of the organization, the focus is on the dysfunctional behaviors of the client; behaviors that may have contributed to their plight.

SUMMARY

There is little wonder that victims have struggled so for rights and services. We are a society that embraces violence while at the same time we fear the very thing we embrace. This fear causes us to find reason to explain the unexplainable.

Barriers to Services

4

Richard B. Ellis and Kristine J. Hart

Crime does not discriminate on the basis of age, race/ethnicity/culture, gender, religion, disability, sexual orientation, or socioeconomic status. Those in the victim assistance field work with victims who come from a wide variety of backgrounds and experiences. As such, practitioners must be able to interact effectively—to be culturally competent—with a diversity of persons in order to provide needed services. This chapter explores concepts of diversity with particular focus on the attitudinal, communication, and physical barriers often faced by crime victims.

UNDERSTANDING DIVERSITY

America could very well be described as a nation that was founded on the principles of diversity—and of violence. This is a nation that supports such tenets as freedom of religion, the concept of a melting pot or a big salad, and the declaration that all men are created equal. But it is also a nation built on the maltreatment of the vulnerable. Our history includes the invasion and displacement of the native population, the enslavement of Africans, and the internment of Asian-Americans. Women and children were once viewed as property, and the disabled and frail elderly were hidden away. America has made progress in dealing with its diversity and protecting the most vulnerable of its members, but we have yet to truly view all members as equal.

This inequality has been apparent not only in society in general, but also in the criminal justice system. While the victim assistance field has made "tremendous progress in securing fundamental justice and comprehensive services for all crime victims" (Turman, 1999), unidentified victims and underserved populations—sometimes known as the invisible victims of crime—are still prevalent. With the enactment of civil-rights legislation, the establishment of the victims' rights movement, and the organization of advocacy groups to give these populations a voice, it is likely that those in the victim assistance field will find themselves working with a diverse group of victims, if they do not already.

"How we interact . . . at any specific time arises from a synthesis of what is happening in the world within us, what is happening in the world around us and how we interpret events" (Miley, O'Melia, & DuBois, 1998, pp. 35–36). Following an ecological view that considers not only the content but also the context of one's experiences, it is imperative to examine the issues of victims who are members of diverse populations. Diversity is inclusive beyond race (including multiracial) and ethnicity. It includes people who differ from the white middle-class norm "who are socially different" (Pinderhuges, 1995, p. 132) such as people who are impoverished, physically or developmentally, or intellectually challenged, people who are gay, lesbian, bisexual, or transgendered, people who are migrant or refugees, or people who are obese, to name a few illustrative examples of diversity.

CULTURAL COMPETENCY

Inherent in this discussion and review of victims in diverse populations is the goal of developing culturally competent practice, interventions, and culturally sensitive community and institutional systems (Lum, 1999; Sattler, 1998; Miley et al., 1998). In this sense, culture refers to the values, norms and traditions of any group of a minority status.

What is cultural competency? Elements include:

- Making active attempts to understand the world view of a culturally different person without negative judgements or stereotyping the person as belonging within the confines of a certain group—variations *within* groups are greater than *between* groups.
- Being aware of one's own values, biases, and preconceived notions or assumptions but also those of the agencies or organizations whom one represents.
- Acquiring culturally relevant knowledge that includes not only specific information about culturally diverse groups but also the uniqueness of one's own experiences and attributes within the group.
- Gaining knowledge about the history of oppression and discrimination and an awareness of how such populations manage these social pressures.
- Developing, maintaining, and applying culturally sensitive and relevant responses in order to achieve a good fit between victim needs and systemic responses (Miley et al., 1998; Lum, 1999; Sattler, 1998).

In order to provide effective services to victims, it is essential that providers become competent in delivering service to people from all walks of life. Being aware of the characteristics of a culturally competent service provider is certainly a beginning; however, due to our own unique cultural values, there are barriers that exist in making the transition to effective work with those that are different from ourselves. These barriers can be divided into three areas: attitudinal, communication and physical.

ATTITUDINAL BARRIERS

Attitudinal barriers are probably the greatest single obstacle individuals from diverse populations face and refers not only to the attitudes that those in the victim assistance and criminal justice fields have about the victim, but the attitudes held by the victim about victim assistance personnel and the criminal justice system. Both sides of this barrier will be explored in this section.

One cause of attitudinal barriers is prejudice—"a positive or a negative attitude towards a person or group of people which is not based on objective facts" (Tucker-Ladd, 1999a). These false notions, or "myths" are "usually based on stereotypes . . . [or] on an emotional experience we have had with a similar person" (Tucker-Ladd, 1999a). Examples include such myths as "Domestic violence only affects younger women"; "People who work in the criminal justice system don't care about minority crime victims"; and "Individuals with disabilities who have been victimized do not make good witnesses in court." In addition to their own prejudices, service providers should also be aware of any prejudices that may be a part of the agency they represent. The bad news about prejudice is that everyone has some type of prejudice(s), the good news is that prejudice is learned and can therefore be unlearned (Tucker-Ladd, 1999b). For example, Nerenberg (1996) reports that many domestic violence programs could be accused of having ageist attitudes because of their lack of sensitivity to the special needs of older battered women (p. 11). She goes on to say, though, that in areas where programs have been designed to meet the needs of older battered women, stereotypes such as, older women are "less likely to take action to stop abuse than their younger counterparts," are being shattered (p. 11).

Another attitudinal barrier is fear. While fear is a common barrier that may affect all victims, for victims from diverse populations, the fear, many times, is that the agency that is supposed to help them in their time of need will set in motion a process that will result in unthinkable consequences. For example, a belief within the Latino community that "social-service agencies will discriminate against immigrants and report undocumented persons to the Immigration and Naturalization Service is pervasive" (Nerenberg, 1999a, p. 215). Other examples include elderly victims who fear that they may lose their independence (i.e., having others take control of their personal affairs and assets or being placed in a nursing care home) if they reveal a deficit in their ability to take care of themselves; and domestic violence victims with disabilities who fear they may risk losing their children to their abusive spouse (courts have been known to award custody to the abusive nondisabled spouse with the assumption that the children are better off there than with a parent with a disability) (Nerenberg, 1999b; Tyiska, 1998).

Fear may also result from the possibility that the victim may be targeted for retaliation or retribution if they seek help. This fear may be acute for some of the most vulnerable members of society (e.g., children, individuals with disabilities, the elderly) who may not be able to defend themselves or escape from the situation. Other victims may not find themselves threatened with physical violence, but exposure (e.g., an immigrant's illegal status or an individual's sexual orientation).

Distrust of the criminal justice system is another attitudinal barrier experienced by some victims of crime. Examples of this distrust include elderly crime victims, for whom there is a pervasive belief that the losses they experienced as a result of the crime will never be returned to them and that they will not be believed even if they do come forward; and many members of minority groups who find themselves "disproportionately represented in the criminal-justice system," and where negative perceptions of law enforcement can be particularly pronounced (Nerenberg, 1999a, 1999b).

The final attitudinal barriers that will be discussed here are socialization and lack of understanding. Attitudinal barriers based on socialization can take a number of forms. For example, women who were brought up to believe that divorce is not an option and therefore refuse to leave an abusive situation and cultures that believe that family issues should stay in the family. Individuals who provide services to victims from diverse populations should always be careful not to project their socialized traits onto those they serve. For example, many western cultures value direct eye contact when listening to another, but in Asian and Pacific Island cultures it is more respectful to deflect direct eye contact (NVAA, 1999a). This example also illustrates how easily misunderstandings may occur. Simply failing to understand something that is important to a victim (e.g., a cultural or religious practice, the hardship of having to travel a great distance to receive services, etc.) can cause a crime victim to turn their back on the services designed to help them.

There are three steps that can be taken in order to break down attitudinal barriers: education/exposure, networking, and outreach. To work effectively with crime victims from diverse populations, victim assistance personnel need to have a basic understanding about the populations they serve. One way to enhance knowledge and supplement education is actual exposure to various groups and cultures. Studies have shown that, in general, exposure makes groups more comfortable interacting with each other than if they remain segregated. For example, one study found that individuals serving together in integrated (African-American and Caucasian) military units liked each other better, than those serving in segregated units. Another study found that college students who had some previous contact with a physically disabled person were more at ease with their disabled peers when compared to those college students who had not had any previous contact (Amsel & Fichten, 1988; Tucker-Ladd, 1999b). In addition to having an understanding about other groups, victim service providers should also make sure that they have a good understanding of themselves, including addressing any prejudices they may have.

In reality, the extent to which service providers can educate themselves about all the important aspects of all the possible populations they might encounter in the victim assistance field is limited. It is therefore imperative that victim assistance agencies network with other agencies in the community in order to be able to obtain resources and information for the victims with whom they work. For example: local disability organizations may be able to provide sign language interpreters; a local area agency on aging may be able to help elderly victims by providing them with referrals suited to their particular needs; or a local ethnic or cultural organization may be able to assist with translating materials into different languages. Other helpful networking resources include counselors who are bilingual or sensitive to the needs of certain cultures/religions/ages/etc.; transportation services that provide accessible transportation alternatives; and assisted living and skilled nursing homes who might be willing/able to provide shelter services for individuals who have daily living or medical needs that regular shelters are not equipped to handle.

Outreach programs are the final way to help break down barriers and increase the likelihood that otherwise underserved populations will access services. There are an abundance of types of outreach programs that agencies can utilize, but in order to ensure that it is successful, there are several aspects that need to be considered. Benton (1999) describes six elements that are common to outreach campaigns that have been successful in reaching minority populations:

- Learn about the community's need.
- Work with formal and informal local resources.
- Focus on respect, dignity, and family.
- Develop outreach materials for the population.
- Prepare agencies for new inquiries.
- Provide follow up and evaluation (p. 58).

Learning about the community needs means taking the time and effort to understand how the target group defines and understands the criminal act being addressed. Working with local resources includes "linking with 'trusted' community leaders . . . , media services, and health and social service agencies" (Benton, 1999, p. 58). The use of nontraditional locations (e.g., beauty shops, meal programs, and pharmacies) and non-traditional means (e.g., utilizing gatekeepers such as postal workers who have frequent contact with certain populations such as homebound elderly) to disseminate information is also suggested. With regard to uti-lizing churches, this avenue is encouraged, but the author cautions against over reliance because of many churches' competing demands. "Without exception . . . programs must focus on how knowledge about a topic or service will strengthen families or increase independence" (Benton, 1999, pp. 58–59).

Brochures and materials should be easy to read, use images reflective of the target population, and contain words that convey respect and dig-nity. Moreover, outreach efforts should not just focus on written forms of communication but also use verbal methods such as music, discussions, and skits (Benton, 1999, p. 59).

One aspect that many agencies overlook when conducting an outreach program is to make sure that their staff is trained to handle inquiries from the population being targeted. If staff is not knowledgeable and sensitive about the needs of the target population, or if the agency is not prepared to handle an influx of inquires and therefore will become overwhelmed and unable to provide a timely response, the program will most likely fail. Finally, agencies should always evaluate their outreach services to ensure that the program is having the intended effect and that the infor-mation has actually reached the intended population (Benton, 1999).

Specific methods that have been found to be effective with diverse, underserved populations include the following: for populations where trust is an issue, "offering services to clients in settings that are familiar, accessible, and acceptable to them" is preferable (Nerenberg, 1999a, p. 219), as is having staff that reflect the make-up of the target group and who have on-going sustained contact with the population in order to gain famil-iarity and build trust (Nerenberg, 1999a); and in cases where the elderly are the target population, "one-on-one contact seems to be more effective than large scale public awareness campaigns" (Nerenberg, 1996, p. 14).

COMMUNICATION BARRIERS

Three skills are essential in helping persons from a culture different from one's own: communication, observation, and ethnic sensitivity. Commu-nication is important with all clients, but especially with someone from a different culture (Schulman, 1991). Communication can be divided into three aspects: (1) the spoken conversation (what is explicitly expressed in both verbal and nonverbal communication), (2) the helper's internal dialogue (what the helper is thinking), and (3) the client's internal dialogue (what the client is thinking). Thus, the internal dialogues of both the service provider and the client reflect both the cultural meaning and emotional issues (Schulman, 1991). Sometimes these internal dialogues become externalized through body language, incongruity of facial expression (frowning when relating to a supposedly pleasant event), racial or ethnic humor, or comments based on stereotyped physical, social, or other characteristics. Slips of the tongue can alter the meaning of what the service provider is saying and reveal associations, motivations, or beliefs the person feels but has been trying to conceal (Goldensen, 1984).

Communication also includes the toleration of silence while the client crystalizes his/her thoughts. The service provider can plan appropriate responses reflecting feelings or content to reassure the client that he/she is listening. Here it is important that the helper clarifies with the client that he/she comprehends the communication according to the characteristics of the clients culture (Pedersen, 1990).

Observation is another basic skill associated with communication. The service provider should develop significant flexibility to differentiate the cultural significance of both verbal and nonverbal cues. Does a client's smile mean anger? Joy? Displeasure? Is the client showing discomfort with the environment, with the interviewer? Is the client expressing psychological distress through body movements? Interpretation of the importance and meaning of these cues depends on ethnic sensitivity and knowledge of the client's cultural value system (Schulman, 1991).

Ethnic sensitivity emerges from the factors involved in the establishment of the client's ethnic identity (Schulman, 1991). Ruiz (1990) describes the stages of ethnic identity development as follows.

Experiences and Emotions

Negative parental messages concerning their ethnic identity or other traumatic events in school or the community may encourage the individual to disaffirm self-identity and self-worth.

Thoughts (Cognition)

The rejection of ethnic identification may be noted in individuals' efforts to assume characteristics of people in the dominant culture because they believe that only by assimilation can they escape the poverty and prejudice that has been evident in their ethnic group.

Consequences of Stages 1 and 2

Alienation from one's ethnic identity and refusal to practice customs may be the outcome of negative experiences and beliefs. Denial, dissociation, or identification with the dominant group are some of the defense mechanisms that may ensue.

Working Through the Ethnic Conflict

The service provider must have the skills to apply knowledge of ethnocultural assessment to discover the source of the identity conflicts from the clients' histories, attitudes, and distress about their ethnic origin. Ethnotherapy conducted by an empathetic service provider helps the client identify negative feelings about ethnic origin and promotes the integration of an ethnocultural self. This does not deny the reality of societal discrimination but reinforces methods of coping with and responding to potentially negative experiences.

Problem Resolution

The ideal resolution occurs with the development of an understanding about the reality of the social forces, the development of a satisfying ethnic, and the integration of the client into a network of support systems that encourage ethnic continuity. The success of these goals depends largely on the value system of the helper. These values should emphasize a positive acceptance of the worth and dignity of the client's ethnicity. In this way the counselor establishes an environment where the client feels valued and supported by the genuineness of the counselor (Schulman, 1991).

PHYSICAL BARRIERS

While attitudes may be the single greatest obstacle faced by crime victims from diverse populations, it should be noted that eliminating attitudinal barriers may not matter if the victims are unable to physically access the organization to receive services. As noted by the Cook County State's Attorney's Office (1994), "All the etiquette in the world does not achieve the equality people . . . deserve without equal access to the function and institutions of society. The priority must always exist to make any activity and facility fully accessible to all persons. Always consider the need for physical access" (p. 10). Physical access to services may be impeded by such things as architectural barriers, isolation, distance and lack of transportation.

Architectural barriers refer to anything in the way a building or facility is set up that might prevent it being accessible to all. Examples of architectural barriers include steps, narrow doorways, lack of signage with braille lettering, unreachable water fountains and telephones, etc. Individuals who may be affected by architectural barriers include individuals with disabilities and the elderly who may experience such things as mobility impairments including those caused by a congenital condition, a spinal cord injury, arthritis, muscular dystrophy, amputation, polio, or the muscle weakness sometimes experienced by individuals with HIV/AIDS; visual impairments; and hearing impairments. In addition to these populations, architectural barriers may also affect individuals who were injured during their victimization (e.g., an individual who requires the use of crutches because they sustained a broken leg from an assault) and child victims whose only option for obtaining services is to go to a facility designed for adults.

For individuals with disabilities, the Americans with Disabilities Act (ADA) of 1990 addresses the issue of accessibility of public entities, public accommodations and commercial facilities, including, but not limited to, police departments, courts, rape crisis centers and shelters. The basic requirement of the ADA with regard to accessibility is that an individual who meets the ADA's definition of having a disability cannot be denied or excluded from receiving services or taking part in a program because of the disability. A detailed discussion of the ADA's accessibility requirements is beyond the scope of this chapter, but the following questions should illustrate some of the accessibility issues that may need to be addressed:

- Is there a path of travel that does not require the use of stairs? Is the path of travel stable, firm, and slip resistant? Is the path at least 36 inches wide?
- Can all objects protruding into the path be detected by a person with a visual disability using a cane? (Note: In order to be detected using a cane, an object must be within 27 inches of the ground. Objects hanging or mounted overhead must be higher than 80 inches to provide clear head room. It is not necessary to remove objects that extend less than 4 inches from a wall.)
- Do curbs on the pathway have curb cuts at drives, parking, and drop-offs? Are the slopes of ramps no greater than 1:12 (for every 12 inches along the base of the ramp, the height increases no more than 1 inch)? Do all ramps longer than 6 feet have railings on both sides that are sturdy and between 34 and 38 inches high?
- Are there adequate accessible parking spaces? For example, cars require an 8-foot-wide plus 5-foot-striped access aisle. Lift-equipped vans require: 16 feet wide with 98 inches of vertical clearance. Are these spaces clearly marked?
- Is there an entrance door that does not have steps, is at least 32 inches wide and has a handle no higher than 48 inches that is operable with a closed fist? (Do not use a service entrance unless there is no other option.)

- Are doormats and carpets low-pile and secured to the floor at all edges?
- Do elevators have both visible and audible door opening/closing and floor indicators? Do the controls have raised and braille lettering? Are the call buttons no higher than 42 inches? Is the emergency intercom usable without voice communication?
- If public or pay phones are provided, is the highest operable part of the phone no higher that 48 inches? Is it hearing aid compatible/ have volume control? Is one of the phones equipped with a telecommunications device for the deaf?
- If a restroom is available to the public, is at least one fully accessible? (U.S. Department of Labor, n.d.).

In addition to the guidelines set forth in the ADA, agencies should utilize organizations in their communities that work with diverse populations (e.g., the local AARP or facilities that provide services to individuals with disabilities) to get feedback about their current level of accessibility and ways they could improve.

Nosek, Howland, and Young (as cited in Nosek & Howland, 1998) note that one area that still needs a vast amount of improvement with regard to accessibility barriers is women's shelters because "it is generally acknowledged that programs to assist abused women are often architecturally inaccessible, lack interpreter services for deaf women, and are not able to accommodate women who need assistance with daily self-care or medications" (p. 2). While this is still a major problem for disabled and elderly women who want to escape their abusive situations, one solution being tried in several cities is to work with the city's assisted living and skilled nursing facilities to provide emergency shelter to elderly victims with special needs (Nerenberg, 1999).

ISOLATION

Isolation refers to being separated from society. That separation can occur by physical means, such as institutionalization or an inaccessible or, in some cases, inescapable environment (e.g., a severely disabled child who almost never leaves their house); or by social means such as an elderly individual with no family or living friends who withdraws from the community, the individual whose language and culture keep them isolated, at times, even from their own families (e.g., the grandchildren of many immigrants who were raised in America do not speak their grandparents' language and thus may not join in their cultural beliefs), or the individual who is ostracized because of their physical appearance/HIV status/sexual orientation/and so forth; or from fear such as that experienced in an abusive relationship, in cases where discovery may mean deportation if the victim happens to be in the United States illegally, or where a mental illness has caused an individual to fear what lies beyond their front door. In cases where the individual has endured pervasive isolation and becomes the victim of a crime, they may be unaware of available services and resources, their legal rights, or, in cases where they have no reference as to what types of conduct are condemned by society, that they have even been a victim of a crime (Tyiska, 1998). Even in cases where the victim may be aware of these aspects of the criminal justice system, isolation as a result of being ostracized by the community in which they live can also hinder their accessibility to services since the service providers are generally members of the community. To break down the barriers isolation causes, those in the victim assistance field can utilize the same types of networking and outreach programs discussed under the attitudinal barriers section.

DISTANCE

Distance as a barrier to services generally affects crime victims who reside in rural areas. Since rural areas typically have very low populations, establishing even basic services for victims of crime presents a challenge. Response times for emergency and law enforcement personnel is longer than in urban areas; traveling to the nearest police station to make a report or to the courthouse for a trial may present a burden to the victim because of the distance they must travel and the time it takes to get there; and services such as counseling and shelters may be many miles and several communities from where the victim resides (NVAA, 1999b). While distance may play a factor for most rural crime victims, there are some instances where it may have an even more dramatic impact. For example, distance may be even more of a factor for American Indians who live on tribal land because of their participation in the federal justice system. It is not unheard of for an American Indian crime victim to have to travel hundreds of miles to reach the nearest agency or to exercise their right to participate in the criminal justice process. For rural victims of domestic violence, escaping their abusive relationship can mean not only traveling many miles to utilize the nearest shelter, but leaving behind any support system they might have and, in cases where there are children, having to take them out of school (NVAA, 1999b).

Remedying distance barriers for rural communities is not necessarily a clear cut issue. People who live in rural areas tend to know their neighbors. While this is generally a positive aspect of rural living, it works against establishing a shelter or counseling services in a rural community because it would not take long for the members of that community to realize which house was the shelter or who was utilizing counseling services, both of which could stigmatize the victim in their own community and/or put the victim at risk since the perpetrator would know where to find the victim. Obtaining funds to support such initiatives in each community is also probably unrealistic. Some of the most promising practices include setting up centrally located victim assistance agencies with 800 numbers, since many of the calls are likely to be long distance from many rural areas and providing outreach to the communities to educate the residents about the services that the agency offers. The piece that seems to make these programs most effective though, is their willingness to help victims with transportation issues, either by personally providing transportation to such things as doctor appointments, counseling services and court dates or by assisting the victim with financial compensation related to travel (NVAA, 1999b).

Transportation is an issue that affects a wide range of victims. For example: victims with disabilities may need accessible transportation; those with limited income or those who do not have access to a vehicle may need money to utilize public transportation; those who are unable to drive such as children or the elderly may need help arranging transportation; and as was previously mentioned, those who reside in rural areas many need assistance with transportation because of the distances they may have to travel to receive services or to access the criminal justice system. A point made regarding architectural barriers bears repeating here, the quality of services available for crime victims in an area are not going to matter if the victims they were designed to serve cannot access them. It is therefore important to inquire about the transportation needs of all victims in order to ensure they are receiving the services they deserve and are able to participate in the criminal justice process as they are entitled.

SPECIAL POPULATIONS

THE ELDERLY

There are a variety of obstacles that may prevent an elderly victim of crime from accessing services. These include: emotional and physical dependency on an abusive care giver; difficulty accessing the courts (e.g., individuals with memory impairments who have difficulty remembering the details of their case, frailties or disabling conditions that may prevent them from getting to court or testifying); fear of losing independence by others taking over their personal affairs or being placed in a nursing home because a personal deficit has been exposed; lack of information about victim services, especially for homebound or non-English speaking elderly; distrust of the criminal justice system, especially for elderly victims who are members of a minority group; and fear of retaliation because of a diminished ability to defend themselves (Nerenberg, 1999). It may also be the case, that the victim's cultural norms or age-related socialization inhibit their willingness to seek assistance. For example: an elderly woman in a domestic violence situation who was raised during an era when divorce was viewed as unacceptable and the thought of breaking up the family unthinkable; an African-American who lived during the enforcement of Jim Crow laws and saw young African-Americans beaten by police during the civil rights movement and is therefore distrustful of the criminal justice system; or an individual raised in a traditional Japanese home who endures elder abuse and does not seek assistance because there is a strong cultural norm against revealing "less than perfect" situations to outsiders (Nerenberg, 1996; Tomita, 1999).

For the most part, victim assistance programs have overlooked the elderly in their provision of advocacy and services despite the significant impact crime on the elderly. For example, few shelters are equipped to accommodate an elderly individual with special, age related needs. This is compounded by staff who have not been trained to work with individuals in this population (NVAA, 1999a). To meet the needs of elderly crime victims, there are several things that victim assistance organizations can do:

- Develop outreach programs that target the elderly. Nerenberg (1999) suggests utilizing churches, meal delivery programs and gatekeepers (individuals who have frequent contact with the elderly, for example, postal workers, merchants) in order to disseminate information to the elderly. The outreach should be age appropriate and culturally sensitive. Finally, all materials should be done in large print and, when appropriate, in a variety of languages.
- Engage in networking with various agencies that provide services to the elderly in order to help identify potential victims, to gain information for the program, and to have resources available for elderly victims.
- Train staff about issues pertaining to providing services to elderly victims.
- Make sure the environment is physically accessible because the older and individual becomes, the more likely they are to obtain an age-related disability.
- In cases where the individual has been financially victimized, explore victim compensation issues and restitution thoroughly in order to make sure that the victim is able to obtain necessities (e.g., medication, care giver services), that, if unable to obtain, would threaten the health, safety, and independence of the victim (Nerenberg, 1999).

CHILDREN

For children who are victims of crime, the accessibility issue may be raised when the environment in which they are receiving services was designed with adults in mind. For example, the furniture may be too big for the child to sit in comfortably, the rooms may seem drab, unfriendly and possibly frightening to a small child, etc. While this does not prevent the child from receiving services, it may affect the child's comfort level, making an already uncomfortable situation seem even worse. In areas where a children's advocacy center is available, all attempts should be made to utilize their services as they have been designed to be child friendly environments. In cases where this is not possible, having a room that has been specifically designed with the small child in mind should be provided.

Gay, Lesbian, BiSexual and Transgender

Researchers have identified homophobic attitudes among a significant percentage of helping professionals. These negative attitudes interfere with helper-client relationships and must be confronted. The social services field in general lacks an integrative approach to the issues of sexual orientation (Lasenza, 1989). Service providers must develop an awareness of their own negative socialization feelings, actions, and reactions toward people with differing sexual orientations. To begin with service providers can gain knowledge about gays and lesbians and the discriminatory practices they face in employment, child custody and visitation rights, and immigration and naturalization (Schulman, 1991).

Intervention strategies with homosexuals are similar to those used with heterosexuals with the additional complications that develop from the self blame of some homosexuals as well as the societal discrimination experienced by many. The development of a positive gay or lesbian identity, an acceptance of and satisfaction with one's sexual orientation, is important for psychological adjustment. This acceptance requires confrontation of the negative social attitudes associated with sexual orientation. It is important for the helper to be comfortable with this discussion.

A second issue to be discussed is that of discrimination experienced particularly in work or career. The helper must be sensitive to these issues as they will compound the experience of the victimization.

Third, the service provider must take into consideration race and ethnic issues. Victimization as a result of living in a homophobic society will be compounded when social class and racial issues are added. Geography and regional differences also affect gay culture and may affect the available resources and networking that can be done. Helpers must be knowledgeable about these issues.

An openly gay lifestyle in a heterosexist society can result in a feeling of isolation for gay and lesbian clients. The service provider must recognize the dangers of an isolated lifestyle particularly as it relates to victimization. Victims tend to isolate themselves out of a feeling of shame. The notion that gay and lesbian clients may have been isolated before the victimization only compounds the problem. The helper must offer support and encouragement to the gay client to develop a wide pattern of interaction with both gay and non gay individuals. Gay people need to affirm the validity of their lifestyles and relationships. Service providers must be aware of the special challenges and the strengths of gay/lesbian couples. They will need to be supportive and open to assisting gay/lesbian couples in this process.

The service provider may find these issues difficult to confront due his/her own biases. Openly communicating with the gay/lesbian client will facilitate not only the well being of the client but of the helper as well.

SUMMARY

All types of people are crime victims. Yet many of the programs and services available have been developed without consideration of differences, and these differences may make access to services difficult. Though not intended, many agencies have not addressed these differences and current policies and practices may even enhance barriers. Victim service agencies of all types are challenged to consider the array of barriers to services that may be present in the community and to be proactive in reducing these barriers so that all victims of crime, regardless of their differences, may have full and complete access for recovery.

The Psychological and Physiological Impact of Stress

5

Dan L. Petersen and Steven D. Walker

It is not what happens to us that matters, but how we perceive it.
—Hans Selye

Victim service providers see many different stress responses to the trauma of violent crime. These physiological, emotional, and social responses are normal reactions to abnormal events. Most often when the crisis subsides so do the stress responses and life goes on, possibly with some residual stress emerging on anniversaries and at other times, though there are times when the stress is so overwhelming that the individual is debilitated. It is essential for service providers to have an understanding of these responses to stress in the context of crime victimization and its impact on recovery.

Humans evolved over a half million or so years in the presence of two major threats to their existence: predators and other hominids (Leakey, 1994). Biological and psychological adaptations across the centuries was inevitable. Harnessing the physiological functions to maximize hyperaroused flight-or-fight responses increased survival. Unfortunately, those same biological functions, which increased the likelihood of survival in early human history, may have resulted in the last hundred years or so in more deleterious outcomes than positive ones. Running from a predatory cat is a pretty clear event. One is either successful or one becomes the cat's next meal. Humans living in a modern society can no longer attack or flee from most events that are perceived as harmful and the clarity of action to take is frequently missing.

Modern culture and society have made it extremely complicated and difficult to escape an abusing spouse or a sexually harassing boss. The biology that was adaptive for flight or fight now appears in many cases to result in a sympathetic nervous system activation that, without an active, intense physical response to convert and utilize the altered biochemistry, can result in harm. In today's world, the fight or flight mechanism, or stress response, is more likely to be triggered by psychological events (e.g., a bullying spouse, the frustrations of working with the criminal justice system, disruptions in life routines, intrusions by the media, etc.). There is no physical fight or flight from these evocative events and in a modern society the evocative events are both immediate and long-term (e.g., financial problems, divorce, litigation, etc.).

It can also be argued that modern man is faced with increasing demands on his/her time and resources. E. F. Schumacher (1973), in a comparative study of technology and culture, argued that as the technology in a society increases the amount of leisure time available to its citizens decreases. Certainly, the stressors of daily life in modern culture would seem to have multiplied over the last century. Traffic jams, commutes to work, pressure on the job, downsizing, keeping up with the Joneses, mortgage payments, car repair, children's college funds, pollution, stock market fluctuations, health insurance, digital phones, call waiting, internet access, e-mail, and so forth, add to the stress of daily living. The number of stressors faced on a daily basis by the average American only seems to be increasing with each passing decade. Of particular note the acts and potential threats of terrorism have dramatically increased the perceived level of threat for most Americans. Such a pervasive stressor within our culture is noticeable and many of its effects are measurable; however, it will take time to assess its full impact on our culture. On the up side, even with all the stressors facing each of us, the average person lives longer and better thanks to modern medicine and nutrition.

DEFINITIONS OF STRESS AND TRAUMA

Selye (1956), the father of modern endocrinology, believed that stress is always with us; it only ends when we die. From that biological perspective stress is any demand made on a person that causes a reaction either biologically or psychologically. From this perspective, not all stress is bad. In fact, some stress is needed to grow and become stronger. Working a puzzle or solving a problem is stressful but not overly so and eventually solving the puzzle or problem teaches new ways to do things. Amusement park rides are stressful but also exhilarating and enjoyable to many of people. A good physical workout is stressful but not overly so and most of us feel good afterwards and our bodies grow stronger.

Stress comes in two forms. One form, called *eustress,* or positive stress, is the result of changes in our environment that provokes us to change.

Putting a muscle under stress when exercising usually causes eustress and if done on a regular basis the muscle gets stronger. The same can be said of some forms of psychological stress where we adapt and become more tolerant.

The other form of stress is called distress or negative stress. Negative stress is often harmful. If too much stress is put on the muscle, the muscle fibers tear, and rather than a stronger muscle, the muscle is weakened. Psychological distress is similar in that it can result in an inability to cope with the world around us and if severe enough it can lead to psychological disorders such as depression and posttraumatic stress disorder (PTSD).

Stress is defined as an organism's total response to environmental demands or pressures. Stress is basically a general term that refers to any demand, either physical or psychological, that is outside the norm and that signals a disparity between what is optimal and what actually exists. That means that stress is part of life and it is normal and impossible to avoid. However, there are events that befall individuals that are intense and commonly recognized as stressful. Suffering a wound in a car accident is stress, and so is the loss of a job. They are not the same, and we respond differently in each situation, though some responses may overlap.

Trauma is the result of severe distress on an organism. If the stress is severe enough to produce noticeable damage, then trauma has occurred. One way of conceptualizing trauma is to picture an airplane wing that has a man standing on the tip of the wing. For a normal airplane wing the man's weight places stress on the wing without causing damage. The wing may bend slightly under the stress of the man's weight but it will spring back to its original position when the man moves off of it. However, put too much weight on the tip of the wing and the wing will break. That result is trauma. Trauma causes damage.

It should be noted that a particular stressor, an event that evokes a stress response, will not have the same effect on everyone. Viewing a particularly bad car accident on television may affect everyone who sees it. Some will forget about it within the hour unless reminded. However, for some individuals, viewing the car accident may affect their appetite and sleep patterns that same evening and for a few the scene may evoke enough fear to affect them for days and even weeks later. The variations in individual response to the same stimulus, or stressor, is likely a function of history, genetics, and current environment. For example, if one person had recently been in a nasty car accident, we would expect their reactions to watching the televised accident to be more stressful than someone who had not personally been in a real accident. Genetically, we know that some people present as more high strung or respond to visual stimuli more than do others. Also, it makes sense that someone riding in a car will respond with more stress than a person watching it from inside their home. We expect that watching the video while riding in a car is different from watching the video in the safety of their home.

Stressors can also be classified as either acute or chronic. For those stressors classified as acute, the primary factor is intensity. A single acute stressor such as the violent death of a loved one is likely to be very traumatic to most people. For those stressors classified as chronic, the principle factors are both intensity and duration. The longer and more intense the chronic stressor the more likely it is to cause severe harm to the individual. Duration of the stressor is a major factor in many victimizations. If enough stressors occur over a long enough time without a chance for the body or mind to adjust and recover, then distress and trauma can occur. Bodily functions and psychological systems will likely be damaged.

No two individuals will respond exactly the same to the same stressor. Even if both demonstrate that the stressor was traumatic, each will exhibit trauma in different ways for different lengths of time. Each person who is victimized by crime must be viewed as an individual who will have individual needs, weaknesses and strengths. An individual's appraisal of the stressor is critical to their psychosocial response (McCann & Pearlman, 1990). When an event does not fit with a person's psychological schema or fails to fall within the framework of their life experiences, the event is likely to be viewed as threatening or traumatic. How a person perceives an event matters greatly.

McCann and Pearlman (1990) outline seven core areas that can be disrupted by stressors. These are: frame of reference, safety, trust/dependency, independence, power, esteem and intimacy. Attacks on anyone or more of these core areas is hypothesized to attenuate or exacerbate the effects of victimization. For example, if a person is the victim of severe physical aggression, the core areas of safety, frame of reference, and esteem would be affected. However, if the perpetrator of the aggression is a loved one, the areas of safety, frame of reference, esteem, trust/dependency, and intimacy would be affected. Interestingly enough, abuse by a loved one is often thought to produce more problems for adjustment than abuse by a stranger.

In summary, trauma can be caused by a severe episode of stress or by stressors delivered over a long enough period of time in which there is no recovery sufficient to handle the strain placed on the individual. It should be noted that for someone who is experiencing trauma, even the most simple of stressors can evoke distress or strain. Events that were easily handled with no visibility of strain can, after a traumatic event, be more than a victim can handle. Victim assistance practitioners should not judge a victim's ability to handle stress based on their own capacity.

BIOLOGY OF STRESS AND TRAUMA

"The brain mediates threat with a set of predictable neurobiological, neuroendocrine, and neuropsychological responses" (Perry, Pollard, Blakley, Baker, & Vigilante, 1996).

A certain degree of stress is normal and a part of every living organism's life. Stress related disease, however, results from excessive and prolonged demands on an organism's coping resources. The presenting symptoms of stress can either be physical or psychological or both. In fact, there is no clear separation of the psychological from the physical. For every psychological activity there is a biological counterpart. Every stressor experienced psychologically by a person has a biological effect as well. Biology and psychology are inseparable. It is important to understand that what events we experience and how we experience those events affect our body, our mind, and ultimately our health. To understand how stress affects our health, a brief review of various stress related research on health is necessary.

Boscarino (1997) found that Vietnam veterans who developed PTSD in response to serious combat exhibited much higher rates of circulatory, digestive, musculoskeletal, nervous system, respiratory, and infectious diseases following military service than other Vietnam veterans who had little or no exposure to combat and did not develop symptoms of PTSD. While the study controlled for many factors associated with physical ills (ie., intelligence, race, income, alcohol and drug use, cigarette smoking, etc.), it did not control for genetic factors that may predispose individuals to develop PTSD or that combat vets may have been exposed to toxins related to combat that other noncombat vets were not subjected to. The important factor, however, is that stress plays a critical role in the development of a variety of health problems both immediate and long-term.

Drugs have been empirically demonstrated to produce durable changes in the neurological system by typically changing neurotransmitter release or more basically the biochemistry within the brain. Repeated administration of a drug can result in the body becoming more reactive to the presence of the drug over time. Sensitization is a biological adaptation well recognized and documented in the psychopharmacological literature. Sensitization occurs when equivalent effects are produced by decreasing amounts of a drug. In simple terms, it takes less drug to produce the same effects. Trauma is argued (Glaser et al., 1999; Luster, 1998; Sapolsky, 1996) to cause changes in the biology of a person's brain such that individual becomes more sensitive to similar events in the future. Future events similar to the original trauma event are argued to trigger behavioral and biological effects in a manner that resembles sensitization. Future events of a less traumatic nature may elicit the same or similar levels of reaction. When this happens, the reaction to the lesser event may be a result of sensitization.

For example, a child or an adult who has been traumatized may develop a sensitized hyperarousal or sensitized dissociative behavioral pattern. If the reaction is hyperarousal the child is poised to react to the slightest threat. If dissociative, the child may show a withdrawal or nonreactive pattern. Such a child may freeze when they feel anxious and refuse to acknowledge an adult's requests for compliance. In such situations the child may either be watching for a specific type of threat (hyperaroused) to the exclusion of everything else or withdrawing and unresponsive (dissociative) to the events occurring around them. Sometimes adults are quick to label these trauma induced behavioral response patterns as oppositional-defiant behavior (Perry, Pollard, Blakley, Baker, & Vigilante, 1996). The child is viewed as having problems with authority. In reality, their problem is trauma induced and as an example, a loud or harsh voice from an adult may be the trigger. In this case it is not oppositional-defiant type behavior but is the result of trauma and a sensitization to certain types of stressors. For example, as soon as something close to the trauma situation occurs, the child freezes and stops responding to the outer world or becomes hyper alert only to that which has been learned to be a threat. They are not being defiant, they are surviving.

It is here that the separation of biology from psychology becomes artificial. The neurobiology of the hyperarousal response has been linked to catecholamine, a brain chemical, which originates in the brainstem (Murberg, McFall, & Veither, 1990). Dissociative type responding has been linked to other neurobiological factors that appear to mimic those of a defeat response in animals (Henry, Stephens, & Ely, 1986; Heinsbroek, van Haaren, Feenstra, & Boon, 1991; Miczek, Thompson, & Tornatzky, 1990). Whatever is happening to the child in our example, it is both psychological and biological in nature.

In general, traumatic events tend to evoke the arousal in the cerebrum (the cerebrum is that section of the brain concerned with higher brain functions, processing of sensory information, and the initiation of movement) which triggers activity in the limbic system (section of brain responsible for emotions, motivation and to some degree memory). Almost immediately the hypothalamus, the section of the brain that regulates fighting, fleeing, feeding, and sexual desire, pituitary gland and adrenal gland release hormones to major systems of the body. These hormones include epinephrine, norepinephrine, and serotonin. The result is an increase in heart rate, blood pressure and blood flow to the muscles. Blood flow is also reduced to the gastrointestinal tract. The organism is charged and is more alert with the stimulation of glucose being released and increased oxygen intake. The organism is ready. Ready to either fight or flee the stressor. A marvelous mechanism for survival has been activated; unfortunately, in today's society we can rarely engage in the physical behaviors for which we are primed and ready.

It is common knowledge today that most stressors produce an effect upon the endocrine system. The endocrine system contains a number of chemical transmitters that are basically hormone producing cells. Hormones are chemical messengers secreted into the blood stream. Specifically, many researchers (Selye, 1956; Luster, 1998; Fischer, Calame, Dettling, Zeier, & Fanconi, 2000) believe that one of these chemicals, cortisol (naturally occurring brain chemical) may be the key to understanding many of the biological stress functions and the illnesses associated with it. Virtually any type of physical or mental stress results in the elevation of cortisol concentrations in the blood. While possibly the important factor in the biology of stress, other biological factors have been discovered that also play a role and any specific chemical has to be viewed as part of a very complex system. However, understanding the actual, rather than just the perceived, impact of stress has important health implications. High levels of cortisol provoked by stress have been linked with memory loss, damage to the hippocampus region in the brain, weakened immunity, and many other negative health consequences (Fischer et al., 2000; Sapolsky, 1996).

Cortisol is released from the adrenal gland and acts to aid in the release of needed calories from stored fat and protein. Cortisol also acts as an inflammatory agent, suppresses the immune function (Luster, 1998), and, it is believed, acts to reduce pain. All of this is extremely helpful in stimulating the body's resources in a fight or flight paradigm. Cortisol has been linked to glucocorticoid receptors in the brain whose concentration levels can be altered by stress. This is important since severe mood changes in the brain have been linked to glucocorticoid levels (Left, 1983; Wolkowitz, 1994). About half of all patients with depression have been estimated to have alterations in cortisol (Wolkowitz, 1994). It might be noted that the relationship of cortisol to estrogen may account for the higher rates (twice as high) of depression seen in women over men. Evidence is emerging that estrogen might not only increase cortisol secretion but also decrease cortisol's ability to shut down its own secretion. The result might be that when women experience high levels of stress in their life that their stress response is not only more pronounced but also longer-lasting in women than in men (Leibenluft, 1998).

How the mechanism exactly works is still unclear but it appears that raised cortisol levels can result in unwanted mood disorders and may, if raised for a long enough period of time, lead to the damage of neurones in the brain and impaired memory (Sapolsky, 1996). Bremmer, Randall, Scott, Bronen, Seibyl, Southwick, et al., (1995) found through magnetic resonance imaging (MRI) that the right hippocampal volume (size of brain structure) of Vietnam combat veterans experiencing PTSD was smaller than those of subjects matched for age, body size, sex, race, education, socioeconomic status, and years of alcohol/drug abuse. Deficits were also found in the PTSD subjects relative to short term memory. The study of Bremmer et al. (1995) correlates the nonhuman primate studies which suggest that cortisol and stress have neurotoxic effects on the hippocampus, a brain structure associated with memory and the ability to learn. More simplistically, high levels of stress appear to affect the brain's very structure in a way that makes it difficult to learn and remember.

Other studies (Herbert, 1995; Buster, 1993) have linked dehydroepiandrosterone (DHEA), a very important hormone that is produced by the adrenal glands in larger quantities than any other adrenal hormone, cortisol, and γ-aminobutyric acid (γABA), the number one inhibitory (i.e., calming) neurotransmitter in the brain to stress and disorders such as depression, cognitive impairments, eating disorders, and others. Both DHEA and γABA are commonly occurring biochemicals that support brain function. It is only when the levels are suppressed or significantly increased that problems appear.

On a more general level, serotonin appears to be activated by stress (Holmes, French, & Seckl, 1995). Serotonin is pervasive in the brain and alterations in the serotoninergic system of the brain have been linked to just about all mood and anxiety disorders. The most commonly prescribed antidepressant medications are designed to affect serotonin reuptake. The serotoninergic system is highly complicated but clearly linked to depression and other mood disorders (Deakin, 1991). While other biochemical substances have been linked to mood disorders, the clinical efficacy of serotonin reuptake inhibitors to significantly reduce the symptoms of mood disorders, suggests a possible strong link.

In a Japanese study, Katakami (1995) found that survivors of the great Hanshin-Awaji earthquake experienced significant increases in metabolic functioning (e.g., aspartate aminotransferase, alanine aminotransferase, and triglycerides changes) that have been linked to both heart and liver functioning. Researchers have been concerned for decades over the relationship between myocardial infarction (heat attacks) and stress (Wolf, 1976; James & Kleinbaum, 1976; Lown, DeSilva, Reich, & Murawskik, 1980). Recent studies continue to demonstrate the existence of a relationship between stress and cardiovascular disease (Fine, 1996; Leor, Poole, & Kloner, 1996; Schnall, Landsbergis, & Baker 1994). Stressors appear to indirectly influence myocardial infarction by affecting heart rate, blood pressure, and lipids in the blood stream. Leor et al. (1996) found that the emotional stress of an earthquake may have accounted for the cardiac arrest rates immediately following the Northridge earthquake.

The full extent of stress and trauma to affect an organism's functioning is only beginning to be understood. It is complex and pervasive affecting many neurologic, metabolic, and biochemical functions in the body. One highly interesting study by Vergano (1996) showed that assumptions based on standard testing was altered radically when stress entered the situation. Vergano studied Israeli soldiers serving in the Gulf War and examined an anomaly where a puzzling number of soldiers experienced adverse side effects to inoculations. The soldiers who were active in the war were given a drug, pyridostigmine, that attaches to nerves outside of the central nervous system. The same drug was given as an inoculation to a comparison soldier group not involved in war activities. The reactions of the two groups to the same drug were very different. The researchers also completed a comparative and highly controlled parallel animal study which yielded similar results to those of the soldiers. Those subjects under stress appeared to have a weakened blood brain barrier. Large amounts of the drug penetrated into the brains of the stressed soldiers as well as the stressed mice. Very few of the nonstressed subjects showed any brain penetration. The subjects under stress showed drug side effects that were not present in those who did not experience the same level of stress. A possible conclusion is that drugs and possibly other events can have different effects than those anticipated when they are given to people under high levels of stress.

Stress has also been demonstrated to reduce wound healing. Glaser (1999) found that psychological stress can have "measurable adverse consequences for key immunologic events at wound sites" (p. 453). Women in his study, who were under measurable stress, showed significantly lower levels of two proinflammatory cytokines important to early stages of wound healing. In the study, abrasions to the skin of subjects showed retarded healing when the subject was experiencing significant levels of stress.

In summary, a number of important factors in human biology appear to be impacted by stress and trauma. These factors are only beginning to be explored by researchers but they do play a role in the health of most people. As researchers learn more about the specific controlling biological factors it may be possible some day to intervene to mediate and lessen the effects of trauma and chronic stress. However, there is no question that stress and trauma can act to alter our health and biological functioning in ways that are adverse.

RISK OF PHYSICAL ILLNESS

Individuals exposed to traumatic events present with health inequalities (Power & Hertzman, 1997; Townsend, Davidson, & Whitehead, 1990; Marmot, Shipley, & Rose, 1984; McEwen, 1997) compared to peers. Read, Stern, Wolfe, and Ouimette (1977) found that a large percentage of women presenting for treatment for specialized health care reported increased rates of stress. They also found that a majority of women presenting at a women's health clinic reported a history of trauma. Of these women, 49% reported having been sexually harassed. In addition, for those women presenting for gynecological problems, more were likely to have been victims of sexual assault and were more likely to report a history of childhood sexual abuse. Trauma victims are disproportionate users of the health care system (Solomon & Davidson, 1997) and the consequences of trauma are enormously costly to victims, the health care system and society in general.

Some of the physical symptoms of stress include reduced immunity to infection leading to frequent colds, coughs, flu, glandular fever, etc.; chest pains and angina; high blood pressure; headaches and migraines; sweating; palpitations; trembling; hormonal problems (e.g., disturbed menstrual cycle, impotence, etc.); physical numbness in the extremities; irritable bowel syndrome; thyroid problems; skin irritations (e.g., eczema, athletes foot, urticaria, etc.); loss of appetite; and gastrointestinal disorders (Gentry, 1984). Even disease activity has been linked to stress. For example, stress has been shown to affect severity in such diseases as Multiple Sclerosis (Mohr, Goodkin, Bacchetti, Boudewyn, Huang, Marietta, Cheuk, & Dee, 2000) and to hasten the transition from HIV to AIDS symptomatology (Leserman, Jackson, Petitto, Golden, Silva, Perkins, Cai, Folds, & Evans, 1999). Kimmerling, Armistead, and Forehand (1999) investigated the relationship between HIV infection and victimization. They looked at 88 inner-city low income women who were HIV-infected. They compared this group to a group of demographically similar group of women who were not HIV-infected. Women in both groups were interviewed and assessed for victimization experiences (i.e., rape, physical assault, robbery/attack). Their results indicated the HIV-infected group were significantly more likely to report a victimization experience. The victim, within the HIV-infected group, reported higher levels of global psychological distress, depressive symptomatology, and greater distress regarding physical symptoms. The HIV-infected victims were diagnosed with higher rates of AIDS-defining conditions than were the HIV-infected nonvictims.

There appears to be a clear relationship between viral related diseases and stress. In a study of college students, Deinzer and Schuller (1998) were able to show that the common stress of academic examinations is sufficient to increase the likelihood of an upper respiratory tract viral cold by reducing salivary immunoglobulin A. Their study suggested that resistance to getting a cold is reduced significantly when we are under stress. In other studies, stress has been associated with viral latency in the herpes virus (Glaser, Kiecolt-Glaser, Speicher, & Holiday, 1985), the Epstein-Barr virus (Glaser, Pearson, & Jones, 1991), influenza vaccine (Kiecolt-Glaser, Glaser, Gravenstein, Malarkey, & Sheridan, 1996), antibody response to hepatitis B Vaccine (Jabaaij, Grosheide, Heijtink, Duivenvoorden, Ballieux, & Vingerhoets, 1993), and others. The exact nature of how stress affects the immune system is still being determined. However, stress is clearly a factor in the body's defense against disease pathogens. The psychosocial stressors that effect victims of violent crime will, in most cases, present a sufficient assault on the victim to potentially weaken the immune system's defense mechanisms. Victim service practitioners should not be surprised to discover that victims get sick a lot more than other people not under the same level of stress.

Stress has also been linked with cardiovascular disease and the risk of stroke and heart attack (Goldstein, 1995). Numerous studies have linked stress with both hypertension and cardiovascular disease (Lown, DeSilva, Reich, & Murawskik, 1980; Wolf, Grace, Bruhn, & Stout, 1976). Reducing stress and teaching coping skills to subjects under stress has been linked to reduced heart rate and blood pressure (Fontana & McLaughlin, 1998). Cancer has also been linked to stress in terms of the course of the disease. Cancer was found to progress much faster in individuals with a stressful emotional/cognitive state (Derogatis, Abeloff, & Melisaratos, 1979).

One final comment on physiological aspects of human stress relates to the ability of individuals to recognize their stress levels. Heightened levels of physiological stress functions may not be discernable by many individuals. In other words, it is very possible that victims of crime may not recognize or relate physical symptoms of stress to the stressor. It can be argued that awareness of a problem is necessary before someone will seek help or attempt to alter patterns of cognition or behavior. Failure to recognize and effectively deal with the problem is likely to exacerbate the consequences.

To summarize, victims of violent crime can be expected to exhibit higher rates of circulatory, digestive, musculoskeletal, nervous system, respiratory and infectious disease following a traumatic event than would their counterparts who had little or no exposure to violent crime. For those victims of violent crime who develop PTSD, the expectation is for much higher rates of physical illness (Linares, Groves, Greenberg, Bronfman, Augustyn, & Zuckerman, 1999). In addition, the literature has multiple examples where stress affects disease by increasing an organism's ability to acquire disease, by increasing the severity of the disease, or by influencing the course (ie., duration, stage acceleration, etc.) of the disease. For service providers in the field of victim services, this means that physical health should be monitored and appropriate referrals made to health care providers when signs or symptoms suggest a problem. If the victim service provider has a directive to support and reduce harm to the victim, then a clear extension of that objective is to at least monitor and educate victims that stress/trauma can result in health problems.

RISK OF MENTAL ILLNESS

For many victims, their reactions to a crime fall within a range of emotions and behaviors that are not deviant or aberrant given the situation. Their reactions, often intense and painful, undergo adaptation and gradually subside; but for some, further problems develop. This section will give an overview of the potential problems, while the next section will analyze the most common diagnosis for victims—PTSD—in depth. This section is meant to be a somewhat basic discussion of diagnostic categories. The major characteristics of each category will be discussed, and the types of disorders in each category will be described (*Diagnostic and Statistical Manual of Mental Disorders DSM IV*, 1994).

ADJUSTMENT DISORDERS

Adjustment disorders are characterized by a clearly identifiable crisis event that overwhelms the person's physical, psychological and/or social resources. The emotional reaction can be varied, ranging from symptoms of anxiety disorders to the extreme symptoms of a psychotic disorder. The key aspect is that this is a short-term disorder, 6 months or less, with the symptoms subsiding spontaneously, often once the crisis is over. One of the original crisis theories stated that these adjustment disorders often had four stages (Roberts, 1990):

- Stage 1: Fight/Flight. The person made the choice to use their resources to confront the challenge or to remove themselves from the danger.
- Stage II: Recoil/Turmoil. The person often was in a state of shock after expending their resources.
- Stage III: Adjustment. After a period of time, the person entered a stage where they seemed to get back to normal. Although the person at least went through the motions of daily living, he or she was still experiencing unexpressed negative emotions due to the trauma.
- Stage IV: Reconstruction. The person got on with his or her life and made the most of the resources that he or she had left. In the terminology of today's victims movement, the person progressed from being a victim to being a survivor.

This original type of crisis theory states that a person proceeds through the stages in an orderly fashion and that each stage was probably longer than the previous stage. There is much debate today about this theory, but it can be utilized to more clearly discuss adjustment disorders with some alterations: progression through the stages may take years and may never be completed. People, places, and events may trigger the cycle again, so the process of recovery is a multicyclical process, not a four-step linear one.

ANXIETY DISORDERS

In the past, anxiety disorders were called neuroses. These disorders are characterized by anxiety and by the behaviors which are designed to escape or avoid it. These mechanisms are only partially successful, and anxiety, in various forms, spills over into the person's life, disrupting their daily routines and personal relationships. Anxiety is a symptom that is found in almost all mental disorders but when it is the main symptom, then it's various patterns and presentations are identified in a separate category called anxiety disorders. There are a number of major types of anxiety disorders.

Individuals with these disorders exhibit anxiety directly in various ways. They may simply appear anxious much of the time and state that they are constantly uncomfortable and feel tense or anxious much of the time (generalized anxiety disorder). They may express great fear of specific objects, people, places or activities (specific phobia or social phobia). They may exhibit repetitive, unproductive activity, or their thinking is interrupted by repetitive (often negative) thoughts (obsessive-compulsive disorder). One type of anxiety disorder that repeats through the trauma literature is that of panic disorder. This disorder is characterized by unexpected panic attacks, often accompanied by intense fear and a sense of imminent danger. PTSD is one of the anxiety disorders and certainly the most researched disorder that relates to victimization (a detailed description of PTSD is provided later in this chapter).

SOMATOFORM DISORDERS

These are disorders in which the primary symptoms surround a physical ailment. For example, the primary symptoms may be pain, a fear of illness, sexual symptoms, gastrointestinal problems, deafness, or numbness or even a combination of many of these symptoms. The hallmark for these disorders is that there is no physical basis for explaining the problem. With conversion disorder or somatization disorder, physical symptoms (paralysis, blindness, deafness, etc.) that seem real to the person have no physiological basis and disappear under certain therapeutic conditions. With hypochondriasis, the person has minor symptoms that he or she imagines to be major diseases. It is the fear of having these diseases that defines hypochondriasis. With crime victims who develop somatoform disorders, there is usually some secondary gain, such as the avoidance of traumatic places or emotions related to a crime. None of the symptoms that define somatoform disorders are feigned or intentional. The symptoms cause the person significant distress or impairment in life functioning.

DISSOCIATIVE DISORDERS

Dissociative disorders often get the most press because they seem so unusual and dramatic. They include amnesia caused by psychological conflicts; individuals forget an event, their identity, their vocation, or some other significant personal factor. Dissociative fugue would also include one of the above and relocation; the person takes on a completely new identity and remembers nothing of their past. Finally, dissociative identity disorder, often referred to as multiple personality disorder, is a dissociative disorder in which the person has identities for each different emotional state or situation. This extreme, and very uncommon, disorder has been thought to be caused by a major physical trauma or sexual abuse in childhood. While some of the anxiety disorders may have symptoms of dissociation, these disorders exist separately because of the prominence, severity and duration of the symptoms. For example, following a major trauma a person may develop the symptoms of PTSD wherein after a month or more the victim may not remember important aspects of their history. PTSD is not a dissociative disorder though as in many other situations, some disorders share presenting symptoms.

MOOD DISORDERS

The major characteristic of these disorders is a disruption of the individual's normal mood or a disruption of the person's usual response to events in their environment. There are two major types of mood disorders: depressive disorder and bipolar disorders.

Depressive disorders involve a pattern of illness related to mood that is experienced as moderate to severe depressive episodes lasting months and even years. These include

- Dysthymic Disorder. Inactivity, listlessness, emotional and physical withdrawal, and negative cognitions of at least 2 years in duration.
- Major Depressive Disorder. Also includes the dysthymic symptoms, but the symptoms are more severe and include depressed mood or loss of interest or pleasure and may include the more extreme reactions of suicidal ideation and behavior.

Bipolar Disorder, also known as manic-depression, is a class of disorders that share the common feature of having either manic episodes (hyperactivity, intense elevated mood, grandiosity, etc.), or hypomanic (less severe or intense than mania). Nearly all individuals with bipolar disorder will experience some episodes of depression. The severity and duration of the highs and the lows tend to identify the particular type of disorder.

- Bipolar I Disorder. Requires at least one manic episode, although there may be a major depressive episode or other depressive symptoms.
- Bipolar II Disorder. Requires that the person experience a hypomanic episode along with a major depressive episode.

- Cyclothymia. Characterized by repeated mood swings that are not severe enough to be diagnosed as major depressive episodes or manic episodes.

These disorders usually indicate a predominance of one extreme behavior or the other with a few instances of the opposite behavior over a long period of time. Many victims may exhibit depression or dysthymia, while a few may be diagnosed with the bipolar type of disorders.

ALCOHOL AND DRUG ABUSE

Current research indicates that in some instances, the victims of violent crime often have twice the rate of alcohol abuse as the average population (Kilpatrick et al., 1992). Historically, four problematic drug groups have been discussed.

- Hallucinogens. Include marijuana, LSD, peyote, mescaline, PCP, and others; their major characteristic is that they alter one's perception of reality and may, at times, also create hallucinations. Except for marijuana, they are usually described as nonaddictive.
- Sedative-Analgesics (Opiates). These sedate the central nervous system and relieve pain. This group includes opium, morphine, heroin, codeine, demerol, and others. They are great pain relievers but are also very addictive. A major problem after high tolerance has been acquired is that the therapeutic dose is very close to the lethal dosage level.
- Stimulants. Increase the activity of the central nervous system, which increases physical activity and emotional reactivity. They include all three types of amphetamines, cocaine, nicotine, caffeine, and others. They are also very addictive, and due to their effect on the heart, even early usage can be lethal.
- Sedative-Hypnotics. These sedate the central nervous system and cause sleep. This group includes alcohol, the barbiturates, librium, valium, and many modern drugs usually referred to as minor tranquilizers or muscle relaxants. This is a group of mainly legal drugs that are very addictive but not usually deadly until after a long period of time—unless various drugs are combined, such as alcohol and valium. The major problem with this group of drugs that concerns our present discussion is that they often precipitate verbal and physical violence. Many crimes occur while individuals are under the influence of alcohol. On the other hand, victims who bathe their negative emotions in alcohol often verbally push others away who would otherwise be available to support them.

This section has been a short summary of the various psychological disorders that some victims can exhibit. When victim assistance practitioners are confronted with any of these, a referral to a mental health professional who has an understanding of victims and victimization, should be made immediately. The most common diagnosis related to victimization is PTSD.

POSTTRAUMATIC STRESS DISORDER

In the original DSM, there was a category called transient situational disturbances, which described temporary disorders that had very clear precipitants, usually a traumatic event. As previously noted, these are now called adjustment disorders.

For many years, these categories were the only ones deemed remotely appropriate for the victims of violent crime, but since a crime was not usually seen as a trauma or crisis, the court often would not accept these as legitimate diagnoses. While an official diagnosis did not exist for many years, there was research in two major areas that eventually led to one: research on victims and research on soldiers' reactions to war.

The major focus on psychological trauma began in the nineteenth century with a focus on a condition called hysteria, in which the person was seen as malingering and faking various types of maladies for some obvious or assumed gain. It was only applied to women, because it was literally translated as wandering uterus. Because it was not seen as a serious illness, it was not evaluated closely until a French neurologist, Jean-Martin Charcot, came to the conclusion that the symptoms of hysteria were psychological in nature. Using hypnosis, he demonstrated in lectures to the public and professionals that the paralyzed could walk and the blind could see. It is apparent today that many of his clients were the victims of violent crime who found refuge and relief in his clinic. His discoveries seemed to continue to indicate that these patients, while ill, were not seriously ill.

Two physicians who were intrigued by his findings, Janet and Sigmund Freud, wanted to go a step further in this study of hysteria and find its cause. Freud had been especially intrigued by the fact that one of Charcot's "cured" patients was a paralyzed man, so the earlier chauvinistic explanations about the female psyche and weaknesses were invalid, and a much broader explanation was needed. Freud and Janet came to similar conclusions almost simultaneously, but Freud stated a much bolder thesis written in a very dramatic style: hysteria was caused by traumatic events that were unbearable and were thus repressed in the unconscious. Since this repression was never completely successful, anxiety over the exposure of these events often seeped into the person's conscious life and created symptoms that had no physiological source.

Freud attempted to use hypnosis to alleviate these problems, but he was not very successful at it. He quickly discovered what he called talking therapy, in which the patient talked about whatever came to his/her mind. Freud found that the patients soon began talking about childhood sexual abuse and other traumas. He later called this new therapy "psychoanalysis." Due to these initial findings, Freud's first thesis (which he adhered to for about 3 years) was that hysteria's roots were in childhood sexual trauma. Because of the constraints of the Victorian society in which he lived, and because of his own personal values, Freud could not entertain this hypothesis very long and thus concluded that all hysterical reactions were rooted in childhood sexual fantasies about the family triangle of mother, father, and child. Despite his earlier experiences as a physician in a Viennese hospital emergency room, Freud could not believe that sexual perversion and abuse were so prevalent; therefore, his clients must be unconsciously lying to themselves by creating these major fantasies—usually about family members. By 1895, the scientific study of psychological trauma pertaining to victimization had ceased.

The other major arena in which trauma was studied was that of soldiers' responses to war. The earliest superficial discussion of war trauma was during the Civil War. Soldiers who could not deal with events in the war zone were seen as weak and having "no heart" for the battle; it was said that they suffered from soldier's heart. For the first time in this war, there was a new drug to manage pain that could be dispensed with a new invention called the hypodermic needle. Because of these two developments, many veterans with physical and psychological injuries returned with "soldier's disease" and addiction to morphine. No attempt was made to understand either one of these conditions.

Finally, both during and following World War I, there was an attempt to describe what came to be known as shell shock. This label was based on the belief that this reaction to the war zone was due to the concussive effects of exploding shells. Later it was evident that this condition could emerge in the absence of exploding ammunition, and therefore, must be the result of psychological trauma. The general belief throughout the war was that shell shock was a sign of inferiority, weakness, or, worse yet, was malingering. No studies were done, and with the end of the war, no further attention was given to the effects of trauma on the human psyche.

During World War II, this condition reemerged as battle fatigue. The relationship between the amount of exposure to the war zone and the subsequent demonstration of symptoms was clearly documented. Attempts were made to intervene by moving the soldier to the back lines for a short period. Although it is very questionable whether this intervention was successful, at least there was some attempt to respond without being judgmental. However, no objective studies were done on the psychological trauma caused by war.

During the Korean Conflict, there was a more concerted effort to remove soldiers from the front who were exhibiting a "transient situational disturbance." They were removed to MASH units and treated for longer periods of time by clinicians, who were involved in larger numbers than in any previous war.

However, the greatest increase in the understanding of psychological trauma occurred because of the Vietnam War. Clinical responses were more adequate and sophisticated during this conflict, but real change was precipitated by Vietnam veterans themselves who started "rap groups" and politically pushed for more research and treatment for the psychological trauma of war.

This research was soon combined with the research on victim syndromes. Crime victims of various types were being studied, leading to the discovery of similar reactions to other traumas. The first was Kempe's description of the child abuse syndrome in 1962. Later, in the 1970s, the rape trauma syndrome and the spousal abuse syndrome were identified and studied at length. This research gave more credibility to victim experiences in the scientific community, but the criminal justice system gave these unofficial descriptions little standing in the court process. All of this changed in 1987 when PTSD became an official diagnosis in the DSM of the American Psychiatric Association. It had been a period of almost 100 years, stretching from victims on Freud's psychoanalytic couch in Vienna to young soldiers shivering in rice paddies in Vietnam, but scientific clarity had finally opened the door for better treatment for the victims of violent crime as well as acceptance by the criminal justice system.

Diagnostic Criteria

PTSD is a response to a major traumatic event in which the person directly or indirectly experiences death or serious injury. This event arouses intense fear, helplessness, and/or horror. The following three sets of symptoms must exist continuously for at least a month (DSM-IV, 1994):

- Persistent Reexperiencing of the Trauma. Thoughts and feelings become cues that trigger flashbacks. Certain behaviors exhibited by others serve as reminders of the trauma. People, places, and things—anything remotely related to the crime—cause various recollections to emerge. Sleep provides no refuge because dreams can also recount the fearful events. The victim must exhibit one example of reexperiencing the trauma.
- Persistent Avoidance of Stimuli Related to the Trauma. Thoughts, feelings, and behaviors that directly or may remotely remind the victim of the crime are avoided, repressed or denied expression. Memories can be locked in the subconscious or deeply in the unconscious mind. People, places, and things that serve as reminders of

the crime are avoided—often through great effort. Because all life now seems very tenuous to the victim, another type of avoidance is the refusal to speak of and plan for the future; to assertively address future issues, one must first deal with the trauma's effect on their life. The victim must exhibit three examples of persistent avoidance of stimuli.

- Clear Evidence of Increased Arousal. The victim is unable to concentrate during the day or unable to sleep at night. They are often irritable and hypervigilant. They may exhibit a startle response to what seems to be minor stimuli. The victim must exhibit two examples of increased arousal.

Table 5.1 provides the specific diagnostic criteria for PTSD.

Many events can trigger PTSD symptoms. Many of them are related to how the criminal case unfolds in the criminal justice system. Having to identify objects, people, or items related to the crime, often many months later, can trigger a reaction. Legal issues and events invariably trigger strong emotional reactions. Anniversaries of the trauma or holidays near the date of the trauma can be cues also. All five senses can betray the person's sense of safety by picking up sounds, sights, and smells related to the crime. Finally, media stories about both similar and dissimilar (with a similar loss of control) crimes can create a PTSD reaction.

Of all the diagnoses noted above, crime victims are at greater risk to suffer from PTSD than any other malady. Current research (Kilpatrick & Saunders, 1997) indicate that 28% of all crime victims have PTSD, while 31% of all rape victims have these symptoms. High involvement with and exposure to the criminal justice system almost doubles the victim's chance of suffering from PTSD.

Negative psychological responses to victimization should be evaluated closely and taken seriously by practitioners. Since it is the most prevalent diagnosis, practitioners should be distinctly aware of the symptoms of PTSD.

TRAUMA AND STRESS RISK FACTORS

As indicated earlier in this chapter, stress in humans results from interactions between the person and their environment that are perceived as straining or exceed their adaptive capacities. Risk factors for distress or trauma are multifaceted. They are often a mix of personal, interpersonal, social and biological factors. Persons who are dependent on others or socially disadvantaged are at particular risk. Children, the elderly, and those with disabilities are often dependent upon others and may have fewer coping strategies and resources. The socially disadvantaged include

TABLE 5.1 *DSM IV* **Diagnostic Criteria for Posttraumatic Stress Disorder**

A. The person has been exposed to a traumatic event in which both the following were present:
   (1) the person experienced, witnessed, or was confronted with an event or events that involved actual or threatened death or serious injury, or a threat to the physical integrity of self or others
   (2) the person's response involved intense fear, helplessness, or horror.
B. The traumatic event is persistently experienced in one (or more) of the following ways:
   (1) recurrent and intrusive distressing recollections of the event, including images, thoughts, or perceptions
   (2) recurrent distressing dreams of the event
   (3) acting or feeling as if the traumatic were recurring (includes a sense of reliving the experience, illusions, hallucinations, and dissociative flashback episodes, including those that occur on awakening or when intoxicated)
   (4) intense psychological distress at exposure to internal or external cues that symbolize or resemble an aspect of the traumatic event
   (5) physiological reactivity on exposure to internal or external cues that symbolize or resemble an aspect of the traumatic event.
C. Persistent avoidance of stimuli associated with the trauma and numbing of general responsiveness (not present before the trauma), as indicated by three or more) of the following:
   (1) efforts to avoid thoughts, feelings, or conversations associated with the trauma
   (2) efforts to avoid activities, places, or people that arouse recollections of the trauma
   (3) inability to recall an important aspect of the trauma
   (4) markedly diminished interest or participation in significant activities
   (5) feeling of detachment or estrangement from others
   (6) restricted range of affect (unable to have loving feelings)
   (7) sense of foresighted future (e.g., does not expect to have a career, marriage, children or normal life span)
D. Persistent symptoms of increased arousal (not present before the trauma), as indicated by two (or more) of the following:
   (1) difficulty falling or staying asleep
   (2) irritability or outbursts of anger
   (3) difficulty concentrating
   (4) hypervigilance
   (5) exaggerated startle response
E. Duration of the disturbance is more than one month.
F. The disturbance causes clinically significant distress or impairment in social, occupational, or other important areas of functioning.

(APA, 1994)

individuals whose resources may be limited due to socioeconomic conditions or educational factors. Other risk factors include discrimination that may lower overall self-esteem and add additional stressors. These individuals may be at greater risk of developing stress related illnesses. Psychologically, these groups may have a greater feeling of helplessness, hopelessness, fear or anger, and distrust of others.

Any crime victim is at risk of health or psychological trauma. Practitioners must take this perspective with each victim. The hope is that the victim will have few and minor repercussions. The role of the victim assistant is to reduce stressors through education and guidance and direct assistance. While rates of trauma are high for crime victims, each client must be monitored for signs of serious mental and physical distress.

In particular, data (Mollica, Poole & Tor, 1998; Mollica, McInnes, Sarajlic, Lavelle, Sarjlic, & Massagli, 1999; Carlson & Rossser-Hogan, 1991) from victims of war related trauma (e.g., being in hiding, sniper fire, torture, refugee experiences) suggest a comparison that might be made to victims of violent crime. While the traumatic events are similar in many cases to violent crimes, the social/environmental conditions under which they take place is different. Again, how an individual perceives their circumstances is critical in terms of how stressors affect them either psychologically or physiologically. While it is difficult to generalize from one population to the other, some similarities are likely. The following indicators were found to predispose war refugees for either physical or psychological disorders:

- previous psychiatric symptoms
- previous trauma
- age (children and elderly)
- physical handicaps
- perceived health status
- education level
- socioeconomic level

Other studies have shown correlations with later development of PTSD or more severe symptoms of distress in PTSD also correlated with greater health risks and such factors as drug and alcohol abuse/dependence and child sexual and physical abuse. Linares et al. (1999) found that women who were protected under a restraining order (RO) experienced higher PTSD-related symptoms and poorer health than a non-RO control group. These women under an RO experienced higher current partner verbal aggression and physical aggression than their dyads. The effects of stressors associated with the RO in these sampled subjects appeared to suggest a cause for increased health related problems.

REDUCING AND PREVENTING TRAUMA

The longer the victim experiences stress, the greater the potential for harm both psychologically and biologically. A victim assistant must be concerned with reducing stressors and should be alert to signs of physical or emotional distress with any victim who is experiencing protracted stress.

Doctors should be made aware that the physical symptoms presented by a victim are possibly either the result of stress or are being exacerbated by stress. Treatments will vary depending on the etiology of the problem. While many healthcare officials may attempt to assess life stressors in relationship to common symptoms of anxiety, it is not clear that many or all will evaluate the role of stress in the variety of physical disorders that can manifest themselves in a person under severe stress. The practitioner may decide to take several courses of action, such as to prepare the victim to inform the doctor of the stress they have been under or provide/assist in writing down for the victim a brief written history of the stressor events and their possible relationship to the presenting symptoms.

There are numerous treatments to reduce stress and while a practitioner should be aware of the techniques and their theoretical and empirical basis, the primary concern is referral. Victim service providers should be aware that not all psychological or psychiatric interventions are equal in terms of effectiveness or efficiency. Also, not all therapists are equal even when they attempt to use the same interventions and operate from the same theoretical perspective. Careful consideration should be given to the professional qualifications, intervention approaches, and experience for those who receive referrals of persons victimized by crime.

Having cautioned the reader on referrals, there are some known treatment procedures that have been successful in the treatment of stress (Foa, 1997). These include prolonged exposure, covert modeling, controlled breathing, deep muscle relaxation, thought-stopping, cognitive restructuring, preparation for stressors, role playing, overt and covert desensitization, flooding, and others. Most successful techniques have derived from cognitive-behavioral treatment approaches. The term *stress inoculation* typically involves teaching clients a variety of these techniques.

Victims can be asked to rate his or her stress level on a regular basis and the practitioner can also observe for stress related signs and symptoms. While each person may manifest stress in different ways, changes in sleeping and eating patterns, and emotional reactivity are good indicators for many victims. If stress is not going down after a reasonable period of time (i.e., weeks), then counseling or an alternative treatment of the client's choosing should be recommended. Many people are afraid to seek help or feel unworthy to seek help for something they feel they should be able to deal with such as stress. The greater the level of distress presented by the victim, the more likely the victim is to develop stress related psychological and health problems of a significant level.

If a victim perceives an event as important, it is. Victim service providers should not be quick to dismiss the small things that may seem trivial but are of great importance to the victim. It is important to take the time to respond to a victim's needs. Sometimes it is the little things that make the difference.

If the victim presents as highly distressed, that victim is more likely to have greater health and psychological consequences. Victims that show low levels of distress are likely to be affected with fewer negative consequences to their health. However, victims who show no signs, whatsoever, of distress may be experiencing dissociation. If the person shows no emotion and appears uninterested in the victimization, the psychological risks to that person may be very great and a referral to a competent therapist should be provided.

Mezey, King, and MacClintock (1998) argued that most victims of violent crime fail to inform their personal or family doctors of the crime or assault. They found in their British study that while women were three times more likely to report any type of assault than men, women rarely reported the assault to their doctor unless the doctor prompted the information. Since the family or personal physician is likely to treat health factors associated with trauma that become manifest after the assault, providing the physician with knowledge of the assault is critical to effective treatment. Often victims will feel heightened levels of stress during the act of describing the traumatic event. Those stress responses are often coupled with emotions of shame, fear, and possible guilt. It is no wonder that victims avoid the retelling of their victimization. Still, they will be faced with demands by the criminal justice system and others to describe (often too many times in the days and weeks following the event) in detail their experience of the crime.

All of this can be helped by explaining to the victim the importance of retelling the episode to certain professionals including their personal physician. Informing the physician can also aid in early detection of both physical and psychological disorders, the provision of better health care treatment, and better allied support in making compensation claims. From a systems perspective, physicians need to be made aware of the prevalence of assault amongst patients so that some screening can be routinely administered. In the British study, Mezey et al. (1998) found that 17% of the patients of general practitioners had been victims of physical or sexual assault. Rates of assault in the U.S. are even higher, therefore warranting the need for physician awareness of a significant variable that may affect patient health. Even if physicians were to ask a few simple questions, earlier detection and better health care services could be provided.

Additionally, it is critical to inform the victim that while they may not experience severe stress in the telling of their victimization experience, many will. Explaining some of the other feelings and emotions that may accompany their victimization, including shame and guilt, can help the victim in their decision making. Hopefully, such preparation will increase the likelihood that victims who need counseling and other services will seek professional help.

Practitioners should be aware that studies (Harrison & Kinner, 1998; Thompson, Norris, & Ruback, 1998) have shown that the greater the trauma, the more likely the victim is to engage in avoidant coping type behaviors that may be detrimental to their health. The greater the distress, the more likely the victim will be unable to utilize coping behaviors they have used in the past with some success. Alcohol and drug use may also present problems for the person who has been victimized. Drugs or alcohol may appear to offer a way to blunt or reduce the existing stress and emotions associated with the victimization. Victim service providers should be careful to watch for signs of excessive drug and/or alcohol use. Numerous studies (McFarlane, 1998; Epstein, Saunders, Kilpatrick, & Resnick, 1998; Stewart, 1996; Ouimette, Wolfe, & Chrestman, 1996) have shown a relationship between trauma and alcohol abuse. Even prescription drugs that have been prescribed for stress/anxiety associated with the trauma can be abused.

While not all victims will suffer from long-term stress, many will react with clear stress responses to stressors that are unavoidable. Victim service providers should be aware of the triggering events that are a part of most crime victim's interaction with the criminal justice system. While the triggering events may be different for each person who has been victimized, the following are a few that are common for many:

- Identification of the assailant
- Media accounts of the crime (may include similar crimes in which the victim was not involved)
- Depositions by the defense attorney
- Hearings, trials, appeals
- Anniversaries of the event, the court decision, etc.
- Any sensory event connected with the crime
- Any time the crime event has to be retold

Preparation of the victim can be very helpful in terms of the stress reaction to the triggering events. Just knowing that triggering events can evoke almost the same fear reactions is helpful to the victim. Often, if the preparation is done correctly, it can reduce the stress reaction.

It is possible for persons who have been victimized to develop a dependency on the victim service provider. In the early stages following the trauma, reliance on the practitioner is to be expected. This may be particularly true for individuals who lack social supports. The victim assistant has knowledge and skills that are essential to helping the person who has been victimized. However, as time passes, the dependent nature of the relationship should change. In the early stages of work with persons who have been victimized, it is not possible to provide quality services and expect the victim to assess all of their needs and state their requests. However, such a situation can be viewed as a goal for the victim as they become more empowered.

ASSESSMENT OF STRESS

Recognizing the multifaceted impact that trauma may have on an individual, practitioners need to be able to assess the individual's functioning in various life areas. An assessment of an individual may reveal issues of concern, but an assessment of stress response is in comparison to the pretrauma functioning. Any previous mental health history should be known to assist the person who has been victimized. Prior histories of mood or anxiety related disorders increase the person's risk of future occurrences of the disorder. Also, previous trauma or victimization should be identified. Studies have shown a high correlation for both physical and mental illnesses related to previous victimizations (Mollica, Poole, & Tor, 1999). If the person has a previous history of victimization, the practitioner should explore with them or the significant others how the person coped with the earlier problems associated with the traumatic event. These coping skills may be modified to help deal with the current victimization. They should also be asked about any medical problems either associated with the previous trauma or that took place following the trauma. A negative outcome from the previous trauma may suggest early intervention and a need for counseling/monitoring by health care professionals. Studies (Koss, 1991; Freedy, Kilpatrick, & Resnick, 1993; Freedy & Kilpatrick, 1994; Orwin, Maranda, & Brady, 2001) have shown that prior victimization of rape victims predicted longer recovery times.

There are many typologies and systems to evaluate a victim's response to stress. Stamm (1966) developed the Stressful Life Experiences Screening form, which can be given either verbally to the client or the client can fill it out. In 1984, Slaikeu developed a profile that encompasses all aspects of the person's life (Andrews, 1992). This Behavior, Affect, Somatic, Interpersonal, and Cognition (BASIC) Profile is useful in that it is comprehensive but easy to understand. It also can be applied to the victim's experience very readily. At issue for the practitioner is when to respond directly and when to make a referral. The sign of a good professional is to be well trained with a breadth of skills and to know the limits of those skills which indicate the need to make a referral. Each letter of the BASIC Profile stands for a different aspect of the victim's existence.

Behavior

The first area to be evaluated is the victim's current behavior. Again, with most victims, there will be few problems indicated by an analysis using this BASIC Profile. The primary question to determine is whether the victim is exhibiting extreme behaviors, based on what is normal for the individual. Simple behaviors that can be noted include motor agitation (they cannot keep still), reduction in normal hygiene, or failure to dress appropriately (i.e., shirt buttoned wrong, wrinkled or dirty clothes, mismatched clothing items, etc.). Other behaviors include lack of activity—do they appear to be listless, inactive and depressed? Or are they overly active, or even manic, well beyond normal activity? The first person may have great difficulty coming to a victim assistance professional's office, while the second person will find a short meeting with the same agonizing.

Victims should be asked about their routines of daily living. Common living routines provide people with a comfort and flow. If the person's life becomes disorganized, the common small stressors of life can start to add to the distress. Routines provide comfort and often help distract from the emotional turmoil brought about by the victimization. The lack or loss of control of one's physical environment is often considered a risk factor (Frey, 1999).

A victim or family may identify that the person is behaving in a manner that is unusual for them. Behaviors may appear normal to the practitioner, but the victim may express great distress over some aspect of their behavior or activity level. In this situation, a referral for further evaluation is appropriate.

Affect

Victimization creates many negative responses that are normal: anger, rage, anxiety, fear, depression, guilt, and so forth. While it is not unusual for these emotions to persist for a period of time, they usually subside in intensity. When this does not happen, and the emotions escalate in the absence of second victimization, a referral needs to be made. This may indicate complicating unseen factors or a history of multiple traumatization. Labile mood swings (i.e., shifts in mood from happy to sad) or affect that is inconsistent with the topic (i.e., laughing while talking about how horrible the trauma was) may be another indicator of problems. While it is possible for any victim to have these feelings and express them, when a victim continues to manifest these emotions across days and weeks, the risk of stress-related illnesses increase (Frey, 1999), as does problems with relationships and overall functioning.

As with the behavioral evaluation, if the victim or their family indicate emotional responses that are unusual for the victim, further questions need to be asked. This unusual emotional response may not necessarily be volatile, but it may be a very uncomfortable emotion for the victim— one which they are having difficulty dealing with.

Somatic

As has been discussed at length earlier in the chapter, victims can have numerous physical or somatic responses to the stress of victimization. When the emotional strain of the trauma is intense or occurs over a period of days or weeks, the risk of stress-related illnesses increase (Frey, 1999). At times, these conditions can become chronic and require medical attention. The physical problem created by stress will vary from person to person. Victimization can disrupt any of the body's systems. Common physiological symptoms easily observable include excessive perspiration for the environmental conditions and shakiness.

Because of society's implicit messages that people should get well quickly and because of their own need to regain control over their lives, victims may minimize an illness and not seek medical assistance. In addition to general questions about health, inquiries about sleep and eating patterns may give clues to overall health. The less disrupted these become the healthier the person is likely to stay. The practitioner's supportive encouragement can overcome concerns about health and help them obtain appropriate medical care.

Interpersonal

Interpersonal problems at home and work and in friendships can be created by victimization. Some major concerns can be addressed which relate to stress by asking the person about their relationship to family members, friends, and coworkers. Isolation and a lack of social support can exasperate the potential for mental and physical health problems. On occasion, a person who has been victimized will push friends away without intending to do so. Victims lose many things through criminal acts, but the greatest psychological loss is diminished trust in others and in the world's order. The basis of any relationship is trust, and when it is absent, the relationship is very tenuous. For many victims, this does not just effect one relationship, but it effects all relationships.

Some research indicates that half of all rape victims have major relationship problems in the year following their victimization (Kilpatrick et al., 1992). Reactions toward supervisors and coworkers can create strained relationships at work. A loss of confidence can make a previously assertive person very passive and unable to fend off incidents of revictimization at the hands of friends, family members, co-workers, professionals, etc. Depending on the situation, a referral may need to be made for individual, couples, or family therapy in order to adequately assist the victim in dealing with these interpersonal problems.

Cognition

This final area refers to the person's thinking. In the 1960s, an American psychologist, Albert Ellis, proposed a theory of therapeutic intervention that focused on common irrational thoughts. He considered these a sign of mental illness, but for the victims of violent crime, they are common thoughts: "I am useless," "I am worthless," "I can't do anything," "I should have . . . ," "It was my fault," and so on. An entire series of negative, self-accusatory thoughts can plague a victim's waking hours for weeks and months. If after a period of time with the supportive input of the victim advocate (and hopefully others) there is no decrease in these cognitions, a referral would be appropriate. In addition to verbalized messages that are self-deprecating or negative, a common indicator of cognitive problems is the failure to track with the conversation by either derailing or tuning out.

SECONDARY VICTIMS

In an insightful study, Sprang (1999) found that many of secondary victims of the Oklahoma bombing who presented postdisaster symptoms, including PTSD, failed to seek mental health services even though in many cases referrals were made by a crisis worker. Many of these individuals expressed embarrassment over their reactions or made comments about feeling guilty asking for help. Examples of comments were, "I feel guilty asking for help when so many others probably need it worse," and "I have been surprised by my reaction." "I should feel lucky but I don't." "I never say anything to anyone about my feelings because I am afraid they would think I was silly." "I didn't lose anyone in the bombing." Secondary victims—individuals indirectly exposed to traumatic events including violent crime—"may not access services based on their perceptions of their own worthiness" (Sprang, 1999).

This suggests that practitioners should be aware of the impact of victimization on family and friends of the person who has been victimized. A brief assessment of how family members are doing can be informative and useful information for assessing the support of significant others to the primary victim. Their level of distress may add to the distress being experienced by the primary victim. Very few, if any individuals, live in complete isolation. Understanding the effects of trauma on significant others in the victim's life may be critical in the provision of effective services. A broader argument could be made that victim service providers should be serving the larger circle of potentially distressed individuals radiating out from the primary victim. From an ecological perspective and one of prevention, services to any victim of crime either primary or secondary is paramount to the health of our society.

Trauma and the Crime Victim

6

Dan L. Petersen

Aknowledge of crisis responding and the potential resulting trauma experienced by a victim of crime is considered by many to be central to the provision of victim services. This chapter is designed to increase the reader's understanding of crisis responding and traumatic stress. The chapter will focus on basic guidelines for interacting with crisis survivors in the immediate and protracted period of time following victimization. It also will identify basic interventions such as protective assessments and victim monitoring. Because of the impact of violence on caregivers, attention is given to vicarious traumatization and issues affecting trauma counselors and therapists.

In a previous chapter, the general effects of stress and trauma were discussed as it affects both the psychological and physiological status of a victim. For a greater understanding of this chapter, the reader is referred to that section of the text. This chapter includes both crisis intervention as well as a more protracted approach to working with victims who are experiencing the negative consequences of trauma.

Hans Selye (1956) is reported to have said that it is not so much what happens to us as how we perceive it that matters. For the most part, Selye was referring to the daily stresses and crises that most of us face in our lives. However, even Selye would likely agree that if the stressors are intense enough, they can disrupt just about anyone's life to the point of distress, if not traumatization. Trauma results as stressors build or the stress is endured long enough that an individual's coping mechanisms are not longer sufficient to protect body and mind. At the point of trauma, some damage has been done. The greater the stressors and the longer they continue to act on an individual, the more likely damage will increase.

Selye and many others contributed to the development of stress theory and its physiological and psychological constructs. Basically, stress theory suggests that individuals exist in a state of equilibrium. Occasionally, this state of balance is upset by stressors and in most situations individuals are able to reestablish equilibrium. However, stressors so traumatic can occur and throw the individual so far out of balance that the individual must struggle usually over time and with immense effort to reclaim some sense of balance.

A parallel theory, referred to as Crisis Theory, also accounts for the disequilibrium experienced by individuals who encounter traumatic events. According to Roberts (2000, p. 7), the term crisis is defined as "a period of psychological disequilibrium experienced as a result of a hazardous event or situation that constitutes a significant problem that cannot be remedied by using familiar coping strategies." If the individual experiences negative outcomes, then trauma has occurred. If the individual is able to quickly reestablish equilibrium through existing coping behaviors, then trauma has not occurred. Crisis theory is behaviorally or psychologically oriented and typically is focused on interventions to prevent or reduce the harm resulting from crisis situations.

Still, Selye was correct in that under the same stressors different individuals will show a variety of reactions. The extent to which a crisis situation is experienced as a traumatic depends on how the person perceives it; the same crisis event for one person may not be experienced as a crisis by someone else (Roberts & Dziegieliwski, 1995). Some will survive the events with little or no long-term deleterious or harmful effects. No trauma will occur. Some will show severe reactions that are both psychologically and physiologically debilitating and where full recovery is at best difficult. In those cases, trauma will be severe. Still others will present with mild to moderate symptoms. If you work with victims, you must realize that no two individuals of the same crime will behave the same. They each have different histories that they bring to bear on the crises they face. They each have learned to cope in different ways with life stressors. They each have different supports in their lives that they can turn to for understanding and support. That is not to imply to the victim assistant that patterns do not exist and that similarities will not be found. Just do not expect everyone to behave in the same manner to the same stressors or type of victimization.

WHAT IS TRAUMA?

When we use the word *trauma*, we are typically referring to damage done to the bio-psycho-social world of the individual as the result of a stressor or stressors. Trauma in an individual can be manifested by physical and psychological symptoms as well as a break down in their relationship with significant others. Physical symptoms of trauma can range from headaches to coronary heart disease. Psychological symptoms of trauma can include such things as anxiety disorders, depression, and posttraumatic stress disorder. Social symptoms of trauma range from a break down in normal ways of relating to isolation from loved ones, divorce, and even hostility and aggression. While separating psychological symptoms from social symptoms is arbitrary, it is important to view not only the individual but also the family, work, and community relationships of the survivor.

Events that result in trauma fracture and shatter the very basic assumptions the victim has about themselves and the world around them. Each of us exists in a world of our making in which we attempt to bring order and meaning to our actions, the actions of those around us and the physical world we inhabit.

We each develop theories about how the world works. For example, I may trust that most people are friendly and act in benign ways. I may expect more good things to happen than bad. I never expect someone to steal my car, or sexually assault me, or kill someone I love. We know these things happen, but most of us assume they will never happen to us. Good things happen to good people. As individuals we rarely think about these assumptions but our actions give proof to their existence. We get up each morning and drive to work or school expecting good things to happen or at worst to encounter minor irritants. We do not wake up each morning into a malevolent world expecting harm and danger to us and our loved ones. If we did, we might never leave the house. When someone becomes a victim of violent crime, the trauma can result in all of their assumptions being shattered and destroyed. The world is no longer safe and bad things do happen to good people. It is often not just a recovery from the specific acts of a violent crime but a recovery that involves a reorganization and understanding of ourselves and the world around us. In any event, the world is no longer a safe place for those who have been victims of violent crime.

OPERANT AND CLASSICAL CONDITIONING

To understand traumatic behavior or crisis responding, it is helpful to view the survivor's behavior from the perspective of a social learning theory. Two models of learning that have relevance are the classical conditioning and operant conditioning models.

In classical conditioning, neutral stimuli are paired with stimuli (unconditioned) that produce a specific response. An unconditioned stimulus is any stimulus or event that produces an autonomic response. The classic example is that of food eliciting a salivation response when presented to dog. As soon as the dog sees the food, it begins to secrete fluids in the mouth designed to facilitate the process of eating and digestion. The sight of food is an unconditioned stimulus. The salivation is an unconditioned response to the sight of food. However, in classical experiments, a sound paired (neutral stimulus) with food (unconditioned stimulus) would after pairing acquire a similar ability to elicit salivation in the dog. What is important is the pairing of these two types of stimuli. Over time, the behavior elicited by the unconditioned stimulus will be triggered or occasioned by the neutral stimulus. As you will see, this helps explain why certain events or stimuli present at the time of a violent crime will later evoke fear reactions from the victim.

The autonomic responses associated with fear can come to be elicited by neutral stimuli that were present when the fear was evoked. For example, a smell or a sound that was present during a sexual assault can later evoke feelings of fear and other emotional/physiological responses present at the time of the assault. This conditioning can theoretically occur with any kind of stimulation from sounds, people, words, things and even ideas. Anything that is seen, heard, or felt at the time of the attack could, through a one-time pairing, evoke almost all the emotional and physiological responses produced by the attack itself.

The sound of a dog barking, if present at the time of the attack, will, days later, evoke a fear reaction when the victim hears barking. A survivor of a drunk driving incident panics at the sight of the red interior of a friend's car. The car she had been riding in when the accident occurred had a red interior. One survivor of a murder/hostage situation recalls taking a walk with her husband years after the victimization. As they walked through a wooded area, she all of a sudden felt afraid and panicked. Later, she remembered that it was in a very similar but distant location that she had run from the killer through a woods to safety. The walk in the woods had evoked similar reactions to the fear she had when she escaped from her abductor years before. While she and her husband often took walks this was the first time since the abduction that she had been walking in a nonurban setting.

While classical conditioning gives us insight into the mechanism under which neutral stimuli come to evoke fear responses, it is operant conditioning that gives us an understanding of the avoidance and escape behaviors victims acquire to protect themselves. Operant behavior is learned and escape or avoidance responses are described as examples of negative reinforcement. Basically, what that means is that as the person operates (omitted behavior) on their environment, responses that eliminate or reduce aversive events will strengthen and be more likely to repeat. For example, if a person has a headache and takes a pain medication and the pain goes away, they would be more likely to take that pain medication under similar headache conditions in the future. Taking the pill resulted in the headache going away. Taking the pill was reinforced by the reduction of the aversive event, the headache.

Some escape behaviors may be hardwired into our genetic structures. The fight or flight response is an example that was talked about in an earlier chapter. Other escape behaviors are learned. The difference between escape and avoidance is whether the aversive event is present at the time the person engages in some behavior to get away from it. For example, if there is a loud or irritating noise and I learn that pushing a green button turns it off while pushing a red button makes it louder, I quickly learn to push the green button. That is escape. The noxious noise is present at the time I respond to make it go away.

However, in this same situation, I discover that just prior to the very loud noise coming on, the green button is illuminated by an internal light. I also learn that if I push the green button when the light comes on, then the noise never occurs. I have learned to avoid the noise by pressing the green button when it is illuminated. This is a discriminated avoidance response. These types or response are very strong and difficult to unlearn, since the individual never comes in contact with the aversive event. The noise could be totally disconnected, but as long as the light comes on, the person will continue to push the green button.

Most phobias are extreme avoidance responses. For example, some people who are afraid to ride in an airplane never get on the plane. Because they never actually experience the harmlessness of the flight, they maintain their fear. An avoidance response such as this could continue for a lifetime unless the person seeks professional help.

It is not uncommon for victims of violent crime who have been traumatized to engage in avoidance behavior or to present with conditioned fear responses. Some of this is easily understood, such as avoidance of the crime scene, a fear of being left alone, and the avoidance of situations or things associated with the specific crime. Other avoidance behavior is less easily understood without a knowledge of conditioning, when victims are unable to leave their houses for months after the crime, or they exhibit fears of situations, sounds, smells, or objects that seem unrelated to the crime.

To help illustrate both classical conditioning and avoidance responding, a woman came for treatment because she was having difficulty sleeping at night. As it turned out she had been a victim of burglary in which her apartment was broken into while she was home. Luckily, she was unharmed, but she was very emotionally upset over the incident. Her response to the victimization was a form of avoidance responding. She had acquired numerous locks that she placed on her door, including a steel rod that attached to the floor and a plate on the door. She also engaged in a lengthy ritual of checking the apartment rooms, closets and windows to be sure she was alone and that the apartment was secure. Her ritual took about 30 minutes to perform. However, once she fell asleep certain sounds would wake her up with her heart beating fast and a fear response in full swing. As it turned out, the sounds that woke her up were sounds similar to those that she had heard just prior to and during the burglary. They included sounds like car doors closing, a neighbor phone ringing, and other normal apartment building noises. When any of these sounds occurred, she would wake up frightened and, to get back to sleep, she would have to go through her safety ritual with the door and the checking of the apartment. Even though certain sounds elicited (classical conditioning) a fear response which woke her up, as long as she could engage in her ritual, she eventually could calm down and began to feel safe (avoidance response). Of course, under these conditions, she only sleeps a few hours at best each night, and her behavior seems odd and unusual to friends and people she knows. And even if those were not problematic enough, she has to experience a life where she wakes up afraid and uncertain about herself and her future. The positive side to this example is that she sought professional help and her situation was improved dramatically.

PTSD AND OTHER PSYCHOLOGICAL DISORDERS

PTSD was introduced as a diagnostic category in 1980. Since that time, the growing body of literature has supported the fact that the experience of violence or other severe traumatic events can lead to the development of a set of symptoms or presenting behaviors that are classified as post-traumatic stress disorder. The DSM-IV lists traumatic events that if experienced directly could lead to PTSD. These include, but are not limited to, military combat, violent personal assault, sexual assault, robbery, mugging, being kidnapped, being taken hostage, terrorist attack, torture, natural or manmade disasters, severe automobile accidents, and others (*Diagnostic and Statistical Manual of Mental Disorders*, fourth edition, 1994). The DSM-IV also lists a series of witnessed events that can lead to PTSD. These include, but are not limited to, observing the serious injury or death of another person due to violent assault, accident, or disaster. It is also stated that learning about an event experienced by another can lead to PTSD. For example, the violent personal assault, serious accident or serious injury of a family member or close friend can result in the development of PTSD. The DSM-IV also goes on to state that the disorder may be "especially severe or long lasting when the stressor is of human design," such as rape or torture.

Victims of violent crime are particularly susceptible to the development of PTSD (Sprang, 1999; Foa, 1997). However, family members and significant others who are personally close to the victim may experience symptoms of PTSD or develop the full disorder. As a victim service provider, it is critical to recognize that others besides the primary victim are also at risk.

Symptoms of PTSD include the following:

- the person must be exposed to a traumatic event,
- the traumatic event is reexperienced,

- there is persistent avoidance of stimuli associated with the trauma and numbing of general responsiveness (not present before the trauma),
- there are persistent symptoms of increased arousal (not present before the trauma).

For more detail refer to the chapter, "Impact of Stress."

PTSD can occur at any age. In most cases, the symptoms occur within the first three months following the traumatic event, though in some cases there have been reported delays of months to years before the disorder manifested itself. The duration of the symptoms varies; approximately half of all individuals diagnosed with PTSD will recover within approximately 3 months. As more research is conducted it appears that the severity, duration, and intensity of the traumatic event predicts to some level the percent of individuals who will develop PTSD. For example, sexual assault victims, who often experience greater invasion of person and higher levels of physical aggression, may be more likely to present with symptoms of PTSD than victims of theft or burglary or even robbery.

Other disorders can result from the trauma of violent crime besides that of PTSD. The literature had suggested that anxiety disorders (i.e., panic disorder, generalized anxiety disorder, phobias, obsessive compulsive disorder), mood disorders (i.e., major depressive disorder, dysthymic disorder), eating disorders (ie., anorexia and bulimia), dissociative disorders (i.e., dissociative amnesia, dissociative fugue, dissociative identity disorder, depersonalization disorder), sleep disorders, adjustment disorder, and others are related to trauma. Trauma can cause a worsening of existing symptoms in most disorders if the person has a mental disorder preexistent to the traumatic event. Trauma can in some individuals be the precipitating event that triggers the development of many of these disorders.

Victim assistants should be aware the relationship between traumatic events and the development of psychiatric disorders. Also, just as important they should be aware that individuals may develop some of the symptoms of these disorders or milder versions of the symptoms related to these disorders. What is critical is to recognize that an individual may respond to a traumatic event in a variety of ways. Some individuals will develop maladaptive and dysfunctional patterns of responding as a result. Crisis intervention is designed to prevent or reduce the harm that traumatic events have the potential to cause. At the same time, if the victim assistant is aware of psychological consequences and presenting behaviors, they may be able to recognize and refer victims to professionals trained to provide therapeutic interventions.

DRUG AND ALCOHOL USE/ABUSE

Research is now showing the correlations between drug and alcohol abuse and that of victimization. One manifestation of trauma in many cultures is the use by the victim of substances that either distract or reduce the symptoms produced by the traumatic event. Previous drug and alcohol use, abuse, or dependence can be viewed as a precursor to more severe or recurrent problems with drug and alcohol abuse later, following a victimization. For example, an individual who drinks more when they are stressed by work or family problems may be more likely to abuse alcohol following their own or a family member's victimization. Some of this can be viewed as escape behavior; if one drinks enough alcohol they can temporarily escape the negative emotions and persistent negative thoughts following the victimization of self or a loved one.

Increased use of drugs and alcohol by victims of crime and/or their family members/significant others is of major concern. Previous abuse histories place the person at a greater risk. Victim assistants should be aware of the potential risks and consider appropriate strategies when inappropriate use is detected or there is an abuse or dependence history present.

MEDICATION

Physicians and psychiatrists will often prescribe medication to assist the trauma victim. In many cases, the use of antianxiety medication and some antidepressant medication may in the weeks and months following a crime victimization be of benefit to the victim. However, there is a potential for abuse with prescription medication just as there is with alcohol and other drugs. Usage of anything that makes the pain go away or that makes the victim feel better is likely to be repeated. If that leads to an abusive or unhealthy use of the medication, then efforts should be made to intervene in the least intrusive but appropriate manner. However, close monitoring of prescription drug use by a family member as well as the responsible physician may be advisable in situations where the symptoms of trauma are severe and evidence of recovery is absent.

WHAT IS CRISIS INTERVENTION?

The term *crisis* was first used as a defined clinical term when Gerald Caplan (1964) responding to current theories and some data that indicated victims of disasters had better outcomes if they received some early intervention. Even though our knowledge of trauma reactions has changed significantly since Caplan, his contribution extends beyond the phrase, *crisis intervention* and into issues of preventive care and advocacy. Crisis intervention is today a staging ground for a plethora of interventions aimed at preventing or reducing negative outcomes to individual, family and community. Today, there is no singular theory accepted by all or even most that defines crisis. Part of the problem in the field is that crisis is defined by what happens to a person, rather than how the person experiences it. In other words, stressors or environmental events often define the existence of a crisis. A violent crime or a devastating fire may define the event as a crisis. Even in the DSM-IV, an individual must be exposed to an extreme stressor. However, there are actually three elements to a crisis. There must be a stressor, a response to the stressor, and changes in either adaptive or maladaptive functioning as result of the crisis. While the stressor must be present, it is the individual's perception and reaction to that stressor that is critical. However, depending upon the crisis and the individual's response to it, changes will occur in the individual that are negative or positive. Typically, a severe crisis will result in reactions that both strengthen and weaken the individual's response repertoire. The individual's perception of these changes and other's perceptions of these changes lead us to label these changes as positive (desired) or negative (undesirable).

Crisis intervention should include assessment, monitoring, interventions aimed at prevention, and, where necessary, referral for therapy to a trained crisis/trauma therapist. The purpose of crisis intervention is to intervene at any of the three elements of a crisis describe above. Interventions should be aimed to eliminate stressors or alter them in some manner to reduce their potential to negatively affect the individual. Interventions should be aimed at assisting the individual in their ability or perception of the stressor(s), and any protracted basis crisis intervention should be focused on altering the individual's reactions to the crisis so as to enhance his or her coping skills and cognitive reappraisal and reduce the development of harmful or negative patterns of responding brought on by the stressor(s) associated with the crisis. One of the more recognized models for crisis intervention is Roberts' (1991) seven-stage approach. Roberts' model, as do others, begins with assessment and ends with monitoring and follow-up.

ASSESSMENT AND MONITORING

In the hours and days following a violent crime, victims not only are faced with a broad array of physical and emotional reactions to the crisis but with the sense of helplessness and loss of control over the world in which they exist (Caplan, 1964; McCann & Pearlman, 1960; Slaikeu, 1990). Victims under such conditions are vulnerable and at risk.

Assessment can be both informal such as the BASIC presented in the prior chapter, as well as formal. At its most basic, it is a series of questions designed to determine the capacity of the victim and their family to recover from the victimization and then assessing or matching what services/supports need to be provided to prevent further harm and facilitate recovery and to meet the demands/stressors that will be confronted with either through the criminal justice system, the media, or any other postcrime victimization demand. At a formal level, it may involve the use of standardized assessment instruments to measure anxiety, trauma, PTSD, and so forth. Some instruments have been evaluated for use by nonspecialists as simple psychological screening instruments (e.g., General Health Questionnaire, see Darves-Bornoz, Lepine, & Degiovanni, 1998; Mezey, King, & MacClintock, 1998). Others should only be administered by trained professionals.

Assessments should be practical and aimed at providing only those services supports that will be necessary to assist the victim and their family to recover. Ideally, assessment should be ongoing so that as resources, supports, and level of functioning changes so does the service plan. Additionally, assessment should be aimed at what will be needed now, tomorrow and several weeks from now or longer.

At its most basic level, assessment should include the following:

- Current level of functioning.
- Support from family, friends, community.
- Available resources.
- Ability to self-evaluate.
- Health risks.
- Mental health risks.
- Family stability and integrity.
- Coping skills.
- Suicide risk.

Frame the assessment and later the interventions in a victim-centered approach. Assessment in this sense is conceptualized as a partnership with the victim and their family. Assess from the victim's perspective as well as from those who know and care about the victim. Following this, the practitioner then adds his or her own professional assessment to the interpretation of the information. However, it is important to keep the conversation open and honest between practitioner, the victim and their family. Often professional concerns can be addressed as questions for the victim to respond to with their own interpretation and perspective. The importance of approaching assessment from a victim-centered perspective is many. First, it allows the victim assistant to frame the victimization, its impact, and the services that will be needed to assist the survivor in the context of the victim's world. This becomes particularly relevant when working with a member of a different ethnic or racial background. One of the problems inherent in working with a person whose values and social structure is different than our own is the tendency to impose our values and assumptions onto them. However, even when attempting to be sensitive to such issues there is a tendency to stereotype or inaccurately interpret the context of the victim's life. Avoid assumptions and approach each victim from a person-centered perspective. The practitioner should allow and set the occasion for the victim and their family to teach them about their values and the context in which they view the world. Allow this assessment of their needs and supports to be directed from the context of their lives. Obviously, the process needs to be interactive with the victim and their family being prompted to participate in all aspects of the assessment and service planning. Victim services should never be a one-size-fits-all program.

The effects of a crisis spiral out from the primary victim to members of the immediate family to relatives and friends to the workplace and community at large. As related in the chapter on the ecological perspective, it is impossible for a single family member to experience trauma from a victimization and not have other members of their family affected. Depending on the intensity and type of victimization, the effects can be far reaching. One of the most notable of these victimizations is the Oklahoma City Bombing. Extensive studies have shown that psychological disturbances occurred in many who had no family members or even friends associated directly with the bombing.

One should not forget that witnesses to a violent crime also may develop symptoms of traumatic stress. They may feel threatened by what they have observed and be vicariously affected. They also may feel as though they are in immediate danger or at risk of threat from the perpetrator or those connected to the perpetrator. Though they are witnesses, they may also be viewed as victims. The same assumptions apply to witnesses as victims. In the DSM-IV it states that post traumatic stress disorder also can be acquired by observing a severe traumatic event. As a result of the Oklahoma bombing, the entire community was tragically affected. Even some members of the community who did not lose friends and loved ones and who did not view in person the bombing were impacted and experienced trauma (Sprang, 1999). The degree of exposure to the event, even among those who were not primary victims of the crime, tends to correlate with the number and severity of symptoms of PTSD (Green, Grace, Lindy, Gleser, Leonard, & Kramer, 1990; Kilpatrick, Amick, & Resnick, 1990; Sprang, 1999). Epictetus said, "Men are disturbed not by things, but by the views they take of them."

Assessment must include members of the immediate family and may extend outward into the community. From an ecological perspective, trauma can be compared to the ripple effect in a pond. If a single member of a family is affected by a traumatic event, it is inevitable that the entire family will be affected in some manner. Family and community systems are dynamic. Affect one member and there are either compensating or reactive effects felt throughout the whole system. That does not mean that the systems reaction will be maladaptive or destructive in some manner. However, it can be. Whole communities can be affected by a violent crime. Families can be broken or develop patterns that will negatively affect the development and growth of its members. How members adapt or compensate for the changes in the behavior of the traumatized member(s) can be either healthy or harmful to both the system and individual members.

Finally, assessment should be viewed as ongoing. Across time, the assessment should look at the victim's ability to cope with stressors. It also should be concerned with assessing social relationship behaviors. A strong indicator of recovering from trauma is the ability to maintain and foster positive social relationships. Deterioration in social relationships may be a sign of worsening trauma symptoms. However, as social relationships improve or as time involved in positive interactions with others increases so is likely the health of the survivor.

EARLY SIGNS OF TRAUMA

Severe stress reactions can produce trauma. The chart below lists signs and symptoms sometimes associated with individuals who are experiencing trauma. The purpose of crisis intervention is to prevent or mitigate the development of serious and adverse psychological reactions or disorders. Recognizing these signs or symptoms in a victim can be important in the early stages of a crisis or in the decision to refer or provide more assistance.

It may be important early on to assess the willingness of the victim to get professional help if symptoms persist or worsen. The following trauma symptoms are listed by the American Counseling Association:

- Reexperiencing the event through vivid memories or flash backs.
- Feeling emotionally numb.
- Feeling overwhelmed by what would normally be considered everyday situations and diminished interest in performing normal tasks or pursuing usual interests.
- Crying uncontrollably.
- Isolating oneself from family and friends and avoiding social situations.
- Relying increasingly on alcohol or drugs to get through the day.
- Feeling extremely moody, irritable, angry, suspicious or frightened.
- Having difficulty falling or staying asleep, sleeping too much, and experiencing nightmares.
- Feeling guilty about surviving the event or being unable to solve the problem, change the event, or prevent the disaster.
- Feeling fears and sense of doom about the future.

Predispositions for Trauma

A significant body of research (Breslau, Chilcoat, & Kessler, 1999) exists that suggests that certain individuals with certain types of histories are more susceptible to trauma than others. Much of this is covered in previous chapters in this text. It is important to recognize that any preexisting condition either psychological or physiological can be worsened by a traumatic experience. For example, if an individual is already experiencing depression or anxiety disorders, the symptoms of those disorders are likely to intensify. However, in summary, research would suggest the following:

- Previous exposure to trauma signals a greater risk of PTSD from subsequent trauma (Breslau et al., 1999).
- Severity of PTSD symptoms was related to increases in alcohol consumption, depressive symptoms, and depersonalization (Sims & Sims, 1998).
- Length of time associated with recovery from PTSD is directly related to a history of alcohol abuse and childhood trauma (Zlotnick, Warshaw, Shea, Allsworth, Pearlstein, & Keller, 1999).
- Childhood sexual abuse related to adult trauma severity (Read, Stern, Wolfe, & Ouimette, 1997).
- Childhood abuse and neglect means greater risk of developing PTSD (Widom, 1999).
- Exposure to traumatic events is related to increases in alcohol abuse (McFarlane, 1998; Stewart, 1996) and alcohol abuse and PTSD (Ouimette, Wolfe, & Chrestman 1996; Dansky, Brady, Saladin, Killeen, Becker, & Roitzsch, 1996).
- A history of childhood rape doubled the number of alcohol abuse symptoms that women experienced in adulthood (Epstein, Saunders, Kilpatrick, & Resnick, 1998)).
- Suicide has been shown to be related to both depression and PTSD (Krug, Kresnow, Peddicord, Dahlberg, Powell, Crosby, & Annest, 1998).

The above list is not inclusive of all variables related to trauma and predispositions for mental health problems. However, it does give a sample of the seriousness of trauma and its relationship to past problematic behavior.

Past coping skills and problematic responses to stressors is highly predictive of how the victim will respond in the current situation. A paucity of coping behaviors or the use of poor coping skills in the past is an indicator that the victim is at risk. On the other hand, if the person has had a success in coping with crises in the past, they will likely have a more successful outcome.

COPING BEHAVIOR

Assessing the ability of the victim to cope with the trauma can give some indication of the severity of the trauma likely to be experienced. Coping refers to the thoughts and acts that people use to manage the internal and external demands posed by a stressful or traumatic event. The literature on coping has divided coping strategies into two major categories; *emotion-focused* and *problem-focused*. Problem-focused strategies are aimed at changing behavior or some aspect of the person-environmental relationship. Emotion-focused strategies are aimed at changing or altering the emotions associated with the stressors or by trying to alter the persons emotional relationship with the stressor (e.g, how the person perceives the event/stressors on an emotional level). Depending on the stressors, it is suggested that a combination of the two types of strategies is the desired process.

Harm to an individual can result in many cognitive reactions. Rationalizations come into play to help rebuild and restore levels of self-esteem (i.e., "It was their fault," "I could not have known," "Most people would have done what I did," "It was impossible to prevent it from happening," etc.). One social strategy may be to convince others around us that we are not as a whole representative of this one incident. Also, note that coping with harm usually contains a heavy ingredient of undoing or reinterpreting what is already past. It also will include anticipatory actions, in which resolutions and plans are made to do things differently in the future. In the process of recovery, coping strategies help us rebuild the world where we are in some measure of control. Where there continues to be some level of threat or perceived threat, the threatened person must prepare for harm that *will* happen or *may* happen. The focus is often on how will they deal with it, prevent it, survive it, tolerate it. Vigilance, itself, often seen in victims of violent crime, can be a form of coping. Vigilance should not be confused with hypervigilance, an extreme form of the same behavior. Hypervigilance should not be considered a coping strategy as much as it may be a manifestation of severe trauma.

Emotion-focused coping behavior has been used to assist victims in recovery. Basically, how one feels better or changes their emotional reactions is the focus of the coping strategies (i.e., positive reappraisal, tension reduction, anger management, etc.). There is some literature (Fontana & McLaughlin, 1998; Fawzy, Fawzy, Hyn, Elashoff, Guthrie, Fahey, & Morton, 1993; Taylor, Peplau, & Sears, 1997) support to indicate that with both men and women, emotion-focused coping strategies leads to reduced physiological variables associated with higher levels of stress.

Problem-focused coping strategies appear to be effective with certain types of stressful or traumatic events. Billings and Moos (1981) first showed the efficacy of problem-focused coping strategies to mediate stress and illness. The tactics employed included problem solving and taking action to make things better. Additionally, they included actions such as talking with a professional person about the incident such as a doctor, someone from the clergy, or a lawyer. Problem-focused coping strategies also have included taking action to become informed and find out more about the situation. Acquiring information can be either emotion-focused or problem-focused depending the use of the information. If the information is acquired to take action to improve things, then it is considered problem-focused. If the information is acquired to support an emotional perspective, then it is emotion focused. Problem-focused strategies can be directed at the challenges and stresses that come with being a victim of crime and are subsequent to the crime. These include dealing with media, defense attorneys, the criminal justice system, and so forth.

Social support can be included as a coping strategy in the sense that the victim uses their relationships with others to find support. Isolation for any length of time from others is typically considered a risk factor for both mental and physical health problems. Social support can serve as both an emotion focused and a problem focused coping technique. Using the help of others to change things or allowing others to provide emotional support and provide emotional feedback is emotion-focused. Numerous studies have suggested the positive effects on stress of social support tactics (Uchino, Cacioppo, & Keicolt-Glaser, 1996; Uchino & Garvey, 1997; Thoits, 1982; Lazarus & Folkman, 1984; Gurley, 1990; Knox, 1993; Knox, Svenson, Waller, & Theorell, 1988). In one study women who were able to speak about their problems with others showed reduced levels of stress (Uchino, Cacioppo, Malarkey, Glaser, & Kiecolt-Glaser, 1995).

The *Ways of Coping Questionnaire* (Folkman & Lazarus, 1988) has been used as both a therapeutic assessment instrument and a research tool in measuring coping skills. It contains a Seeking Social Support scale, which breaks social support into various categories. These include seeking informational support, tangible support, and emotional support.

Some coping behaviors are generally considered inappropriate strategies. However, it may not be the specific coping behavior as much as how long and under what conditions the coping behavior is exhibited. For example, many experts believe that involuntary recall and avoidance behaviors immediately following terrifying experiences are adaptive ways of dealing with the situation. These may be normal defenses particularly when the person is undergoing the trauma itself. For example, a rape victim may dissociate from the event by imagining they are elsewhere or pretending it is happening to someone else. They may not feel anything for a period of time immediately following the rape. However, when these coping responses become chronic and persist, then typically the victim is at great risk. If these reactions persist, it delays recovery and may lead to PTSD (Harrison & Kinner, 1998). In the most severe cases, a victim may exhibit partial or total loss of memory. In cases of prolonged abuse, these mechanisms for coping may lead to fragmentation of identity or cognitive processes such that dissociative identity disorder (formerly known as multiple personality disorder) develops. While there is controversy over the validity of dissociative identity disorder as a set of separate or distinct personalities, the presenting behaviors appear real in many clients.

Avoidant strategies have been found to increase blood pressure and rate heart indicators in male hypertensive (Holroyd & Gorkin, 1983; Morrison, Bellack, & Manuck, 1985). Distancing or denial is often considered a poor response to stress or trauma. However, the empirical evidence is either absent or equivocal on these events. Denial, as an example, may have adaptive and even functional attributes to it. In one study (Greer, Morris, & Pettingale, 1979) of terminal cancer patients, subjects who denied the existence of the cancer did better than a control group who accepted the inevitability of the disease but experience higher levels of anxiety of related to their terminal condition. In severe trauma situations, some denial may occur in the early period following the victimization. If the denial continues to persist into weeks and months following the crisis, then most therapists would agree that denial at this stage is damaging or antithetical to recovery. Denial may reduce perceived stress but may also result in necessary actions not taken which can have greater stressful effects later on.

Parents of children with a terminal illness who present with some denial of the terminal condition may do better during the child's illness than those parents who acknowledge the inevitable death. However, parents who use denial-like coping behaviors tend to do more poorly after the death of their child. At the very least it should be recognized that coping changes over time and that what seems to work at one point in a process may have negative consequences later. Another way of conceptualizing denial is to separate denial of fact from denial of implication. Denial that one's child is sick or that one was raped is unlikely to result in positive outcomes for the parent or the child. It may not be an efficacious coping strategy. Denial of implication may be, in some cases, a functional and efficacious strategy. "My child is sick, but I am not going to accept that he will die," could have utility for both the child and the parent. Denial of implication when events are ambiguous can be advantageous.

Distancing is also considered a type of emotion-focused coping behavior. However, distancing (Fontana & McLaughlin, 1998) has also been associated with increased levels of physiological stress factors (blood pressure and heart rate indices). In distancing, the person creates a dissociation or separation between thoughts and feelings about a stressful event. This helps the person evade the emotional implications of the stressful event. Distancing is not uncommon in the very early stages of a traumatic event. It is questionable whether this is functional or even healthy on any long term basis. Some have argued that distancing and denial have a purpose in that the individual is not ready or capable at the time to cope in any other manner. Even if one accepts that argument, the need to intervene to teach ways to handle stress and new coping skills is paramount.

DOCUMENTATION

As in all systems of helping others, documentation is an important element. Documentation has both therapeutic as well as legal implications. From a therapeutic perspective, documentation provides a mechanism for recording and review of client change, hypotheses proven or defeated, reminders of actions to be taken, and an ability to communicate process and outcome related events to others who have a legitimate need to know. From a legalistic perspective, documentation will verify in writing the incident and its impact on emotional, physical and financial levels. Such information may be useful for prosecution and restitution.

INTERVENTION

Crisis intervention is the term used to describe efforts to intervene in order to reduce the harmful effects of a potentially traumatic event. It is possible to conceptualize crisis intervention as having two phases which are distinguished by the needs of the client. The initial phase occurs immediately after the occurrence of the crisis event and is often characterized by acute reactions, which can manifest in a wide range of presenting behaviors. Crisis reactions refer to the behaviors presented during the initial or acute phase following a crisis event (Roberts, 2000). Effective responding to crisis reactions takes training and a clear understanding of the needs of the victim at such a time. As a beginning, safety and control are considered two major foci in crisis interventions with victims of crime during the initial phase.

SAFETY

If a victim service provider needs to remember anything it is the concept of safety. Because of what has happened to the victim of a violent crime, the first and primary actions that can be taken by a responder is to make the victim feel safe. For an individual who has survived, safety for themselves and those close to them (family, coworkers, friends, etc.) will likely be of utmost importance. Until those factors that relate to safety are addressed, very little is likely to be accomplished either from an advocacy perspective or even meeting the concerns of a law enforcement official.

Some steps that can be taken to insure some degree of safety for the victim:

- Indicate a concern for physical safety and medical needs. Ask victims if they are hurt or in pain. They may not tell you unless they are asked. So as a matter of habit, ask each victim the basic questions: "Are you safe now?" and "Do you have any injuries?" Also, depending on the crisis or crime, do not assume they are okay simply because they respond with a negative to your question. Victims can be seriously hurt and unaware of the nature of their injury until the body's protective functions decline. This can take from minutes to hours after the crisis for the victim to become self-aware enough to assess their own physical needs. However, you need to ask the question. Doing so conveys concern and hopefully places the crisis responder into the category of support and possible protector. Someone should do a physical examination of the victim who is trained to assess for injury. However, a systematic visual examination of the victim to be sure no gross injuries are apparent.
- Assess to find out if the victim is in immediate danger.
- Assess to discover if the victim's family or others the victim knows are in danger.
- Ask the victim if there is anything that can be done to make them feel safer or more secure.
- Ask if there is someone you can contact whose presence may make the victim feel safer or more comfortable.
- Assess to see if the victim is able to learn. Strange as that may sound, victim in the immediate aftermath of the victimization may be so traumatized that memory and learning are impaired (Jenkins, Langlais, Delis, & Cohen, 1998). In the very early stages (hours to days) following the traumatic incident conversations with the victim may or may not transfer critical information to the victim. It may be very difficult to share vital information and have it retained and remembered at the necessary times. Repeating frequently and keeping instructions simple are standard procedures for working with victims in crisis. However, it is suggested that the victim assistant should put critical information in writing and share that information with the victim's significant others.

CONTROL

When victims just lost control over their lives, the service provider needs to help restore it. The practitioner cannot give back to them what they have lost; however, they can assist them in gaining back some measure of the control they believed they had over their lives.

- Allow the victims to have input into and voice their concerns over the decisions that are being made with respect to them. Where possible and where it does not interfere with criminal investigative procedures or their safety, give them the opportunity to share their concerns and to make decisions that affect them and their family. One small way to do this is to ask. Ask them if they would like to _____ , ask if they feel able to _____ , ask if you may _____ . It is not just being polite; it is allowing the victim to have some measure of control. They may not care about many of the things they are asked about, but not asking them is risky and they may take offense. Asking them gives them some control over what is now happening in their lives. Even the smallest event that appears trivial to most of us, may in the aftermath of the crisis be important to the victim.

• In the days following a victimization, try to let the victim return to the routines of daily life. Routines of daily living involve the basic repeatable patterns of our lives. Routines involve such activities as picking out our clothes, getting the morning paper from the lawn, making coffee or breakfast, household chores, and cooking meals. Many of these things are done in daily routines that bring an order and control to our lives. Washing the dishes may be as important to the recovery of an individual as anything a friend or relative can say to them. Routines give comfort and a sense of control over our lives. Routines of daily living give an order and balance to our lives that are often taken for granted. Simplistic as this may seem, the victimization has brought about a disruption in life events. The security found in taking control over one's life begins with taking back the routines that support our lives. Friends and relatives should only take over those aspects of the victim's routines of daily living that are freely given up. Even then the victim should be encouraged to assist or take back those basic routines as soon as they are ready. Ask— start small and then take bigger steps with the survivor as they move to more self-reliance in their daily activities.

One final consideration is the use of routines of daily living to give control and support to a victim. In some cases the traumatic event may so affect their lives that routines of daily living that existed prior to the crime may not be possible to reinstate following the crime. In such cases, a system of routines that supports the current life patterns of the victim may need to be suggested. The victim needs to show the way to do this. Suggest the identification of simple routines to get through the day successfully accomplishing those tasks the victim sees as important to them. They should lead and the practitioner should follow with suggestions and ways to implement, guide and support. Unless absolutely necessary, avoid taking control away from the victim.

The view that people vary in the degree to which they can control their lives got its major thrust from the work of Rotter (1966). Basically, Rotter's assumptions were that individuals varied in their perceived level of control over their lives based on their history of socialization and experiences. Rotter found that some people believe they can control desired and undesired outcomes in their lives, while others believed that such outcomes were beyond their control. This was referred to as locus of control, either internal or external. Further breakdowns of personal control have included cognitive control, decisional control, behavioral control, and emotional control. In general, it is thought that individuals with a greater sense of control over their lives do better psychologically and physiologically. However, the factors of control should be considered in the context of the demands placed upon an individual. For example, can giving someone too much control too soon, lead to increases in stress and result in greater levels of distress? The best current answer is to be sensitive to the needs and reactions of the victim. Ask them if they are ready; ask them what they want; observe and support.

In brief, the intervener in a crime related crisis should be concerned with the safety of the victim and with subsequently allowing the victim to achieve some control over the events in his or her life. Remember to make sure the victim feels safe. Ask them if they are and what you can do to make them feel safer. Give them as much control as they are capable of assuming. Think small in both concerns over control and safety. Asking them if you can get them a glass of water rather than just bringing them one is an example of a small way of giving the victim control. The little things do count. Ask them what name they would like to be called when addressing them. Ask them where they would like to sit and even where they would like you to sit when you talk to them. These are questions that for most victims are easy to answer, and this gives them a sense of control over events.

Privacy is something that should be addressed and acknowledged as a concern for each victim. The degree of need for privacy will vary from individual to individual—based on the particular situation, the number of strangers to the victim who are in contact with them, their family concerns, the type of crime, personality type, culture and ethnicity, and other factors idiosyncratic to the people and the incident. The professional needs to protect and keep the victim and their family as safe as possible. Protecting them also includes protecting their need for privacy. The issue of confidentiality arises with the concept of privacy. It may enhance the victim's feelings of security, if they are told that their reactions, emotions and comments will be kept confidential. Confidentiality helps in the establishment of a relationship of trust as well as a sense of safety.

Advocacy and support for the victim should include some degree of nurturance. For example, during police questioning a victim assistant may intervene to verify that the victim, who may be shock, is understanding what questions are being asked. Getting the victim to repeat the questions before answering is one method that may be helpful in making sure they understand the questions. Support may also include attempting to educate others as to the condition of the victim so that others may become more sensitive and understanding in their interactions with the victim. If the intervenor has been with the victim prior to the police questioning them, it is helpful to prepare the police officer as to the victim's cognitive and emotional state. This can be both helpful to the victim and the police officer.

If possible, attempt to keep media and nonessential persons from harassing the victim until the victim is ready and willing to deal with them. When and if they are willing to talk to the media, assist them in responding to the questions. Prepare them for what is likely to happen and the type of questions the media will pose.

Keep the victim informed. For most victims, it is important to know what is being done to apprehend the perpetrator or what has happened to the perpetrator. This may also help assure them of their safety. If the person is apprehended or even dead, the victim will likely want that information. Keep them informed about the extent of any additional threat. If the perpetrator is still at large then let the victim know what is being done to bring them into custody. Also, let them know what will be done to keep them safe. Even if you believe there is absolutely no chance the perpetrator will attempt to make contact with the victim, the victim may not believe such is the case. Assist them in achieving a level of real as well as perceived safety.

The terms ventilation and validation are used frequently in the field of crisis intervention. Ventilation is used to cover a broad topic that relates to trauma and recovery. Victims, in most cases, will want to tell their stories. They will want to do this over and over again. The repetition is important and helps the survivor integrate the crisis into their life and reappraise the events and their life after the crime or crisis. Telling their story is a way of coping with the trauma. Recognize that victims will be searching for words and phrases to describe what has happened to them. As they retell the story of the events, it will evolve in terms of how the event transpired to how they reacted both behaviorally and emotionally to it. Often, the meaning and importance of the traumatic event will undergo change as the trauma results in changes to the victim.

In some cases, it is important to use exact words to describe the events. For example, Mothers Against Drunk Driving (MADD) is insistent on referring to a collision with a drunk driver as a "crash" and not an "accident." They believe that it is important to the victim that the criminal nature of the incident be emphasized.

It is helpful for victim assistants and advocates to acquire listening skills. Reflective listening skill can be very helpful in validating the emotions. Listen to the words the victim uses to describe the incident and their emotions surrounding it. The practitioner can then reflect their comments using their words in many situations. This can be helpful in avoiding comments back to the victim that in the perception of the victim diminish or incorrectly identify what happened to them. Attempt to recognize the intensity of emotion felt by the victim. Validation of their emotions and outrage can result in the victim feeling as though they have been given permission to feel such intensity. This can be liberating and provide a sense of release for some victims.

Validating also includes letting the victim know that what they are experiencing is a normal reaction to a horrific event. To do this, it is recommended that the victim assistant be content-specific and respond with exactness and detail. For example, rather than saying, "I can't imagine how sad you are," it would be better to say, "I can't imagine how devastated you are over the death of your daughter in that senseless shooting." Again, be very careful in the words you use. In some cases, no matter what you say it will be met with a negative reaction. Such reactions are common with some victims and should not be viewed as a personal attack. However, the more wisely the words are chosen the less likely there will be an unintentional affront to the victim. One useful suggestion is to let victims know that their situation is unique and anything but common. Again, listen to the words victims use to describe their emotions and situation.

To facilitate ventilation and validation, ask the victim to describe the events. On occasion, the practitioner may want to ask the victim to give more detail to parts of what happened by asking questions such as, Who was there? What did you see? What did you hear? What did you touch, say or do? Victims should also be asked to describe their reactions and responses. From both an assessment and support perspective, the victim assistant may want to ask victims to describe what has happened to them since the incident. Ask about family, friends, and relatives. Ask the victim to describe the reactions these individuals have had to the crime. In this situation, victims are prompted to view the event from the perspective of others, assisting them in understanding not only their reactions, but how others have reacted. This also sets the occasion for victims to assess how their behavior may be affecting others.

Let the victim talk as long as he or she feels a need and as time allows. As an intervenor, if time begins to run out, let the person know early that you will have to leave at a certain time. The victim should not be made (even accidentally) to feel that what happened to them is not important. Finally, if there is a need to interrupt their telling of the incident and its outcomes, make a plan to meet and continue where things were left off.

One other reason to have victims retell their story is to allow them to remember the events. As time passes, most victims will remember things that were forgotten immediately after the crisis. What the victim remembers immediately following the incident may change. This is not uncommon and is just part of the process of putting events into a temporal sequence and under less stressful and emotional conditions remembering more detail. Expect at times for there to be inconsistencies between what may have been told to police and others right after the incident and what is remembered days and even weeks later. It is perfectly normal for arousal and stress to interfere with memory. It is therefore, normal for the victim's story to unfold and to become a more detailed and consistent recreation of the event. However, the victim advocate should never lead or add suggestions as to what might have happened. Memories can be affected by the input of others. Avoid contaminating the victim's memory with any hypothesis or suggestion. Listen and probe for detail, sequencing and feelings. Allow the victim the ability to remember under conditions of support and safety and understanding.

A sometimes useful technique is to suggest that the victim write about the event or use audiotapes to record their experiences. Keeping a journal can be both useful as well as productive in ventilating the experiences. A journal can provide a base for remembering and keeping certain facts about the case organized and clear.

Some common things to say and avoid saying when talking to the victim:

- Do not say things such as,
    - I understand.
    - It sounds like . . .
    - I'm glad you can share those feelings.
    - You're lucky that . . .
    - Don't worry, it's going to be all right.
- Do say things such as:
    - You are safe now (only if true).
    - I'm sorry it happened to you.
    - I'm glad you are talking to me.
    - You are not going crazy.
    - Things may never be the same, but they can get better.

It only makes sense that if someone has been a victim of crime, the more stressors they experience, the more potential there is for additional harm. The job of a victim assistant or intervenor must include efforts to reduce the stressors or their impact on the victim. In the days, weeks, months, and sometimes even years following the crime, victims will be in need of information. Educating them on the criminal justice system and other events subsequent to the crime can be significant in reducing stress. Victims require practical information. Such information allows the victim to predict what may happen and in response to upcoming events prepare. Education involves many factors depending on the situation. For example, in a rape case or sexual assault a forensic examination by a medical person may be required. Understanding why and what will happen can assist the victim in ameliorating the stresses attendant with such events. In other cases, they may be asked to view a body or return to the crime scene, there may be a need for an autopsy, or funeral arrangements will need to be made.

In many cases, victims are likely to be approached by the media. Media have a history of revictimizing survivors. Help victims understand what the role of the media is in their situation. Educate them so they can understand their rights and how the media can be used to their advantage. Help protect them when they desire privacy.

Most people have never been involved in the criminal justice system as a victim and need to understand how it works and their role in the process. Understanding the protracted nature of the process is important. It can, in some cases, take years before criminal judicial proceedings are completed. Understanding the law, the prosecutor's role and their rights is essential. If the victim has legal consequences related to the incident then those must be addressed also. Be honest with victims and keep them informed.

More immediate in crisis work is to make sure that the victim is planning for any immediate consequences resulting from the crime. Areas that need to be addressed include but are not limited to medical concerns (sexually transmitted disease, injuries, etc.), finances, resources, relocation (if necessary), and lost time from work. Help the victim make lists and check them twice.

TYPES OF TREATMENT

Studies (Foa, 1997) have shown that various therapeutic interventions appear to be efficacious in the treatment of trauma related disorders. As a general rule those therapies that utilize cognitive behavioral approaches (Forbes & Pekala, 1993) are likely to be more effective and efficient than those that do not. These include such therapies as:

- Solution-Focused Therapy. Probably, one of the most effective crisis counseling interventions is solution-focused therapy (Greene, Lee, Trask, & Rheinscheld, 2000). This therapy views change as a constant in life and emphasizes the finding of solutions rather than just solving the problem. The therapy does not pathologize but assumes that clients ultimately are capable of making healthy decisions and resolving their problems.
- Prolonged Exposure Treatment. The client is asked to relive the traumatic memory and recount the event in detail. The description is audiotaped and the client is asked to listen to the audiotape across time. In vivo exposure to feared objects may also be incorporated.
- Stress Inoculation. Usually involves the teaching of a variety of techniques to manage anxiety such as controlled breathing, deep muscle

relaxation, thought-stopping, cognitive restructuring, preparation for stressors, covert modeling, and role-playing. All of the aforementioned techniques are efficacious treatment procedures used alone or in combination with a skilled therapist.

• Multielement Therapies. Those that use cognitive behavioral approaches appear to be effective and package assessment, dynamic family interactions, and other proven treatments together (Henggler, Schoenwald, Borduin, Rowland, & Cunningham, 1993; Frueh, Turner, & Beidel, 1996) have been effective at working with abused youth and their families. Originally, developed to work with delinquents and drug abusing adolescents and their families, the multisystemic therapy treatment package shows promise with victims and their families.

• Group Therapy. While many trauma victims will need individual therapy, group therapy can be helpful. In group therapy, trauma victims can find others with similar experiences. These therapist-managed interactions can help the victim reach an understanding relative to the experiences of others. Additionally, group therapy allows the victim to help others and learn from the failures and successes of others. There is often reassurance provided in groups as other talk about their own recovery and such groups provide a level of understanding and tolerance that is difficult to achieve with friends or, in some cases, family members.

Beware of any treatment that promises success after only one or two sessions. Any treatment that provides such promises is likely to be bogus and a waste of time, emotion, and resources for both the victim and the victim assistant. EMDR and other related therapies have come under greater research scrutiny in last few years. Long-term outcome studies do not suggest that EMDR is effective with certain populations (Devilly & Spence, 1998; Devilly, 1996).

REFERRAL

In a review of the literature on the epidemiology of trauma, Solomon and Davidson (1997) indicate that while trauma victims are disproportionate users of the health care system, they are reluctant to seek mental health treatment. This suggests that getting a victim to access mental health care may be difficult. There are numerous barriers to seeking mental health supports. However, when the victim is willing it is likely that they will ask for a recommendation or the names of therapists.

Choose a therapist wisely. Not all therapists are created equal. Before referring a victim to a therapist, there should be some knowledge about certain things, such as specifics about the therapist's training, qualifications to work with crime victims, and whether they gone through inservice training that qualify them to work with trauma patients or victims of crime. If a therapist takes offense with questions about their qualifications, they should be politely thanked for their time but should not be used for referrals. If a therapist is that defensive of their training or they believe themselves to be beyond some level of scrutiny, then chances are they may have problems relating to clients. In any event, they are not likely to be a collaborative member of a treatment team.

Remember that in all professions there is a range of competence. It is important to find the most competent therapist to refer victims to for therapy. Do not be afraid to ask clients about their satisfaction with a therapist. It is good information to accumulate. However, the fact that clients like certain therapists is a positive and essential element. The ability of a therapist to promote change is not guaranteed by consumer satisfaction. Find therapists who can do both.

Another way to find out who may be a quality professional is to ask other therapists who they respect and who they feel is competent and trained to work with victims. Being respected by fellow therapists may not mean that they are the best therapists to work with victim. However, it is one way of screening the field, and it usually correlates with competence.

Also, choose a therapist who is likely to cooperate with other professionals. This person should be willing to be a team member in the process of helping the victim. Using a team approach to service delivery is preferred. It maintains important levels of communication that prevents omissions of services needed and avoids duplication of services through a lack of communication. It also allows various professional perspectives and insights to be brought into the treatment plan. Interdisciplinary approaches have been known to be more effective and efficient than multidisciplinary approaches.

RECOGNIZING CULTURAL AND ETHNICITY WORLD VIEWS

Though addressed extensively in chapter 4, "Barriers to Services," cultural and ethnic sensitivity in trauma response is critical and warrants further emphasis. It begins with understanding that each individual is different and unique. To be responsive to the needs of any individual, stereotypes based on skin color or dress or origin of location must be avoided. The victim assistant must recognize that they will be ignorant of the cultural and ethnic backgrounds of many of their clients. It is appropriate to ask the victim or the family to educate you to any cultural or ethnic considerations that you should be aware of. The biggest problem individuals can have in providing services that are insensitive to multicultural/diversity issues is making assumptions and being afraid to ask.

Of course, there are some important self-instructional efforts that can be made. If one works in an area that has a significant minority group, then actions such as asking a member of the clergy in the community to teach how to be sensitive to the groups needs or learning the groups language and customs may be taken. One should never presume, however, that learning the language or dialect grants some great insight that lets you assume you are one of them. Unless a person grew up in the culture, faced their problems, their discriminations, their struggles, then one can only grasp elements of what it might be like. But increased knowledge will contribute greatly to sensitivity and respect of differences and the worth of the individual.

Interventions must be framed in the context of the life of the victim. Cultural, traditions, community, and racial contexts must be assessed so that interventions can be directed with the support rather than the opposition of such contexts. In some cultures, it is important not to have family or friends observe a victim during an emotionally distraught time where their presentation of grief, loss, or lack of control may be seen as a loss of dignity. Understand the culture and the victim's personal context within it.

The bottom line is, do not assume. The practitioner should ask the victim to lead in a process that will help the victim assistant to help them. Wrap services around the person and center the planning of services around victim.

VICARIOUS TRAUMATIZATION

Vicarious traumatization is described as the presentation of symptoms similar to posttraumatic stress disorder and the disruption in cognitive schemas in clinicians and victim professionals who are exposed to the material of their clients (Brady, Guy, & Poelstra, 1999; Pearlman & Saakvitne, 1995). Victim assistants come in contact with some of the most emotionally demanding and stressful client situations that exists in the helping field. Victim assistants are thought to have broad shoulders and be capable of withstanding all sorts of trauma experiences without being affected. Often, others expect victim assistants to operate without complaint and to take on huge case loads. As most victim assistants know, the job can be extremely rewarding but it can also be frustrating and highly anxiety provoking. The vivid and sometimes graphic descriptions of a client's brutal victimization or terrible loss contributes to vicarious victimization. The cumulative effect of one case after another, one story of less and pain after another, and the inability to sometimes change patterns of abuse can result in professional stress and trauma. Caregivers sometimes have a hard time in knowing when they should be taken care of and when to seek assistance.

The weight of the work can lead to both physiological and physiological problems. Agencies can establish protocols to facilitate the health of their employees. Critical Incident Stress Management (CISM) has been implemented in various trauma programs to attempt to reduce the impact of vicarious traumatization caused by critical incidents (e.g., severe violent crimes, death scene responders, death notification). CISM usually involves a multielement approach to stress reduction.

While the jury is still out on the efficacy of debriefing alone, some system to reduce the effects of stressors on staff is highly recommended. Research on critical incident stress debriefing is not as conclusive as it might be. While some studies have argued its effectiveness at reducing or preventing negative client outcomes, other studies suggest that there is minimal effect or the positive effects can be attributed to other factors such as peer support (Hytten & Hasle, 1989). The department of Behavioral Science, Ben-Gurion University, Israel, conducted a study of 15 women who were not physically injured in a terrorist attack. All the women participated in a group debriefing with brief group psychotherapy. No clear effects could be attributed to the debriefing alone. Other studies (McFarlane, 1988; Stephens, 1996; Kenardy, Webster, Lewin, Carr, Hazell, & Carter, 1996) have suggested that when variables such as staff predispositions for trauma are controlled for little or not benefit was observed as a result of the debriefing. These studies raise some concerns about the efficacy of such brief interventions. However, it may also be that such techniques as debriefing are only effective if used in the context of other stress management techniques along with follow-up procedures (Corneil & Kirwan, 1997). Management of critical incident stress may be the more appropriate way to approach the stress of a trauma worker.

Some professionals have argued that efforts should be directed at teaching preventive skills to trauma workers rather than applying a universal brief intervention immediately following the trauma event. In any event, the utility of CISD has yet to be fully explored and explained.

There are things the professional should consider to protect themselves. First, be aware of changes in emotional state. Increases in emotional outbursts and emotional sensitivity may be signs of increasing stress. Monitor self and your body. Changes in sleep patterns may also signal a need to deal with work related trauma. Increases in health related issues (e.g., increased colds, aches, stomach/digestion problems, and headaches) may signal a need to seek assistance. Discuss with a professional thoughts, dreams and images that refuse to fade and continue to cause anxiety.

Recommendations for staying healthy:

- Learn how to relax. Most people do not know how to get physiologically relaxed. Learn one of the available techniques and practice it until you become proficient. Then work time into your schedule to take time to relax.

- Spend time enjoying friends and family. Keep connected to other people and use that time to have fun.
- Eat well and take care of diet. Stress affects nutrition and a poor diet will only make things worse.
- Set boundaries between work and home. Do not take your work home. Recognize there are limits. Plan to be in this profession for the long haul and do not allow yourself to be overburdened and burnt out.
- Play. Take time to have a hobby or participate in sports. Exercise has been shown to reduce stress. Play. When we play we are usually smiling. If your time away from work results in a frown or more stress, change your recreational events.

SUMMARY

As a summary to this chapter it is important to point out that the relationship between the victim assistant and the victim is contractual. The contract may be verbal and informal or it may be written and formalized. However, the relationship is defined there is a responsibility or burden on the victim assistant to provide the best service and support to the victim that they can.

There are a host of ethical issues that this chapter cannot address. However, an essential ethical practice inherent in this chapter is informed consent. The victim assistant's relationship to the victim requires honesty and trust. An essential element of both honesty and trust is fully informing the victim of one's professional abilities, purpose, and limitations. If information is keep on the victim, then she or he needs to know what the information is about and who will have access to it. Keep victims informed and allow them to make decisions. At its basic level informed consent is easy to understand. Inform and educate victims and always check with them to be sure they are in agreement with the actions to be taken. At another level, the elements of informed consent are complex, subtle and easily forgotten in the attempt to help. Keep victims' needs first and involve them in planning decisions. Let them know what the possible outcomes are for any action taken. If there are restrictions on professional behavior imposed by the employing agency or other entity, make sure the victim understands those restrictions. For example, in prosecutorial based programs, victim-witness coordinators function under the prosecutor's umbrella. Confidentiality is limited and must include the theoretical sharing of all information with the prosecutor. The victim must know that up front and may need to be reminded. Educate and inform and seek consent.

The Justice System and Victims

7

Thomas L. Underwood

J ustice is not a simple concept. It involves the rights and interests of the accused, the victims, the public, and the agencies that make up the justice system. Due process as a constitutional protection focuses on the rights of the accused against arbitrary and unjust treatment. However, many individuals "believe that the justice system focuses on the criminal to the detriment of the victim" (National Center for Victims of Crime [NCVC], 1997). Yet, the justice system draws from the classical school that considers crime to be an injury to society and the responses of the system are intended to be utilitarian in nature (Williams & McShane, 1998; Allen & Simonsen, 1998).

The criminal justice system is the social institution that provides the most hope for victims of crime as well as the most criticism. This chapter explores the concept of justice as it is played out through the various components that make up the criminal justice system. The complex labyrinth of the system is analyzed in terms of the conflicting relationships between the systems components and the uncertain and often tenuous balance between the rights and responsibilities of offenders, the community, and victims.

HISTORICAL CONTEXT OF JUSTICE

A system of justice has existed since the earliest of times. In early primitive societies, victims sought personal retaliation or private revenge as remedy of wrongful injury or property loss. This retaliation was probably not based so much on justice and the belief that wrongdoers should be held accountable, but rather it was a survival response: Aggression was a defense against regression. As the clan or tribe became more organized, private retaliation was augmented by collective retribution in which the victim's clan took revenge on the offender's clan. These were called blood feuds, and though the feuds could be quite violent, the term blood feuds did not refer to the bloody nature of the retaliations but rather to the social control of the kindred, where an offense against one member of the clan was considered an offense against the whole group. Again, the primary function of these responses was probably more a reflection of survival than justice. However, the basic foundation of lex talionis—eye for an eye—continues to be a principle of most legal systems.

As individual and collective retaliation practices escalated into endless, socially disruptive battles or vendettas between parties, a system of laws evolved to manage the disputes. As cultures became larger and more economically stable, a system of compensation developed in which goods or money could be paid in place of blood vengeance. Atonement for wrongs by payment to appease the victim's family or tribe (known as *lex scalia* or *wergeld*) is still in effect in many Middle and Far Eastern countries where the compensation is dependent on the extent of injury, the status of the injured party, and the status of the offending party (Allen & Simonsen, 1998).

Codification of these customs are evident as far back as about 2000 B.C. The Sumerian Code, the Code of the King Hammurabi of Babylon, and the Mosaic (Law of Moses) Code are some of the oldest. These codes defined individual responsibility and redress for wrongs committed. The codification of Roman law by Emperor Justinian was "one of the most ambitious early efforts to match a desirable amount of punishment to all possible crimes" (Allen & Simonsen, 1998, p. 7). The Code of Draco in Greece allowed citizens to prosecute the offender for the sake of the injured party, reflecting the public interest of the social order.

As society became increasingly economically complex and urbanized, people became less independent and self-sufficient. With social complexity, the social contract or relationship between the state and the citizenry also changed. The philosophy of social contract is that individual rights and freedoms are minimally compromised in order for the government to protect the majority of society (Williams & McShane, 1998). Thus, the state assumes responsibility to protect the citizenry from harm.

The power and authority of the state grew, and crime was increasingly viewed not merely as an offense against an individual but as an offense against the state. Offender compensation for the victim injuries and losses was replaced by public fines rather than restitution. Further, the "advent of penitentiary further diminished the use of restitution as a criminal sanction (Smith & Hillenbrand, 1997). "Concentrating that power also led to a tendency to ignore victims and their losses, while concentrating on the crime and criminal" (Allen & Simonsen, 1998). Thus, the victim became an incidental observer in the justice process. The system that at one time served the goals of restoration of the victim no longer served that function. Legal compensation to the individual became a separate field of law: Civil law.

PERSPECTIVES OF JUSTICE

As the social institution responsible to implement the concept of justice, the component agencies that compose the justice system can be characterized as a nonsystem of criminal justice. Segmented and often isolated from each other, the agencies seem to work in contradictory directions and operate with "different goals and needs" (Wallace, 1998, p. 42), and with "the only thing they have in common is the fact that they all deal with the same clientele" (Albanese, 1999, p. 134). Yet it is a system, since the segment of one system directly impacts the workload of the other components. Increased arrests mean more cases for prosecution, and, in turn, increased judicial docket. Presuming these cases are adjudicated, there is further impact on probation departments and correctional institutions. Of course, increased workload on probation and correctional institutions, without the commensurate resources to handle the cases, increases the likelihood of decreased effectiveness. These dynamics of contradictory goals, segmentation, and isolation breed distrust between the component agencies, yet "they must attempt to act together if justice is to be achieved" (Albanese, p. 135).

What is the role and responsibility of the criminal justice system? The traditional paradigm of crime is that it is "a conflict between the offender and society. Viewed as such, crime generates not an obligation to the victim, but a debt to society" (Fattah, 1997, p. 259) and the criminal justice system functions to uphold the authority of the state (Van Ness and Heetderks Strong, 1997). Thus, under this traditional paradigm, there is no place for the victim, and the criminal justice system holds no obligation to the victim other than that toward society in general. As such, victims, and the services intended to support victims, are often viewed by the justice agencies as an imposition, believing that compliance with victim rights will impede the efficiency of case processing and will usurp the professional autonomy of the agents. Furthermore, attitudes regarding victim contribution or provocation of their victimization affect interactions between justice agents and victims. The conceptualization that the victim bears greater responsibility for their victimization than does the offender is not uncommon (Peterson, 1991).

Contrary to this traditional paradigm, *New Directions from the Field: Victims' Rights and Services for the 21st Century* notes that "the agencies that make up our criminal and juvenile justice system have a moral and legal obligation to respond. It is their responsibility not only to seek swift justice for victims, but to ease their suffering in a time of great need" (1998, p. 45). This quote calls on the system to seek justice—but what is meant by justice? Is justice retribution, rehabilitation, or restitution?

RETRIBUTION

As presented earlier, punishment has a long history in the justice system dating back to the earliest codes. Punishment is usually justified on the utilitarian grounds that it serves as a deterrent to future criminal activity both for the individual (specific deterrence) and as a warning to others (general deterrence). Punishment is also justified as a moral practice of vengeance, or *lex talionis*. This "eye for an eye" approach rights the wrong through making even the score; by inflicting proportional and equitable harm to the offender to reestablish the social harmony and moral order (Allen & Simonsen, 1998; Karmen, 1996; Albanese, 1999). Retribution is not future oriented. It does not consider the aspect of change by the offender, only the offense and the retributive actions deemed appropriate by society.

Individual victims may express fantasies of revenge and retribution, a normal reaction of crime victimization grief (NCVC, 1999). Karmen (1996) notes that revenge fantasies can sustain a person and give direction and purpose, but "the thirst for vengeance can destroy victims as well" (p. 164) if it becomes a preoccupation that flames the painful memories of the victimization. The literature suggests that, contrary to fears and stereotypes of criminal justice agents, not all victims thirst for vengeance and often are less punitive in their desires than is the justice system (Kelly & Erez, 1997).

REHABILITATION

Rehabilitation as a goal of justice values interventions that help offenders become productive, law-abiding citizens. Rehabilitation assumes that criminal behavior is a manifestation of some personal or social impediment or shortcoming. It also recognizes that most offenders will either remain in the community under court supervision or, if incarcerated, will eventually reintegrate back into the community. As such, interventions are necessary and appropriate for the interests of society. Rehabilitation activities may take the form of counseling, medical services, education, or other psycho-bio-social interventions. Rehabilitation may be particularly favored by those victims who know the offender.

RESTITUTION

Offender restoration of the victim's financial condition places the victim as a priority in the system. Support for restitution as a goal of justice has been generally positive by the public and victims, especially as a condition of probation for nonviolent offenders.

Karmen (1996) identifies divergent arguments in favor of restitution:

- Repayment. Offers an incentive for victims to get involved in the criminal justice system.
- Rehabilitation. Offender learns about the injurious consequences of the criminal action and through efforts to repay the victim understands personal responsibility and social obligation.
- Reconciliation. The restitution amount may be determined through a mediated process where both the victim and the offender agree to be fair and constructive.
- Punishment. Restitution viewed as a penalty that should be imposed after the debt to society has been paid (pp. 301–303).

Thus, restitution as a goal of justice can be congruent with the other goals of retribution and rehabilitation. The criminal justice system's emphasis on compliance is related to the amount of restitution paid by offenders. In other words, payment tends to be better if restitution is emphasized as a priority in the court and by corrections (Smith & Hillenbrand, 1997).

Along with the call for justice, the quote from *New Directions* previously cited stated that the system was obliged to ease the pain of victims. This consideration of victim needs reflects a different paradigm of criminal justice. It is a paradigm that establishes the purpose of law and the justice system agencies to "heal the injury, repair the harm, compensate the loss and prevent further victimization" (Fattah, 1997, p. 79). This reflects the values, at least in part, of restorative justice, wherein crime is viewed not only as an injury to the government but also to individual victims and the community and the role of the criminal justice system is to "help repair those injuries . . . [and that] victims, offenders and their communities also must be involved at the earliest point and to the fullest extent possible" (Van Ness & Heetderks Strong, 1997, p. 31). Victim involvement may be a key in alleviating victims' "frustration with and alienation from the system" (Erez & Tontodonato, 1990, p. 452).

AGENCIES OF JUSTICE

As discussed, the various components of the criminal justice system have goals and needs that are not always consistent and may be contradictory to the goals and needs of the victim. Each of the various segments will be explored in terms of function, relationship to victims, and public perceptions.

LAW ENFORCEMENT

In most cases, law enforcement is the first contact crime victims have with the criminal justice system. There are various law enforcement representatives in which a victim may have contact: dispatch when a call is made; uniform officers at the crime scene; and detectives investigating the case. The initial impressions a victim has of these first contacts with the criminal justice system will likely be long lasting.

Law enforcement serves a dual role. From a strictly legal perspective, it is the responsibility of law enforcement to investigate crimes and arrest alleged offenders. To do this effectively, police need victim cooperation. The other role is that of the service provider, whose task is to "ensure that victims are treated with sensitivity and provided essential information and emergency assistance in the aftermath of victimization (New Directions, 1998, p. 47). Thus, there is an interdependence between the crime victim and the police (Jerin & Moriarity, 1998).

Law enforcement may become involved with a crime victim either through direct observation of a criminal act or through the reporting of a crime by a victim or other person. The likelihood of direct observation is very rare, and since less than half of violent crimes and about a third of property crimes are reported to police (U.S. Department of Justice, 1999) it is obvious that victims exercise a lot of discretion about their involvement in the system. The decision not to report may be based on a variety of factors. These reasons may be internally focused, such as embarrassment and fear of social stigma, feeling partly responsible, perceiving the crime to be a private matter, or perceiving the crime as too insignificant to bother reporting. The reasons not to report may also be externally focused, such as fear of retaliation and a lack of confidence or regard for the justice system (Kennedy & Sacco, 1998; Jerin & Moriarity, 1998; Freedy et al., 1994).

General dissatisfaction with law enforcement is a combination of culture as well as personal experiences. Neighborhoods characterized by poverty and instability tend to be more dissatisfied with police (Sampson & Bartusch, 1998). In a survey of residents from 12 cities, about 30% reported contact with police in the past year. Of these, 98% reported satisfaction with the police in their neighborhood though satisfaction was higher among those who had not experienced a violent crime (Smith et al., 1999). Thus, prior experiences with the justice system, especially if they were negative, may affect the decision to report (Erez, 1990), though, generally negative perceptions about police do not play much of a role in the decision to report.

Law enforcement has made significant strides the past several years in their interactions with crime victims as well as the community. Law-enforcement-based victim assistance units address the dual role of law enforcement through the allocation of resources specifically designed to address the specific needs and rights of crime victims. Multidisciplinary teams, directed collaboration between law health, social services, law enforcement, and others address the holistic needs of victims, especially those with special needs. Community policing strives to connect the police officer with the neighborhood to address crime and community problems in a proactive manner (New Directions, 1998).

PROSECUTION

The rights of the accused and the rights of the victim are brought into play at the prosecutorial stage of the justice system. The prosecutor represents the public—not the individual victim. While this does not preclude the prosecutor from representing the interests of the individual victim, if "the public interest comes into conflict with that of the victim, the former prevails" (Erez, 1990). In spite of this obligation to the public, it was recommended in the 1982 President's Task Force on Victims of Crime that prosecutors represent the victim's interests in all court appearances, plea negotiations, restitution and sentencing. Other recommendations from the Task Force for prosecutors include keeping victims apprised of their case status from the initial charging through parole, protecting victims from harassment and intimidation, resolving cases as quickly as possible by minimizing continuances, and returning property to victims as soon as possible.

These recommendations are addressed, in part, through prosecutor based victim/witness programs that exist in most jurisdictions. These programs provide an array of services, but this has not necessarily translated to victim satisfaction.

The types of services provided can generally be described as witness-oriented and victim-oriented. Witness-oriented programs focus on providing "the kinds of services necessary for a crime victim to become a reliable witness for the prosecution of the offender" (Jerin & Moriarity, 1998, p. 53) and focus on comfort and cooperation of victims. Victim-oriented programs focus more in intervention and recovery assistance. Crisis intervention, counseling, referral and financial assistance are examples of victim-oriented services. While prosecutor resources must be considered, victim satisfaction may be affected if the victim feels like a peripheral concern that serves only to enhance the management of the case prosecution. Furthermore, many services are limited to only select victims and some of the services provided may be relatively unimportant to victims (Erez, 1990).

The prosecutor has very broad discretionary powers, and it is the prosecutor's decision whether a case merits further action. A decision to proceed with a case depends on the legal sufficiency of a case, such as evidence of a narrowly defined unlawful act and the presence of criminal intent. In other words, is the case winnable? The decision to prosecute may also be influenced by an array of extralegal factors like department policy, such as "no-drop" policies for domestic violence cases, or automatic diversion for certain types of first time offenses. The cost of prosecution is another factor; that is, is the case worth the expenditure of time and money resources due to either the nature of the offense or for the anticipated return of the investment? Characteristics of the victim, as well as the offender, are additional factors. Some of the victim characteristics that research suggests increase the likelihood of charges being lodged against defendants are the following: The victim is middle-aged or elderly, white, employed, and has no prior arrest record (Myers & Hagan, 1979; Williams, 1976).

The overwhelming majority of criminal cases are resolved through plea negotiations. According to the U.S. Department of Justice, over 90% of felony convictions occurring within one year of arrest were obtained through a guilty plea. A common perception among the public and crime victims is that plea negotiations reduce the consequences of the criminal actions committed by offenders. Studies suggest, however, that most plea negotiated sentences are equivalent to those that would have been received upon conviction by trial (Karmen, 1996; Allen & Simonsen, 1998). A negotiated plea also means that the victim does not have go through the traumatic ordeal of the court hearing and the inherent risk that the defendant may not be convicted. These facts should not preclude victim involvement in plea negotiation discussions as is required in the majority of the states and the federal government and "if the victim is adamantly opposed . . . the prosecutor should seriously consider not going forward with a plea negotiation (Wallace, 1998).

The opportunity to submit a victim impact statement is probably the one option for victim participation that is the most common and formalized. In spite of the broad establishment of victim impact statements, only a small percentage of victims actually complete them. The lack of participation in this process may be because victims can only participate that in which they know about. The extent to which a victim submits a statement "depends on the court officials' level of enthusiasm towards such reform" (Kelly & Erez, 1997, p. 241). Even though a court officer may have told a victim about the impact statement as a matter of advisement, victims are typically overwhelmed with information and may not remember or realize the nature of the report. Further, this right may be resisted by prosecutors and their staff due to ideological or practical considerations.

DEFENSE

Defense attorneys function in the adversarial system of justice as representatives for the rights and interests of the accused. The right of an accused to be represented by counsel is clearly established in the Sixth Amendment of the U.S. Constitution and extends to both felony and misdemeanor offenses.

The Sixth Amendment also guarantees the right to a speedy trial. If the defendant is not in jail pending court, though, there may be an incentive by defense counsel to stall proceedings in an attempt to reduce the commitment by victims and witnesses to cooperate with the prosecution of the case. According to data from the U.S. Department of Justice (Reaves, 2001), the median length of time for case processing from arrest through adjudication is 79 days, though the length was twice as long for rape defendants and over a year for murder defendants.

Another aspect of the defense procedures that may conflict with victims is the cross-examination of victims as witnesses, often calling into question victim behaviors that may be judged as contributory or provocative in nature. Fortunately, most victims do not have to go through this revictimization since trials are relatively rare events.

JUDICIARY

The role of the judiciary is to provide oversight of the court proceedings in order to ensure compliance with judicial procedure and that individual rights are protected. While judges enjoy judicial discretion, the majority of the decisions made by judges, from bail to sentencing, are shaped by statute, case law, or administrative procedures.

Judges do have control of courtroom protocol and, unless prohibited, can include victim presence and input throughout the judicial process. For example, judges can invite victim comments about safety concerns prior to bail consideration. Judges can also recognize the victim's role in the judicial process by recognizing their rights and by facilitating their right to be present (New Directions, 1998).

The judiciary can also support victim participation though encouragement of victim impact statements and allocution. Victim impact statements can provide an additional method of documenting objective information of the physical and financial impact of a crime as well as the social and psychological impact. Thus, the statements can provide useful information to judges regarding the need for restitution and may improve the likelihood that it will be a part of the judicial order as a sentencing condition.

Victim impact statements are also intended to provide a venue for victims to express their wishes regarding disposition of a case. Research, though inconclusive, generally suggests that victim impact statements do not significantly impact sentencing decisions (Erez & Tontodonato, 1990; Davis & Smith, 1994). These decisions tend to be legalistic and consider variables like severity of the offense and prior record. However, victim input may be valuable in the determination of community supervision requirements.

This does not mean that there are not other benefits in victim participation through impact statements. For some, the chance to voice their account of the crime may serve their sense of duty in the pursuit of the ideal of justice; for others, it may be a psychological catharsis. Regardless of the personal benefit, victims should not be led to believe that participation through impact statements will significantly influence sentencing outcomes when in fact it probably will not. Victim satisfaction may be enhanced if they are provided accurate information about sentencing legal parameters, including truth-in-sentencing, which advises the earliest possible release from prison.

CORRECTIONS

Corrections as a segment of criminal justice system includes community and institutional based supervision of offenders. While incarceration rates in America are among the highest in the world, most offenders are supervised in the community.

Two primary concerns of community corrections regarding victim interests. One is protection from the offender in terms of harassment and further harm. Recognizing that the offender knows the victim in most violent crimes, keeping an offender away from a victim is not always an easy task. The offender and the victim may have common associations, such as school, work, and even family.

The other concern for victims is the payment of restitution as ordered by the court. Though restitution is embraced as a concept that is an appropriate obligation of offenders, it "remains one of the most under-enforced victim right within the criminal and juvenile justice systems" (New Directions, 1998, p. 357) with only a portion of the restitution amount ordered ever paid (Smith & Hillebrand, 1997; New Directions, 1998). Poor compliance with restitution is due, in part, to the limited resources and ability of most offenders to pay. In spite of these limitations, compliance is generally better when offenders perceive restitution as important. Perception is influenced by judicial and corrections attitudes and strategies to collect, such as payment plans and sanctions for failure to comply.

These same needs, protection and restitution, are also important in the institutional element of the correctional system. Prisons and jails also are obliged to keep the victim notified of an offender's status regarding release and transfer. Parole boards also should notify and invite victims to participate in parole hearings, either in person or through written victim impact statements.

In addition to the rights and recognition promoted in these areas, victim participation in corrections has increased in other areas. Crime victims serve on program advisory committees and are involved in programs

such as victim impact panels that educate offenders how crime has affected them. Victim-offender reconciliation programs are another example of
restorative justice initiatives that increase victim involvement in the justice
process and may enhance victim satisfaction (Umbreit & Bradshaw, 1995).

TYPES OF JUSTICE SYSTEMS

A discussion of the American justice system would not be complete without recognizing that it is a system of, not one but many, jurisdictional systems. Each with its own unique, yet overlapping, focus. This section
offers a brief overview of these systems with notable issues as they pertain to victim services.

STATE AND LOCAL

The majority of government services, including criminal justice, are offered
at the local and state level. Law enforcement, for example, is made up of
about 90% local and state and over three-fourths of this is local police and
sheriff officers (Bureau of Justice Statistics, 2000). As another example, of all
persons incarcerated, about 30% are in local jails, and about 90% are in
state prisons (Beck, 2000).

Local control of government functions has a firm historical basis in the
United States. The development of the criminal justice system resulted
from a "progression from small, religiously and culturally similar communities to larger towns and cities with more diverse populations"
(Albanese, p. 136). Judicial systems were established in each of the original
colonies. During the Revolutionary War the courts in these autonomous
systems were "used as a forum to fight unjust laws" (p. 264). "This independence continued after the American Revolution and resulted in wide-
spread differences among the various states, some of which still exist
today" (Wallace, p. 37).

Even within the confines of a limited geographic area there may be
numerous local jurisdictions subject to overlapping, and possibly conflicting, turfs. Within a county, for example, there may be several cities or
towns, each with its own law enforcement, judiciary, and even detention.
Add the aspect of numerous counties and communities within a geographic
area of a state or territory, the jurisdictional issues can be significant.

Certainly it is at the local and state level where some of the most innovative justice programs for victims occur. The concepts of policing,
prosecution, courts, and corrections that are community-based speaks
to the values of local involvement in the justice process. These concepts
all involve a collaborative approach in the prevention and intervention of
victimization.

FEDERAL

The federal criminal justice system functions to address criminal activity that is in violation of federal law. A criminal act may be in violation of federal as well as state statute.

Federal law enforcement consists of many different agencies, some of which include the Immigration and Naturalization Service, the Federal Bureau of Investigation, Drug Enforcement Administration, the U.S. Marshals Service, and the U.S. Postal Inspection Service. There are 89 federal judicial districts in the fifty states. District courts also exist in Puerto Rico, the Virgin Islands, the District of Columbia, Guam, and the Northern Mariana Islands.

Attention to victims in the federal justice system came about in 1982 with the enactment of the landmark legislation called the *Victim and Witness Protection Act.* This act formally recognized the responsibility of the federal government to ensure that rights for victims of federal crimes were established. In response to this, victim service programs, predominantly in the U.S. Attorneys Offices, were developed. The Attorney General Guidelines for Victim and Witness Assistance expands the scope of victim services to include all departments "engaged in detection, investigation, or prosecution of crime" (2000).

MILITARY

The United States military has its own justice system to deal with offenses involving military personnel. Military commanders possess considerable discretion on how to proceed with a case, that is, whether to take no action, to take some level of administrative action, or to refer the case for court martial. Though there are different types, a referral for court martial is similar to a civilian court trial. If found guilty, a conviction may be appealed. This process may, theoretically, go to the U.S. Supreme Court.

Department of Defense directives issued in 1994 provides "statutory requirements for victim and witness assistance and provides guidance for assisting victims and witnesses of crime from initial contact through investigation, prosecution, and confinement" (NVAA, 2000a). In addition, each branch of the military has a Family Advocacy Program that is designed to prevent and provide intervention of family violence.

TRIBAL

Criminal victimization against Native Americans is a significant concern as that population experiences twice the violent crime rate as the rest of the population (Greenfield & Smith, 1999). Tribal justice systems exist to address criminal victimization that occurs in Indian communities. These

justice systems range from those that mirror the structure of state and
federal courts while some maintain an indigenous structure. According
to the Bureau of Justice Statistics, there are 135 tribal law enforcement
agencies. In addition to law enforcement services, American Indian
tribes and the Bureau of Indian Affairs operate 69 jails in tribal areas
(Ditton, 2000).

Tribes do not have exclusive jurisdiction over criminal matters. Certain
crimes and processes are regulated or managed by the federal government. This shared jurisdiction can create problems, such as decisions
regarding enforcement and prosecution of crimes considered important
by the tribe, the ability to prosecute non-Native Americans who commit
crimes on tribal lands, and the overall sovereignty of a people to determine solutions in their community based on the values and customs of
that population. In essence, the question of jurisdiction depends on "the
identity of the victim(s), suspect(s), the seriousness of the offense, and the
state in which the offense was committed" (NCVAA, 2000b). In addition
to these complex legal issues regarding jurisdiction, the philosophy of
justice held by many Native American communities may be quite different from traditional Anglo concepts.

There has been increased support by the U.S. Department of Justice to
support justice initiatives for Indian tribes and organizations. For example, the Victim Assistance in Indian Country initiative, supported by the
Office for Victims of Crime, has funded the development and enhancement of victim assistance programs that includes, in part, crisis intervention, court advocacy, and bilingual counseling services. Similarly, the
STOP Violence Against Indian Women discretionary grant program has
supported tribal justice response to domestic violence.

JUVENILE JUSTICE

The juvenile justice system evolved from the belief that needs and
issues of children who violate the law are different from that of adults.
"According to this view, minors who broke the law were actually victims of improper care and treatment at home" (Albanese, 1999). The
state, under the doctrine of *parens patriae,* was the ultimate parent and
was therefore required to assume responsibility to intervene in the best
interest of the child. In order to maintain a separateness from the justice
systems that addressed criminals, a distinct justice system, different in
intent and function, developed. This included different laws that guided
the system response.

The format of the juvenile system generally reflects that of the criminal
justice system though, as suggested, under different laws and, often,
under different governmental structures. At least in larger jurisdictions,
it is common to find a juvenile division of law enforcement, detention,
prosection, court, and probation. For example, in a study of large law

enforcement agencies, defined as 100 or more sworn officers, 66% of police departments and 49% of sheriff departments had special juvenile crime units (Snyder & Sickmund, 1999). Federal guidelines discourage securing juveniles in adult jails, so many jails have special jurisdictions operate local or regional juvenile detention facilities. About a fifth of the delinquency cases processed by juveniles courts are detained and 28% are adjudicated juveniles are referred for residential placements (Snyder & Sickmund, 1999).

As a system that operated under the philosophy that favored rehabilitation more so than punishment, certain protections were afforded to juvenile cases. A significant protection was that of confidentiality. This protection has traditionally meant that juvenile cases were not open to the public, including the victims.

The philosophy and practices of juvenile justice have come under considerable scrutiny. Increasingly, a law-and-order approach has replaced the concept of *parens patriae*. Laws and policies pertaining to juvenile justice have become more criminal oriented and, as a result, many of the protections, including confidentiality, once afforded juvenile offenders have lessened. Many states now allow victims and/or the general public access to information and to attend hearings. Thus, victims of crime, once excluded from juvenile justice system, are increasingly more involved.

In spite of this trend toward a more criminal oriented approach, a rehabilitation philosophy—that is, recognition of the potential for change—continues in many innovative juvenile offender programs, as evidenced by victim-offender mediation programs, restorative community service, and education programs.

SUMMARY

The role of the victim in the process of justice has varied from direct, intimate involvement to that of an obscure bystander. The victim rights movement has shifted the balance so that victims once again have a role, albeit sometimes it is minimal. Regardless of the formal rights afforded to victims by statute or policy, real involvement in the justice system is more a reflection of attitudes; attitudes of acceptance and respect by the justice agents. Policies and regulations may eventually influence attitudes, but mandates without endorsement are shallow.

The justice system is challenged to balance the rights and responsibilities of offenders, the community, and victims. To bring about this balance, "there is a need for all criminal and juvenile justice personnel to ensure that the voices of victims are heard throughout the criminal justice process so that justice agencies are able to develop effective, victim-sensitive polices and programs (New Directions, p. xiii).

Victims of Sexual Abuse and Assault: Adults and Children

8

Nancie D. Palmer and Christine N. Edmunds

S exual assault. These very words invoke a kaleidoscope of images and responses from those who are victims to those who serve to assist them. In the twisting and turning over of these images are ever-changing perspectives of just what is sexual assault and just who are the victims? This chapter seeks not to provide the definitive answers but, rather, to provide an overview of the issues relevant to this vast topic. The hope is that those who assist victims of sexual assault—both individuals and systems—will become more aware of and responsive to this population.

While estimations of prevalence vary among researchers and professionals, one thing is evident. Sexual assault is underreported and crosses every socioeconomic and demographic dimension of society. No other form of assault is more psychologically invasive and difficult for victims to manage against a backdrop of values and norms that foster shame, secrecy, and silence. The inherent challenges of managing the experiences of sexual assault are magnified when viewed in the context of the victim's lives. Add to these dimensions the impact of oppression and disenfranchisement, and the kaleidoscope of the pieces becomes even more multifaceted. By providing an overlay, an ecological perspective, these multiple dimensions are presented for viewers to see and understand with, hopefully, greater clarity and appreciation for the impact of such experiences. Implications for systemic, organizational, and institutional responses are reviewed in this chapter.

OPERATIONAL DEFINITIONS

Definitions of what constitutes sexual assault as it pertains to children and to adults present a vast range of options from federal and state statutes, to instruments for reporting such acts (Finkelhor, 1986; Hunter, 1990; Gil, 1996; Sakheim & Devine, 1992). For purposes of discussion, however, it is useful to provide a working language of the territory. The National Center for Victims of Crime (NCVC) includes in its definition "any unwanted sexual contact or threats," which includes but is not limited to "touching any part of another person's body in a sexual" manner (even through clothes) without that person's consent (NCVC, 1998). Sexual assault includes rape and attempted rape, sodomy (oral and anal sexual acts, or sexual contact with an object or animal), incest, child molestation (including fondling), sexual exploitation of a child (including forcing or enticing a child to participate or watch others engaged in sexual activity with children or adults), forcing a child or adult to be photographed for sexually explicit pictures.s At its extreme, in ritualized abuse (which may include Satanic cult practices), "some survivors report having been stimulated sexually while forced to watch or participate in atrocities. . . . The end result is a tormented individual who views him or herself as evil, culpable, and dangerously out of control" (Sakheim & Devine, 1992, p. 320).

The concept of sexual assault, however, expands as it is less anchored in laws and statutes and more attached to the actual experiences of child and adult survivors. For example, Hunter (1990) takes a broad definition of sexual abuse to include, "intentional, repeated invasion of privacy" and other forms of covert behavior; that is, behavior that involves deceit or the intention to hide activity that is sexual in nature (p. 4). Hunter's (1990) examples include a parent requiring periodic "bug checks," in which the child (in this case a male) is stripped naked and the parent then proceeds in "running her or his hands over the boy's body, lifting his penis and scrotum, and inserting a finger into his anus" (p. 5). Other examples, include such practices as bathing an older child or adolescent, sexualizing the relationship, stripping to hit or spank or child or youth often publicly in the presence of siblings, other adults, or those in close proximity), or treating the child as a pseudo or surrogate spouse such as being privy to intimate information or sexual talk (including phone sex), or invited to sleep with the parent to comfort the parent. In these instances, although there may be no overt sexual activity, there is a sexual tension, and expectation on the part of the child or youth that "something else might happen." (Hunter, 1990, p. 7). (See also, van der Kolk, McFarlane, & Weisaeth, (Eds.), 1996; Carlson, 1997; Sakheim & Devine, 1990).

A central feature in the experience of sexual assault, whether the victim is a child or adult, is the negative valence of such events. Valence refers to the prescribed or psychological meaning of the experience by the victim. Negative valence includes physical pain and injury, emotional pain or despair, and incidents perceived as likely to cause physical or emotional pain or injury. There is damage or threat of damage to the individual's psychic integrity or sense of self (Carlson, 1997, p. 29). Another central feature is the real or perceived lack of control (Alan, 1995; Wallace, 2002; Sakheim & Devine, 1992; Carlson, 1997). "There is considerable evidence to suggest that because protection from harm is a basic component of human (and animal) survival, people seek to control their environments so that they can protect themselves from harm" (Carlson, 1997, p. 32). (See also De Becker, 1997). Valence is also affected when oppression and discrimination are present.

DEFINITION SUMMARY

Multiple definitions which are shaped according to

- federal, state, and local statute,
- social institutions and organizations that serve and respond,
- victim's perceptions and ascribed meaning, and
- ecological influences such as gender, race, age, orientation, and status.

What constitutes sexual abuse of a child is shaped according to

- statutes that define a child according to age,
- statutes that distinguish between age, age of consent, and adult,
- statutes that define relationships,
- those who investigate and respond, and
- those who provide treatment and care.

Forms of sexual assault include unwanted or contact without consent that may include

- physical or psychologically forced vaginal, oral, or anal penetration,
- previously and commonly referred to as rape,
- sodomy (oral, anal, other sexual acts with objects or animals),
- lascivious acts such as child pornography, voyeurism, photographing of children and/or others in sexual or sexually suggestive/simulated acts,
- indecent contact,
- indecent exposure such as displaying sexual organs, or masturbation,
- touching another sexually without consent or through coercive means,
- fondling, caressing, other wise violating body integrity in a sexual manner
- forms of sexual assault with limited definitions—that is, acts covered by statutes/policies to address
  - stripping of children under disguise of punishment or body searches,

- sexualizing a parent-child relationship or through other intimate means,
- nonovert sexual activity with sexual overtones and tension,
- intentional, repeated invasions of privacy, and
- making fun of a child's sexual development, organs or preferences.

CHILD VICTIMS

THE CHOREOGRAPHY OF CHILD SEXUAL ABUSE

Essential to understanding the hows and whats of a sexually abused child are the relationships and interactions between abuser and victim. Frequently, current understanding is shrouded in mythology and misconception. Examples follow.

MYTH: Children are likely to be sexually assaulted by a stranger.
FACT: 75%–95% of offenders are known (familiar) or related to the child.

MYTH: Children lie or fantasize about sexual activities with adults.
FACT: In developmental terms, children cannot make up explicit sexual information.
  - Children must be exposed to sexual situations/speak from experiences.
  - Primary indicators of a child "making up stories" include the following:
    - Lack of specificity.
    - Inability to describe in explicit detail.
    - Inability to illustrate the act.
    - Lack of related/corresponding language.
    - Grossly inconsistent account.

MYTH: Most child sexual abuse is a single incident.
FACT: Most child sexual abuse is repeated and progressive (Finkelhor, 1986, Hunter, 1990).

MYTH: Nonviolent sexual contact with a child is not damaging.
FACT: Nearly all victims experience shame, guilt, confusion, anger, and loss of self-esteem (Gil, 1996; Hunter, 1990; Shirar, 1996).

MYTH: Child molesters are homosexual men.
FACT: Most child sexual abuse is by heterosexual men who find same sex adult relationships undesirable. Pedophiles and homosexuals are not the same (Groth, & Birnbaum, 1978; Newton, 1978).

MYTH: Children and youth "really want it" or they would say no.

FACT: Children need adults or others to survive. They accommodate to please, to survive, to receive desperately needed attention. They may be coerced/enticed or threatened or rewarded (Hunter, 1990; Shirar, 1996; Gil, 1996; Carlson, 1997).

MYTH: Children who become aroused must "like it."

FACT: The human body does what it was designed to do. There is an inherent need to avoid pain and threat of harm (Carlson, 1997; De Becker, 1997).

MYTH: If a boy and a woman have sex, it's the boy's idea and he is not abused.

FACT: Boys can be just as devastated by abuse as girls and, as children, are just as powerless. Sexual abuse in disguised form is likewise upsetting and confusing (Lew, 1988; Hunter 1990).

MYTH: All sexually abused children, particularly males, will abuse as adults.

FACT: Only a portion of child victims abuse. Protective and other factors may increase resiliency and recovery (Groth, 1978; Finkelhor,1978; Palmer, 1991; Palmer, 1997).

MYTH: Children who are sexually abused should know place, time, and details

FACT: To tolerate or accommodate abuse, particularly that which is painful and terrifying, victims may dissociate (i.e., develop altered states of consciousness). Developmental factors may also inhibit. Children may be drugged as well (Shirar, 1996; van der Kolk et al., 1996; Sakheim & Devine, 1992).

MYTH: Females, as children or adults, do not sexually abuse others.

FACT: There is a growing body of evidence that females (children as well as adults) sexually abuse others (Hunter, 1990; Lew, 1988; Wallace, 2002; Allen, 1995).

MYTH: Siblings just engage in acts of curiosity, not sex.

FACT: Sibling abuse is any form of physical, mental, or sexual abuse. It manifests power and control in age and other physical differentials (Wallace, 2002)

MYTH: Sibling sexual abuse is not harmful to the victim.

FACT: Sexual abuse is power over and violation of body integrity. Sibling sexual abuse can be just as damaging and distressing to the victim (Carlson, 1997).

CHILD VICTIMS AND RELATIONSHIP TO SEXUAL ABUSERS/PREDATORS

Just as there is *no* one profile of people who sexually abuse others, adults and/or children, there is no one profile of a child victim. Various researchers such as Finkelhor (1986) have developed theoretical models, such as *The Four Preconditions Model of Sexual Abuse*, which present the personal and social context (Wallace, 1999) for expression of sexually abusive behaviors. While this model is valuable to our understanding the behavior of perpetrators, the perspective does not wholly include the rich and dynamic inner life of the victim. For example, three of the four preconditions focus on

1. motivation to sexually abuse (the perpetrator),
2. overcoming internal inhibitors (the perpetrator), and
3. overcoming external inhibitors (primarily the lack of protective parental figures or environmental conditions).

The final precondition considers

4. overcoming child resistance.

To more fully appreciate and understand child victims of sexual assault is to be aware of certain biological/psychological factors that are a part of every child.

Discussion of sexual assault, initially presented in this chapter the notion of a kaleidoscope of images and responses, is integrated within an ecological framework. Such an approach can identify personal, interpersonal, and environmental features that interact and influence each other in significant ways. Thus, a choreography or thematic dimension is created to enhance our understanding and awareness of a victim's experiences, including the dynamic inner life of the child victim.

THE INNER LIFE OF CHILDREN: PERSONAL AND INTERPERSONAL DIMENSIONS OF CHILD VICTIMS

Guiding our understanding is a profound observation of Dr. Margaret Mead, who observed that despite best efforts to understand children, we are forever limited because "we have no idea at all what the world is going to be like 40 years from now" (Klein, 1975). In other words, "a child today is at the center of his (or her) own 'becoming" (Klein, 1975). Adding to this idea the fact that responders of whatever profession are always outside the inner life and actual experiences of the victim would indicate that caution is advised in developing any model of explanation. Our charge is to connect with child victims as we become students, that is, learners, of their experiences, rather than to overlay our notions of what we think they experience in their inner and outer worlds. That said, certain internal features are part of our human makeup.

Biology: The Forgotten Element in the Experience of Child Trauma

While research and corresponding literature has emerged concerning the biology of trauma, the information seems to focus on adults rather than on specifically considering children and youth. Thus, we must consider the biology of trauma as it is linked to two critical factors:

1. The influence of biology as it is connected to the physical self.
2. The influence of biology as it is linked to attachment as a critical emotional or psychological phenomenon of all human beings.

It is the very essence of our humanness that makes anyone a potential victim of sexual assault. Children are most vulnerable because "trauma experience(s) can hit us where its hurts most—it strikes at our mammalian core" (Allen, 1995, p. 23). For example, the limbic system among other biological attributes is wired to facilitate the attachment process between infant and parents (most often the mother or mother figure). The concept of *attachment* is a critical factor which has emerged in the study of trauma (Allen, 1995; Fonagy, Steele, Steele, Higgit, & Target, 1992; Stein, Fonagy Fersuson, & Wiseman, 2000). Attachment, both physiological and emotional or psychological is crucial to survival. In fact, the limbic system is exquisitely developed to signal distress in response to separation enabling the human to "generate the 'separation cry' to produce reunion" (Allen, 1995, p. 28). Universal stressors in mammals may include such things as painful stimuli, electric shock, cold or heat, restraint, frightening or threatening situations, or intrusion. Attachment is indispensable and provides the basis of safety and security in the world; thus, the drive for a human being to bond with a caregiver is powerful (Melody, 1997).

Biology also has a particular psychological impact on a victim who may experience pleasure (including orgasm) during an assault (Gil, 1996). Victims most frequently feel responsible for being sexually abused, "many youngsters have difficulty with their bodies' responding with pleasure to the abuse. They believe that if they had physical sensations, this means they were responsible" (Gil, 1996, pp. 115–116), or consenting to the sexual assault. What professionals and volunteers often fail to do is recognize that human physiology is doing exactly what it was designed to do. Gil (1996) has used in treatment of victims of sexual assault, the analogy of an onion, which when cut produces tears of those near by. Gil observes, "I'm not sad, you're not sad, and there is nothing to cry about. And yet, when our noses smell the onion, our eyes leak tears . . . (p. 116). It is a way of helping victims (children and adults, male or female) understand that pleasure, including orgasm was not compliance with sexual assault, but a way in which one's body responded to sexual stimulation (Gil, 1996). It is this biological reaction that may, more than any other, keep victims silent or reluctant in sharing their experiences.

To speak of the biology of life is to also speak about the dimension of death. When "we have built our lives on assumptions that enable us to feel safe and secure, we tend not to concern ourselves with our physical existence. And yet, we become painfully [excruciatingly] aware of our fragility as physical beings through traumatic events (Janoff-Bulman, 1992, p. 56). Van Derkolk, Weisaeth and Van DerHart cite Lifton's description of the basic survival threat as the "death imprint; that is, a jarring awareness of the fact of death . . . and confrontation with one's own mortality" (p. 480). Through the continued study of trauma, a second biological function of attachment has come to light, namely, the regulation of physiological arousal (Allen, 1995, p. 46) and "as a regulator of various neurochemical metabolic sleep-wake, cardiovascular and endocrine systems (Meloy, 1997, p. 10). Putman (1997) provides an excellent discussion of the "ways in which behavioral symptoms map onto biological systems known to be affected by traumatic experiences" (pp. 128–129). At the core of each traumatic experience is the profound sense of helplessness and lack of control. The impact is that long after the assault is over the victim often experiences a physiological arousal through such phenomena as intrusive memories, flashbacks, and nightmares (Allen, 1995). In sum, our very humanness (biological/mammalian core) creates a paradox of facilitating attachment and sexual response and yet creates greater vulnerability both physical and emotional for human contact. Perhaps this vulnerability is best understood from the child's inner world in these ways:

- Children need adult caregivers (physical *and* emotional) in order to physically survive.
- Children need attachments to significant adults in order to have a secure base and safety from which to physically and emotionally develop.
- Children who are not attached or who are poorly attached (often because of physical and emotional absence, violence, or inconsistent caregiving) are not only insecure but may, because of deprivation, be starved both physically and emotionally for attention and affection. This "starvation" is biologically driven and is our human imperative to fulfill often by any means.

- Children need to trust and please their caretakers in order to obtain what they need for physical and emotional survival.
- Children need, as all humans do, physical human contact and may have some pleasurable responses to sexual stimulation during assault.
- If the assault is accompanied by stimuli that invokes a sense of annihilation/impending death, then it becomes a defining feature of the survival experience.

These neurobiological needs and responses are inextricably integrated with psychological needs and processes, thus making children (including youth) a particularly vulnerable target for sexual predators. In these situations, resistance may be low, the need to have some kind of human attachment is great, and a child's repertoire of coping responses extremely limited. If the environmental context is also challenging, oppressive, unyielding, or threatening, then attachment is compromised at best and most likely devastating.

Interpersonal Dimensions of Perpetrators in Relationship to Children

Perhaps the most detrimental misconception of a person who sexually abuses and assaults children is the image of a stranger who is male. It is the very "normalcy" of the perpetrator that makes him or her a clear threat to a child (DeBecker, 1997). Two factors are important to consider in understanding the choreography of assault, including sexual assault:

1. Responders must be aware that trauma, such as sexual assault, will most likely be at home, or familiar places by people familiar to the victim.
2. Assault will likely be repeated and protracted.

Given these two critical dimensions, the concept of captivity is crucial to understanding the interaction between perpetrator and his or her victim. Captivity means that another has both psychological and physical control and power over the victim. (This concept will receive greater explanation in chapter on family violence).

Complicating the understanding of victim's experiences is that it is likely that the perpetrator of sexual assault, blames the victim. The criminal justice system and practice of an adversarial process (legal system) may unwittingly through lack of sensitive response or through vigorous defense, further traumatize and blame victims. Studies (Lev-Wiesel, 2000, p. 3) indicate that offenders justifications fall into general categories:

1. A restricted lack of understanding of violence against children (lack of empathy for).
2. Tolerance of and for violence.
3. A distorted sense of attribution (personal characteristics such as mental illness, alcohol, evil), according to which the perpetrator is absolved of responsibility or guilt or the seductiveness of the victim.
4. Circumstantial conditions such as unemployment, marital problems, or the death of one's spouse.

The Child Sexual Abuse Accommodation Syndrome: Forensic Implications

Activation of protective systems, such as civil and criminal justice systems, requires report and disclosure by a child or adult victim. However, "the disparity between child experience and adult acceptance is compounded by the fact that child victims tend not to complain about victimization because they are fearful about repercussions of disclosure" (Summit, Miller, & Veltkamp, 1998, p. 43). The child sexual abuse accommodation syndrome" (CSAAS), initially developed by Dr. Roland Summit (1983), provides a useful framework bridging the child's inner world with outer realities that touch on the ecology of the child's environment, such as family, extended family, close relationships, and social or institutional systems designed to address maltreatment and child distress. Such a framework as the accommodation syndrome is critical for "understanding what otherwise appear to be illogical and irrational responses to various types of stressful life experiences" (Summit & Miller, 1998, p. 44). Additionally, it is critical for responders to understand the extremely limited options for coping that a child has in the face of prevailing adult indifference or disbelief. In essence, "in the course of processing the trauma which occurs during sexual abuse there is a compromise not only by the intrinsic victim perpetrator interaction but also by the isolation and psychological distancing (orphaning) unwittingly imposed on the child by adults who fail to recognize that child sexual abuse is occurring (e.g. mother too intimidated to intervene in abuse of children)" (Summit et al.,1998, p. 45).

CSAAS is made up of cognitive, emotional, and behavioral characteristics that in sum are designed as mechanisms of survival in the face of impossible odds: the failure of parental or social systems to respond and protect. Components are:

- Secrecy.
- Helplessness.
- Entrapment and accommodation.
- Delayed, conflicted, unconvincing disclosure.
- Retraction.

Each component or phenomenon serves a useful protective function for the child and highlights the enormous challenge of disclosure—"A dilemma faced by the child victims in attempting to communicate their experience to those who may potentially help them" (Summit et al., 1998, p. 45).

Secrecy, "the cornerstone of sexual abuse" (Davies and Frawley, 1994) is imposed by the perpetrator with threats and promises that ensure the child's acquiescence (p. 36). Secrecy is "nearly universal", is enforced by the isolation of the child victim, and "most profound" . . . a "paralyzing confusion produced by the context of the abusive experience" that is "different from any human interaction" (Summit et al., 1998, p. 46). Children succumb to the power of adults who control and create their reality (Allen, 1995; Summit et al., 1998; Gries, Goh, Andrews, Gilbert, Praver, & Stelzer, 2000).

Helplessness reflects that "No child is a match for the test-proven blandishments of a child molester" (Summit et al., 1998., p. 47). When a child is subjected to assault/trauma over time, by a trusted parent or adult, even a more powerful sibling, it is overwhelming to the psyche and fuels the very real human fears of annihilation and sense of abandonment.

Delayed, conflicted, or unconvincing disclosure refers to the child's stewing in "fearful ambivalence . . . of wishing to prompt rescue yet desperate to keep the secret" (Summit et al., 1998. p. 51). Typically children are highly reluctant to disclose and may, at best, only hint at distress. Seligman (1975) hypothesized that all humans are fearful, that is, terrified of consequences when threatened, and therefore need a safety signal as a means of gaging the risks. Likewise, it is unusual for a child to experience relief upon disclosure, particularly if systems fail to provide (add parents or parental figures) a real sense of safety and security or protection. Without these realities in place, a "child may simply return to the treacherous security of the secret" (Summit et al., 1998, pp. 50–51). A child, may, in order to survive, give partial information or distorted information or may dissociate during the trauma and have limited information consciously available. The net effect is that delayed, conflicted, or unconvincing disclosure, while very normal under the circumstances of a child, is "regarded by skeptical adults as contradictory to normal, credible victims behaviors" (Summit et al., 1998, pp. 45–46). In other words, a child victim is placed by responders in the position of acting like a nonvictim. This leads to retraction.

Retraction occurs when the child, overwhelmed by the lack of validation, the repeated assaults of disbelieving or skeptical responding social institutions and/or parents (parental figures), has no place to emotionally go but to retreat to what is perceived the only place to go, that is back to the secret. The very nonsupportive and nonvalidating reactions, particularly coupled with the aggressive cross-examination in a criminal justice system, reinforces the predictions of doom and harm a child was initially threatened by. Responders must view retraction as diagnostic and "not the final word," which "ironically is the child's best efforts to appease adults that elicits the most empathic adult distrust" (Summit et al., 1998, p. 53). In the wake of retractions, adults may angrily react at what they perceive as a child's "deceit."

Note. Similar dynamics occur in situations of sexual assault of adults, particularly with "different" diverse populations, including male victims. See discussion on Special Considerations.

ECOLOGICAL DIMENSIONS IN RELATIONSHIP TO CHILD VICTIMS

The criminal justice and civil systems may further reenforce (albeit unintentionally) responses that essentially blame the victim. For example, the following may occur:

• Lack of understanding and empathy for the inner experiences of children (Lev-Wiesel, 2000). This creates comorbidity in their experiences of trauma. Such things as, leaving them in abusive situations or failing to remove the predator/abuser from their environment, accompanied by sufficient emotional support for the victim, and actions that reassure him or her that what happened is not their fault. That it is adults responsibility to nurture and protect the child. Removing a wounded child further reinforces the "punishment" threatened by their abuser(s) and may contribute to a retraction as a desperate move to maintain secrecy and "approval" by parent or authority figures and thus remain "attached" to the family.

• Tolerance for violence (Lev-Wiesel, 2000). There is currently a lack of clear, swift actions by civil and criminal justice systems that convey real messages that violence will not be tolerated. Such tolerance reinforces the sense of helplessness as described in the CSAAS model.

• Lack of clear understanding by the civil and criminal justice systems of what a child is, what bio/psycho/social factors are present, including a child's experience in the larger social environment that may condone blame and/or oppression and discrimination or disenfranchisement if he/she is "different." And, correspondingly, understand that a child's responses are ones of attachment and survival. These dimensions are reflected in the CSAAS model.

• Civil and criminal justice systems may minimize a child's trauma and suffering in the wake of holding offenders unaccountable or minimally accountable for their actions through the justice process—that is, the pressure of creating "true/false" in an adversarial legal system may also create disbelief by authorities and make it impossible for victims to adequately describe their experiences in ways more appropriate to clinical interventions. Or, attributing the alleged abuse to offender situations (ill spouse) or attributes (mental illness, alcohol abuse), thereby creating the phenomenon of delayed, conflicted, or unconvincing disclosure.

CHILDREN AND MEMORY: A CHALLENGING ISSUE

When victims are particularly challenged through the process of the civil and criminal justice systems, issues of the child's recollection or memory emerge. The false memory syndrome has been one such defense (belief that memories are fabricated or induced by influential people such as therapists). Thus, victims, especially children, are subject to scrutiny the likes of which would be daunting to even seasoned professionals. The very notion of true or false as used in the criminal justice systems fuels the debate, because memories are reconstructions of past experiences. What victims are trying to achieve and maintain are coherent narratives for describing traumatic events. "Yet, as apt as the term 'false memory' may be for legal purposes, it starts scientific and clinical discussion off on the wrong foot" (Allen, 1995, p. 84).

As with all human experiences, there are many avenues of "knowing" what happened. Therefore, it is destructive to put memory into a dichotomous equation of either/or. The true extent of false memories is unknown, because there is no empirical evidence to support or account for it. As Allen (1995) observes, there is an abundance of empirical evidence that indeed individuals are traumatized. Terr (1994) gives considerable weight to symptoms of trauma through her now well recognized studies of children. The strength of Babcock's (and Palmer's 2000 revision of Babcock) conceptual and clinical protocol to reach reasonable clinical certainty that child sexual abuse has occurred is the requirement of diagnostic material in multiple areas.

Gaarder (2000) observes that the "so-called memory debate" appears to focus almost entirely on females, especially women, and characterizes them as mentally ill, crazy, hysterical, and attention-seeking, although one in six males are among the victims. Additionally, women are characterized as "vengeful, suggestible, and prone to fantasize about sexual violation (Herman, 1994, p. 54). Likewise, therapists targeted in the debate are primarily women (Gaarder, 2000).

The criminal and civil process of demanding that a child report and repeat over and over again, his or her experiences to multiple people in authority is illustrative of systems not supporting victims in their efforts to achieve a safe environment and corresponding attachments to people who can protect and nurture them (see also previous discussion on child sexual abuse accommodation syndrome).

SEXUAL ABUSERS AND THEIR CHILD VICTIMS

Most research suggests that child abusers do not fit any stereotype. While theories vary, it is useful to identify some conceptual framework in order for responders and treaters to understand the choreography between abusers and their victims. Finkelhor (1986) established four factors present in the incidence of sexual abuse. This theory is called the four preconditions model of sexual abuse. The value of this model is that it creates a context of personal and social behaviors where sexually abusive actions are expressed. In addition, this model, complements and illustrates examination of victimization from an ecological perspective. Further examination adds to our understanding of the victim's experience within the choreography of the relationship and experience between victims and their abuser(s).

Finkelhor's (1986, pp. 86–87) preconditions include motivation to sexual abuse, overcoming internal inhibitors, overcoming external inhibitors, and overcoming the child's resistance. Examined further, each precondition includes additional features.

Precondition I: Motivation to Sexually Abuse

- Emotional congruence. Satisfy a need to relate to a child in a sexual manner. Children learn about social behaviors from others. They may become sexualized and socialized to engage in sexual ways.
- Sexual arousal. The child is a source of gratification. Children may likewise be sexually aroused. This adds to the child's confusion, shame, guilt, and loyalty (see also Brady, 1979).
- Blockage. Alternative forms of sexual gratification are not present/available or less satisfying. (Note, care must be taken not to blame others, especially females, for this reason).

Precondition II: Overcoming Internal Inhibitors

- Use of alcohol or other drugs by the abuser and victim who may be forced to ingest substances.
- Lack of empathy or ability to see victim as a person.
- Weak criminal sanctions and legal responses (few perpetrators are charged and successfully prosecuted).
- Inability to see child as frightened, confused or having other feelings.
- Psychosis (rare).
- Reenacting own victimization & trauma (should not be excused but treated).

Precondition III: Overcoming External Inhibitors

- Type and amount of supervision a child may have.
- Lack of parental figure close by to protect.

- Lack of protective/nurturing adults (Palmer, 1997).
- Unusual sleeping or living arrangements (see also section on children and diversity).
- Lack of social support for mothers and family.
- Erosion of family networks/social support systems.
- Socialization and sexualization of children in the media.
- Social tolerance of violence & force as a method of problem solving.

Precondition IV: Overcoming Child Resistance

- Children need adults/more powerful others to survive.
- Children want to please adults.
- Child may be deprived and starving for affection/attention.
- Children feel powerless and helpless (male victims exhibit as well (see Moi San & Sanders-Phillips, 1997).
- Children trust the abuser.
- Children need physical human contact.

To summarize, as the issue of sexual assault is more closely examined, the pieces of the kaleidoscope become more clearly seen in relation to each other. Sexual assault occurs when there are combinations of environmental, social, personal, and child factors, which in movement together result in assault. This is the ecological perspective. It must be emphasized that victims are never to be blamed but rather to understand factors of vulnerability and risk for the victim and opportunity for victimizers.

THE DISCOVERY OR IDENTIFICATION
OF CHILD SEXUAL ASSAULT

Child sexual abuse is often "discovered" in relation to other presenting features. Most texts tend to discuss indicators of child sexual assault and thereby imply that discovery is inductively concluded (Wallace, 2001; Hunter, 1990). This approach has limitations because indicators, in and of themselves, are not necessarily conclusive. A protocol developed by Dr. Elizabeth Babcock (1985) provides a substantial approach for reaching what she refers to as "reasonable clinical certainty that sexual abuse had occurred." This protocol has been expanded upon (Palmer). The strength of this approach is that it does not rely on stand-alone elements for concluding that a child has been sexually assaulted. Rather, it is a formula or equation that first clusters indicators and then secondly combines the clusters into a formula, the strength of which requires all elements to be present and accounted for.

The formula for diagnosing or reaching reasonable clinical certainty that child sexual abuse has occurred also lends itself to meeting the

Cluster I + Cluster II + Cluster III = Reasonable clinical certainty/child sexual abuse

FIGURE 8.1 Formula for clear and convincing standard.

Cluster I + Cluster II + Cluster III + Medical/Physical Evidence = Child Sexual Abuse

FIGURE 8.2 Formula for beyond reasonable doubt standard.

standard of clear and convincing evidence used to address child welfare issues in civil proceedings and contributes substantively to the standard of 'beyond reasonable doubt' in criminal proceedings. The latter standard of reasonable doubt is further enhanced by the presence of medical and/or physical evidence. Using a formula that requires multiple examples of evidence significantly meets the challenge of accusations of fabrication of child sexual abuse, a common response by perpetrators and/or the legal representatives. Regardless of the presence or lack of legal action, it is essential for intervention and treatment purposes to have substantially supporting information. In this regard, an ethical approach to child sexual abuse is maintained in response and practice.

It must be also noted that reaching reasonable clinical certainty that a child has been sexually abused does not mean that there is a corresponding identification of the offender(s).

The Formula of Child Sexual Abuse: Civil Action and Clinical Treatment provides discovery and identification, and provides substance for standard of "clear and convincing." This formula is illustrated in Figure 8.1.

The Formula of Child Sexual Abuse: Civil and Criminal Proceedings and Treatment provides discovery and identification, provides substance for standard of "clear and convincing," and provides substance for standard "beyond reasonable doubt." This formula is illustrated in Figure 8.2.

REACHING REASONABLE CLINICAL CERTAINTY OF CHILD SEXUAL ABUSE

Cluster I: Presenting Symptoms/Problem

Includes but is not limited to the following characteristics:

- Sleep (too much or too little or night terrors).
- Has abnormal appetite (eating too little, too much, hoards, is bulimic or anorexic).

- Hyperactive or withdrawn.
- Wets/soils bed.
- Hostile/aggressive/given to sudden rage.
- Presents somatic symptoms (frequent headaches/stomach aches).
- Oppositional/defiant.
- Sets fires/destroys animals.
- Exhibits phobic behaviors/avoidant.
- Steals/lies.
- Exhibits global fears/anxiety.
- Clings.
- Regresses.
- Runs away.
- Commits self-destructive acts (including burning, cutting, mutilating biting self).
- Commits disfiguring acts (some victims make themselves larger by eating or otherwise disfigure their appearance).
- Dissociates (separates from conscious awareness).
- Presents depression (emotional constriction or flat/bland affect).
- Exhibits hyperarousal (extreme sensitivity to people and environment).

Note, these presenting symptoms/problems may be explained by a host of contributing factors, including family problems, such as divorce, death, or moving to a new location; physical or emotional abuse; neglect; learning disabilities or developmental delays; physiological and medical problems/illnesses; school or peer difficulties; other life altering events, or sexual abuse.

Cluster II: Sexual Specificity

Includes but is not limited to these characteristics

- Has knowledge of sexual activity beyond age.
- Initiates sexual activity with another—especially younger—child.
- Simulates adult sexual act(s).
- Excessively masturbates.
- Stimulates self with objects, inserting objects/fingers, rocking in public.
- Asks to be sexually touched and stimulated.
- Shows seductive or sexualized behavior.
- Uses explicit words for body parts and sexual activity.
- Is fearful of being touched—especially genitals—or fear of baths.
- Refers to sexual activity between children.
- Has a preoccupation with cleanliness or refers to genital areas as "dirty."

- Displays pseudo maturity (adultified child).
- Exhibits otherwise unusual behavior with sexual overtones.

It is not uncommon for offenders to allege that a child saw some adult sexual act, such as when walking into a bedroom, "accidentally" saw some pornographic pictures or movie, or is "lying or making it up." Researchers and clinicians maintain that children must be explicitly exposed and involved. The discovery or identification of child sexual abuse is further substantiated by the third cluster: the child's report.

Sexual specificity may also be substantiated through medical and physical evidence, although such evidence is often not available or attainable (Wallace, 2002). In addition the presenting symptoms or problem(s), when combined, are especially diagnostic.

Cluster III: Child's Report

Disclosure by a child may take many forms. Generally, children, when they already perceive that a parent or adult is otherwise unavailable (not responsive to a child's general well-being, needs, or distress), may be very reluctant to report or disclose sexual abuse. In addition, children are often threatened by the offender(s) with abandonment or removal of themselves or parent or significant other. Children may be threatened with destruction of their favorite things or pet. Often, an offender entices or coerces a child. Sexual abuse may be progressive, ranging from less physically intrusive acts such as voyeurism, fondling, and exhibitionism, to acts of physical contact and penetration. Considering the preconditions, a child may be starved for attention or affection, thus making him or her even more vulnerable to the attention of an adult or other offender.

Children may blame themselves for what is frightening, confusing, and sometimes sexually arousing to them. "Society can reinforce the victim's self blame in several ways" (Hunter, 1990, p. 71).

Self blame that is reinforced includes

- Removal of the child from his/her home.
- Subjecting the child to adverse legal and investigative proceedings.
- Subjecting the child to repeated questioning by multiple investigators.
- Being told directly that the child is to blame.
- Being told that the child is lying.
- Believing that a loving parent/person could not be harmful/hurtful.
- Being forced to keep a secret (inducing shame and guilt).
- Being admonished as to the "evil" of sexual acts, threats that "You're going to hell."
- Having other diagnoses applied.

Examples of Child's Report or Disclosure

- Child states someone removed his/her clothes.
- Child states someone else exposed self to him/her.
- Child states someone touched/penetrated (poked, punched, hurt) bottom.
- Child states s/he witnessed sex acts between adults, adults and children, and so forth.
- Child states someone s/he was made to touch someone's private parts.
- Child states someone made him/her touch the person's bottom or mouth.
- Child states that objects or sharp objects where put into him or her.
- Child hints about sexual activity, complains that someone is bothering him or her.
- Child states s/he witnesses sex between children, children and adults, adults and adults, adults and animals, children and animals.

Children of varying ages, development, and circumstance may likewise not directly disclose through explicit and direct reporting. Many children may reveal themselves and their experiences through drawings or other expressive medium (Shirar, 1996; Malchiodi, 1998; Brett, 1992; DiLeo, 1970; Wohl & Kaufman, 1985; Webb-Boyd, 1991). These drawings are often explicit in nature depicting sexual acts, injured body parts particularly the genital area, sadness, fear or terror, and despair. Drawings may exhibit great anxiety, with emphasis on genital areas or mouth (Wohl & Kaufman, 1985; Malchiodi, 1998). Drawings may reveal other explicit activity such as children or adults having sex with people or animals or defecating or urinating. Although this "disclosure or report" is not in a voice medium, qualified professionals can present evidence as to their power and validity. For purposes of assessment, or "discovery," it is critical that any drawing(s) be conducted by a trained professional accompanied by a clinical interview. Figure 8.3 illustrates the formula for reasonable clinical certainty that child sexual abuse has occurred.

Physical and Medical Evidence

Many discoveries or disclosures of child sexual abuse are not accompanied by corresponding physical or medical evidence. However, careful observation, and physical examination by a sensitive and qualified medical professional may reveal evidence that such activity has or is occurring.

The Formula: Diagnosing Child Sexual Abuse

CLUSTER I
Presenting Symptoms/Problems*
(often calling attention to the child)

    PLUS
    CLUSTER II
    (Sexual Specificity)

        PLUS
        CLUSTER III
        (Child's report)*

            EQUALS

                REASONABLE clinical certainty that
                child sexual abuse has occurred.

FIGURE 8..3 Formula for reasonable clinical certainty of child sexual abuse.

Indicators or observations of physical and medical evidence includes:

- Child relaxes rather than tenses rectum when touched.
- Child has relaxed anal sphincter.
- Child has anal, or rectal lacerations or scarring.
- Child has enlargement of vaginal opening.
- Child has trauma around the genital area.
- Child has vaginal laceration or scarring in females.
- Child has sore penis.
- Child shows evidence of sexually transmitted disease.
- Reports of the child displaying anger/rage/agitation around toileting.
- Child has chronic constipation due to avoidance of using the toilet.
- Child is preoccupied with feces or urine.
- Child has a history of soiling another child or environment with body wastes.

SPECIAL CONSIDERATIONS: RITUALISTIC ABUSE

Although the phenomenon of ritualistic abuse is a controversial one, there appears to be significant evidence that it exists (Wallace, 2002). Clinicians' reports bear significant similarities of presenting symptoms and sexually specific or related behavior (Sakheim & Devine, 1992; Shirar, 1996; Wallace, 2002). This particular form of child abuse is particularly destructive to children. Within the practices and experiences of ritualistically abused children is the total destruction of their psyche through the committing of atrocities that compromise their sense of self and goodness. "For example survivors report being buried in the ground (sometimes in a coffin with a dead animal or person) after being severely abused. The reported abuse usually involves some type of mutilation that would result in severe hemorrhaging" (Sakheim & Devine, 1992, p. 30). This ritual is followed by pronouncing the child or adult as born again as evil or unto Satan. A child may be branded or scarred showing cult ownership. Children may be stimulated sexually while being forced to watch atrocities. Other practices include eating feces or drinking blood or urine. A child may be actively involved in killing or mutilation of another child or animal.

Additionally these activities are accomplished and accompanied by sleep deprivation, threats, starvation, and forced use of alcohol or other mind and mood altering substances. These practices are essentially those used with prisoners of war or by terrorists focused on mind control.

Ritualistic abuse poses a particular threat to children (and adults) because of their indoctrination into practices that are considered barbaric and evil by society. The ever present exposure to mutilation, death, blood, and other atrocities, creates a pronounced and very real belief in immanent annihilation by the forces of Satan or the cult. Children will do whatever it takes to survive physical and psychological horrors and as such will engage in the unthinkable. Because under such extreme distress, children may dissociate or already be under the influence of mind altering chemicals, accurate disclosure is also made very difficult (Sharir, 1996; Sakheim & Devine, 1992).

Indicators of Ritualistic Abuse

- Child fears ghosts, monsters, witches, devils, evil spirits.
- Child believes evil spirits inhabit his/her closet, house or body.
- Child reports evil spirits or the devil watching him or her.
- Child sings or chants odd songs.
- Child does odd, ritualistic dances that may involve circles or other symbols.
- Child sings songs with sexual, bizarre or "you better not tell" themes.
- Child is preoccupied with occult symbols such as a circle, pentagram, number six, horn sign, inverted cross.
- Child fears occult symbols or becomes markedly agitated/upset.
- Child states that s/he has prayed to the devil, made potions, performed ritualized songs, did magic.
- Child may costume self in red or black.

Problems Associated with Small Spaces or Being Tied Up

- Child fears closets or being locked in a closet.
- Child fears small spaces, elevators.
- Child closes pets or other children in closets or otherwise traps/confines.
- Child expresses fears of being tied up or states someone else was tied.
- Rope burns are evident on the child.
- Child attempts to tie other children or pets up or hang upside down.
- Child states s/he was 'practicing' to be dead.
- Child may talk frequently or obsessively about death and dying.
- Child may fear doctor's office and express receiving bad shots or drinking blood.
- Child upon physician's exam may be overtly frightened or invite sexual contact.
- Child acts out death, killing, cannibalism, and burial themes.
- Child's play involves bondage, pretending to eat body parts, weddings, other ceremonies or rituals or drugging.
- Child fears own blood and may become hysterical.

SPECIAL CONSIDERATIONS: MALE CHILD SEXUAL ABUSE

There have been relatively few studies of male children who have been sexually abused and far fewer of diverse male child victims (Moisan et al., 1997; Kuhn, Arellano, & Chavez, 1998). The struggle of male victims mirrors the "disparity between sexual victimization and societal stereotypes of masculinity" (Gil & Tuffy, 1997) which creates in victims "an overwhelming sense of failing to meet perceived requirements, i.e., a 'real male' would have been able to protect himself" (p. 32).

The added dimension of a rural setting for such abuse further compounds the experience of trauma because of geographical isolation, lack of resources, and additional stress due to poverty, poor housing, and morbidity rates (Champion, 1999). Male child/youth victims when compared to female child victims generally are

- More likely to be abused by a wide range of perpetrators.
- More likely to be victims of anal and physical abuse.
- More likely to become sexual abusers/predators.
- More likely to have symptoms ignored/or minimized.
- More likely to be blamed.
- More likely to struggle with issues of sexual identity (not the same issue as sexual orientation, which does not seem to be generally an issue or empirically considered a cause of homosexuality) (Gil & Tuffy, 1997).

- Less likely to be taken seriously.
- Less likely to have a trauma history taken.
- Less likely to be prosecuted (Champion, 1999; Moi San et al., 1997; Kuhn et al., 1998).

SPECIAL CONSIDERATIONS: SEXUAL ABUSE OF ELDERS

No discussion of sexual abuse concerning children or adults would be adequate without recognition that a significant portion of all victims is largely unnoticed or ignored. "What has been much less well recognized is that the distress from traumatic experiences may be persistent, disrupting for decades, the lives of those burdened by it" (Hunt, Marshall, & Rowlings, 1997, p. 2). A reexperiencing of trauma may occur after decades and is more likely to be attributed to dementia or old age (Hunt et al., 1997; Schreuder, 1997) Given that elders are seen as pioneers and were not growing up in an era of mental health, the notion of trauma may be foreign to them as well, even though their bio-psyho-social history and symptoms may present otherwise (Hunt, 1997; Herman, 1994; Schreuder, 1997). Such an example is illustrated by an 80-year-old grandmother who brought her granddaughters to a mental health clinic upon court referral for the father's incest. "During the process of education about incest, the grandmother's eyes reflected a new awareness as she softly murmured through her tears, (to the clinician) 'Honey, I'm so glad you are here for my granddaughters.' Pausing and grasping my arm, she looked at me with deep sorrow and said, 'there was no one there for me" (Palmer, 1991, p. 69). The real life threatening situations and emotional or physical losses may trigger or reactivate earlier trauma. Consequently, a competent social and trauma history taking is in order.

SPECIAL CONSIDERATIONS:
POPULATIONS WHO ARE OPPRESSED AND DISENFRANCHISED

"Victims are threatening to nonvictims, for they are manifestations of a malevolent rather than a benevolent one" (Janoff-Bulman, 1992, p. 148). To encounter a malevolent universe is to encounter experiencing our very real human fears. As human beings striving to survive and belong, we are faced with universal fears and needs. These fears are

- Fear of annihilation and/with threat to life.
- Fear of abandonment.
- Fear of disintegration with loss of identity.
- Fear of fusion with loss of identity, or being consumed.

In the face of oppression, which may be openly hostile and violent or subtle and silent, these fears become realized by anyone viewed as different.

Accompanying experiences such as those described in this chapter results in an exacerbation of isolation and absence or loss of resources. To be traumatized and alone is the most excruciating and terrifying of all human experiences (Herman, 1994; Allen, 1995). Threaded through out this most profound of all human experiences is the realization that oppression communicates a clear message to the victim who is different; "You are expendable! Your life is not worth anything [loss of life]. We do not want you in this society [abandonment]. We do not like you or who you are/represent (disintegration/loss of identity), and In order to secure the support, resources, life needs, you need, you must be like us [fusion]. " The total effect of oppression is not only the traumatic event(s) itself but the experiencing in reality of one's most profound fears. Victims who are oppressed and disenfranchised suffer the most extreme of all human conditions.

INTERVIEWING CHILDREN

Children live and grow in social contexts that significantly impact and influence their lives. Social contexts include their family (and can include extended family members, kin networks, godparents, and community), their cultural context, and particular interpersonal experiences (including cults). Each of these personal contexts frames the child's world of shoulds, oughts or otherwise expected behavior. Children, in their need to survive, be loved, and protected, will accommodate those on whom their survival and needs for protection and nurturance depends.

If their world gives explicit or implicit instructions in not disclosing or revealing certain experiences or information (often accompanied by threats of various kinds), then children are in a particularly excruciating situation when outsiders ask and expect them to reveal parts of their private world. Such actions on the part of helping responders or investigators then present a situation that is cognitively and psychologically distressing. Additionally, children who are abused and/or neglected have already learned that the world is not to be trusted. First and foremost is the child's need for physical and psychological safety, the latter taking extended time and effort to achieve.

Such considerations must be kept in mind with any interview.

Interview Time

Age appropriate—

- PreSchool: 15–25 minutes
- School age: 25–45 minutes
- High school: 45–90 minutes

Interview Place

- Must be free from interruptions.
- Must be physically comfortable.
- Furniture must fit the age of child.
- Must be ideally suited for multiple interviewees to see and hear yet minimize numbers of people who will be wanting the same/similar information.
- Ideally, it should represent the child's cultural environment.

Focus First on Rapport

- Presented as a joint undertaking.
- Child given undivided attention.
- Interviewer conveys willingness to listen.
- Interviewer conveys willingness to hear whatever information is given without judgment.
- In child's native or first language.
- Convey trust, patience and putting child's needs first.
- Give reassurance but not false promises.
- Listen openly and nonjudgmentally.
- Attend to messages of your (interviewer's) nonverbal behavior.
- Speak slowly, clearly, with warmth and care.
- Work from a position of cultural understanding and competence.
- Do not threaten or otherwise pressure child into confession.
- Do not ask leading questions.

How to Encourage a Child Without Leading Questions

- "What happened then?"
- "Go ahead—you are doing fine."
- "I'd like to hear more."
- Use child's name frequently.
- "Please go on."
- "What were you thinking or feeling?"
- "So, what you are saying is . . ."

What to do if Child is Quiet or Silent

- Stay quiet—give the child some time.
- Ask, "Is it hard to put into words?"
- Say, "For the last few minutes, you've become pretty quiet. I'm wondering what you were thinking."

How to Respond to a Child's Anxiety

- "I know it's difficult to talk at first. I'm wondering what some of your concerns or worries are about being here today?"

- "It's hard to talk about personal feelings (or experiences) is there anything I can do to make it easier?"
- "Something makes it hard for you to talk about what happened. Can you tell me what makes it hard?"
- "Are you afraid of what I or others will think or do to you?"

Handling Crying or Agitation

- "What's it like to talk to me?"
- "You seem sad right now." (Observation)
- "You seem like you are trying not to cry. It's OK to cry here."
- "What were you thinking about when you were crying or tearful just now?"

Seeking Clarification

- Ask the child to identify who s/he is talking about.
- Ask child to explain what any term or nickname means.
- Ask, "what do you mean by that?"
- Say, "tell me more about . . ."
- Paraphrase: "So, what you are saying is _____ is that right?"
- Do not ask "why" questions.

With any interview or assessment, a child at any given time may be weighing out his or her risks. The need to survive takes precedence over everything else. Additionally, children fear the loss of others upon whom their need to survive and grow depend. Children who are abused, particularly sexually and especially ritualistically, are particularly vulnerable and fearful of abandonment, annihilation, or loss. Responders must understand and appreciate this at all times. Work must proceed at the child's pace.

Child victims may be in a compromised state through dissociation or ingestion of alcohol or other mind altering substances. Great care must be used with the utmost in professional responses and interventions.

ADULT VICTIMS

Previous introductory comments on general features of sexual assault apply here. In addition, it should be noted that adults likewise may be victims of ritualistic abuse that most frequently includes forms of sexual assault.

Estimates vary among researchers regarding the prevalence of adult victims of sexual assault which still remains one of the most underreported crimes in the United States. Sexual assault can happen to anyone. It is estimated that one out of every three or four females and one out of every seven to ten males is sexually assaulted sometime in her or his life time (Finkelhor, 1986). Because society does not typically think of men as victims (Lew, 1988), a separate discussion of male victims is included. "Statistics like this tend to distance us from the tragedies that surround each incident, because we end up more impressed by the numbers than by the reality" (de Becker, 1997, p. 9). Sexual assault can be devastating. Victims experience not only an invasion of their body, the assault attacks their total sense of well-being. When added to the backdrop of the social environment, recovery may be compromised.

Sexual assault is a violent crime that is committed without consent or with someone under legal age. Sexual assault can occur within a marriage or living-together relationship; it can be an act against someone of the same sex; and it can be committed by a friend, acquaintance, or relative (familiars), or by a stranger.

Sexual assault is committed

- By acts of physical force or psychological coercion.
- By taking advantage of a victim who is unconscious or physically powerless.
- By taking advantage of a victim who is incapable of giving consent because of
  - a mental condition (emotional or intelligence)
  - a disease or injury
  - having ingested substances (voluntary or forced)
  - another condition that precludes informed consent
  - age
  - the victim's belief that she or he is undergoing a medical procedure

Unlike sexual assault of a child, most often adult victims of sexual assault are blamed (Wallace, 1999). Additionally, within the context of social norms and pressure, victims often blame themselves (de Becker, 1997; Hunter, 1990). Women may blame themselves because they are socialized to be responsible for the character of their relationships. Likewise, they are also socialized to "act like a lady," to "be nice," and "not to offend anyone." Essentially, humans, particularly women are socialized to ignore their very survival signals. "No animal . . . suddenly overcome with fear would spend any of its mental energy thinking, 'It's probably nothing'" (De Becker, 1997, p. 30). Yet women are socialized to be very attractive targets of sexual assault.

"To study psychological trauma is to come face to face both with human vulnerability in the natural world and with the capacity for evil in human nature" (Herman, 1994, p. 7). While victims of sexual assault may experience events differently given their own particular psychological/ physical make up, circumstances and environment, there are certain fundamental attributes we all share as human. Our need to survive, for human attachments, a coherent sense of meaning, for a sense of value and belonging, are universal. "The fundamental stages of recovery are establishing safety, reconstructing the trauma story, and restoring the connection between survivors and their community" (Herman, 1994, p. 3). The stages of recovery then mirror our basic universal human needs. To relate and respond to victims is to confront our own humanness-fears and vulnerabilities. This is the real work of responders and their systems.

CHOREOGRAPHY OF SEXUAL ASSAULT

While sexual assault takes many shapes and forms, when studied in the context of the larger society, the factors of gender socialization illustrate how females are particularly vulnerable. De Becker (1997) provides some illustrations of the choreography of assault, which includes the following:

Forced Teaming

An effective way to establish premature trust because of a "we're all in the same boat" attitude is hard to rebuff without feeling rude. Forced teaming is intentional and directed. It is one of the most sophisticated ways to establish trust. The detectable signal is the projection of a shared purpose or experienced where none exists. The use of the word "we" is a powerful word to females socialized to see themselves in relationships.

Charm and Niceness

Charm is a directed instrument, which, like rapport building, has motive. To "charm is to compel, to control by allure or attraction" (p. 56). "He was so nice," is a common example of a victim's reaction to a charmer. "A woman is expected, first and foremost, to respond to every communication from a man" (p. 58). "A woman who is clear and precise is viewed as cold, or a bitch, or both" (p. 58).

Too Many Details

Too many details are designed to confuse or redirect a person (woman) so that the real intention or the real context of a situation is not perceived.

Typecasting

This involves labeling a woman in a critical way, hoping she will feel compelled to prove the opinion is not accurate. Comments like "You're probably too snobbish to talk to the likes of me" (p. 59) always involves a slight insult, usually one that is easy to refute. Given the need to be nice and to be liked, women find typecasting particularly painful.

Loan Sharking

Doing something to place the victim in his or her debt. Offering assistance . . . while it could be anybody, the "predatory criminal who imposes his counterfeit charity into someone's life" has a motive (p. 60).

The Unsolicited Promise

"The unsolicited promise is one of the most reliable signals because it is nearly always of questionable motive. Promises are used to convince us of intention" (p. 61).

Discounting the Word 'NO'

"Actions are far more eloquent and credible than words. . . . Particularly when it is offered tentatively or without conviction" (p. 62). "Declining to hear 'no' is a signal that someone is either seeking control or refusing to relinquish it" (p. 62).

"The criminal's process of victim selection . . . is similar to a shark's circling potential prey. The predatory criminal of every variety is looking for someone, a vulnerable someone who will allow him to be in control, and just as he constantly gives signals, so does he read them" (De Becker, 1997, p. 63). Also, if a victim is of a diverse population or in the United States illegally, her or his vulnerability is magnified against a backdrop of disenfranchisement and oppression.

MALES AS VICTIMS

Throughout the general introduction and the discussion on children, it was emphasized males can very much be sexually assaulted. Yet, prevailing myths abound:

- Males cannot be raped or otherwise sexually assaulted.
- Women don't rape or sexually assault males.
- He really liked it.
- An older female and younger male is desirable—in fact, this is a "conquest" for the male.

THE CHOREOGRAPHY OF MALE SEXUAL ASSAULT

A central dynamic of sexual assault is coercion and power. Males who have been socialized to be masterful and in control feel particular shame and emotional pain as victims. The social environment likewise, enhances a predators opportunities to assault (See Finkelhor, 1986, Preconditions).

The most common sites for male sexual assault involving postpuberty victims are out of doors. Other common sites include remote areas in automobiles. Males in their early teens or who are passive or nonassertive are also more likely victims (Wallace, 2002).

Gang rape is more common in rape of males, as is physical force. Multiple acts of sexual assault are more likely as is the display of weapons. The common forms of assault commonly include penetration of the male victim both anally and orally. Complete domination and control is sought by the predator(s). An attack is considered extremely successful if ejaculation by the male victim occurs. Ejaculation creates great confusion with the mistaken belief that somehow the male liked or consented.

Males have particular difficulties in disclosing or reporting. The "suppression of knowledge of male rape is so powerful and pervasive that criminals such as burglars and robbers sometimes rape their male victims as a sideline solely to prevent them from going to the police" (NCVC, 1997). Further, males victims of rape greatly fear that they will be perceived as homosexual (Groth, 1978). Male sexual assault has nothing to do with sexual orientation of the predator or the victim, just as same sex assault does not make that person gay. The majority of all forms of sexual assault are done by heterosexual males (Groth, 1978; Newton, 1978).

SPECIAL POPULATIONS

GAY, LESBIAN, BISEXUAL, OR TRANSGENDERED

"The myth that lesbian relationships are more peaceful and egalitarian than heterosexual unions has been shattered by the reality of lesbian battering" (Renzetti & Miley, 1996, p.2). Likewise, the presumption that gay male relationships are more "enlightened and sensitive" or are less violent than their heterosexual counterparts is not accurate (Renzetti & Miley, 1996). While projected rates vary (Lobel, 1986; Renzetti & Miley, 1996; Cruz & Firestone, 1998), the existence of same sex violence is a reality. Same sex violence often includes sexual assault, although this aspect has received little attention. "While antigay attitudes permeate American society, they seem to have an extreme affect on the homosexual community" (Cruz & Firestone, 1998, p. 162). People who are bisexual or transgendered are often ostracized by the gay community as well and are even more disenfranchised by society as a whole.

THE CHOREOGRAPHY OF SEXUAL ASSAULT: SAME SEX VIOLENCE

"On the last day she used force against me; would not let me leave the bedroom until I agreed to do what she wanted" (Kate Hurley in Lobel,

1986). "Since all battered lesbians have engaged in extensive efforts to protect the batterer from exposure as a terrorist and from the consequences of her violence, battered lesbians may continue 'taking care' of the batterer by blaming herself" (Lobel, 1986, p. 184). It is essential to remember that the phenomenon of same-sex assault is "not a gender issue, but a power issue" (Renezetti & Miley, 1996).

Men likewise have their particular challenges as well. "Rape and sexual assault are often an integral part of a perpetrator's violence. . . . A man who will beat and/or sexually abuse his partner is not likely to care enough to protect him from HIV infection" (Renezetti & Miley, 1996, pp. 72–73). A common denominator among gay males, lesbians, bisexual, and transgendered people is that they are expendable in the eyes of society. In fact, these populations are not considered as belonging in the category of human; they are frequently considered freaks of nature or sinners not worthy of consideration. Additionally, "a major problem is the inability or unwillingness of other people to accept their victimization as legitimate" (Renzetti & Miley, 1996).

Not reporting or disclosing violence by same-sex partners or by familiars and strangers is significantly reinforced by threats of *outing* (revealing publicly that someone is gay, bisexual, or transgendered). Threats of calling the Immigration Service may accompany assault to persons of color, even if the legality of their living situation is not known.

THE AFTERMATH OF SEXUAL ASSAULT

Regardless of the age, gender, relationship, degree of force, or acts themselves, all forms of sexual assault are stressful, and most are traumatic. How a child or adult responds to sexual assault varies with the circumstance, the environment, and the individual. Sexual assault, regardless of its form, is violent, and it violates both the body and the psyche. "When someone has been sexually assaulted a crisis has happened" (Palmer, 1996, p. 10). A crisis is a devastating emotional state the results from some event(s) perceived as having a negative valence. A crisis is uncontrollable, and may be sudden or at least unexpected.

The negative valence, that is, the ascribed meaning to the victim, may include injury that is physically painful or injurious, that is emotionally painful or terrifying, and may be perceived as likely to cause physical pain, injury, or death (Carlson, 1997). This includes threats to life and limb or exposure to grotesque, violent, or sudden loss of a loved one.

The sudden or unexpected events of sexual assault create the experience of loss of control to varying degrees

- Capacity to cope may be overwhelmed.
- Disorganized in thinking/response.

- Little or no time to cognitively process the event(s).
- Environment is experienced as unpredictable and therefore dangerous.
- Others once trusted (even slightly familiar) are no longer trusted.
- Sense of safety is significantly lost or compromised.

The trauma may initially result in shock. It may also cause intense fear, including the fear of dying. Extreme emotionality may be countered with a numbing of affect. Do not interpret calmness and an appearance of being unattached or composed as a sign of the victim's being unaffected by the assault. This may instead be shock or a dissociative state.

RAPE TRAUMA SYNDROME

While there are great variations to the experience of sexual assault, the rape trauma syndrome is widely recognized as a way of understanding a victim's response and processing of the assault.

First Phase: Acute

- Extreme emotionality or shock.
- A change from one extreme to another emotionally.
- Great terror and anxiety.
- Great confusion.
- Disbelief.
- Extreme suppression of all emotion.
- A display of physical injuries/trauma.
- May be suicidal.

Second Phase: Extended Reaction

- General soreness, bruising especially the throat, neck, thighs.
- Genital or rectal tears or bleeding.
- Body tension and hyperarousal or sudden awakenings.
- Startled reactions (edgy or jumpy).
- Other physical/somatic symptoms.
- May repress or suppress seeking help or reluctance to talk about it.
- Desire to return to normal life.
- May start or increase abuse of substances.
- May be suicidal.
- There may be forms of dissociation.

Third Phase: Resolution or Unresolved Trauma

- Intense resurfacing of emotion or reexperiencing the event(s).
- Flashbacks (may appear in second phase as well).

- Feelings of guilt, disbelief, anger or other intense emotions.
- Assess for suicidal ideation.
- Through support and treatment, resolution and reintegration.

Ongoing legal processes may prolong the reexperiencing of the events even if legal resolution is sought or desired. Victims who are survivors of early or other trauma may be particularly vulnerable to the effects of assault. Add to this the overlay of oppression and disenfranchisement, and victims are increasingly challenged in their healing and recovery.

ADDRESSING THE COMPREHENSIVE NEEDS OF SEXUAL ASSAULT VICTIMS

Approximately 2,000 organizations have been established to provide support and services to sexual assault victims (New Directions, 1998). Developing a comprehensive community response to sexual assault should begin at the point of victimization and should include a number of individuals and agencies that provide services and assistance to the victim:

VICTIM SERVICES

- Medical.
- Mental health.
- Law enforcement.
- Prosecution.
- Courts.
- Institutional and community corrections.

Working together, these agencies can create a model response to rape victims that accomplishes the following:

- Allows and supports the need of sexual assault victims to assume control over their own lives.
- Recognizes and responds to the immediate short- and long-term mental health impact of the trauma.
- Provides accompaniment/transportation to emergency medical treatment and pays for all forensic rape examinations.
- Vigorously investigates all cases.
- Apprehends offenders and aggressively prosecutes cases in a timely fashion.
- Informs victims at each stage of the proceedings.
- Vertically prosecutes cases within prosecutors' offices.
- Gives victims the opportunity to express a preference for what they would like to see happen to the offender.

INNOVATIVE INTERVENTIONS TO SEXUAL ASSAULT VICTIMS IN THE MEDICAL COMMUNITY

Sexual Assault Nurse Examiner (SANE) programs offer an innovative approach to handling the medical/evidentiary aspects of sexual assault and child abuse cases through the use of technology, nurse examiners, and specialized settings. Instead of having doctors handle these cases in busy emergency rooms, SANE programs create a special environment for victims and use trained nurse examiners to conduct the evidentiary medical examination and present the forensic evidence at trial. According to the Tulsa Police Department, the nationally recognized Tulsa SANE program has substantially improved the quality of forensic evidence in sexual assault cases. The Sexual Assault Resource Service of Minneapolis is developing a guidebook for starting SANE programs for use by communities (New Directions, 1998).

SIGNIFICANT FEDERAL LEGISLATIVE REFORMS IN RESPONSE TO SEXUAL ASSAULT

Within the last decade, significant federal laws have been enacted that address rights for sexual assault victims, recognize new classifications of sexual crimes, and provide funding and support for the criminal justice response to sexual assault. The major federal legislation includes the following (National Victim Assistance Academy, NVAA, 1999):

THE VIOLENCE AGAINST WOMEN ACT OF 1994

The Violence Against Women Act offers an important source of new funding for programs that address the needs of sexual assault victims. While this law has been described in other chapters, it is important to point out that for victims of sexual assault, certain provisions of the act are pertinent:

- To qualify for the available funding, states have to pay for forensic rape exams.
- Female victims of violence can now sue in federal court for damages resulting from violent attacks.
- Federal funding is providing for coordination, investigation, and prosecution of crimes against women.

Appropriated and authorized funds to implement provisions of the Violence Against Women Act for domestic violence and rape prevention and intervention programs represent a significant increase in federal support. The impact of this federal law will be seen for years to come.

THE CAMPUS CRIME SEXUAL ASSAULT BILL OF RIGHTS OF 1992

Because of a nationwide problem of sexual assault on college campuses—which was traditionally handled by campus security, rather than through outside law enforcement and as a criminal justice matter—and because very often there was pressure on the student-victim not to report to outside authorities, a bill of rights became necessary for college rape and sexual assault victims. In addition to requiring that campus authorities treat rape victims with respect, give them information about their criminal and civil justice options, and establish procedures for assisting victims, rape prevention education is required.

THE STUDENT RIGHT-TO-KNOW AND CAMPUS SECURITY ACT OF 1990

Due to a long tradition of handling crime on campus internally and not reporting crimes to local law enforcement, the extent of campus crime across the country was underreported for many years. Rape is among several on-campus crimes that now must report to local law enforcement under this law. Equally important, the law requires colleges and universities to provide information on safety-related procedures for the student.

THE HATE CRIME STATISTICS ACT OF 1990

This law requires the reporting of crimes that are motivated by prejudice, race, religion, sexual orientation, and ethnicity. Women are not considered a protected class under the law; however, information is collected about crimes against women within protected categories. For the first time on a nationwide basis, sexual assault and rape statistics covering many types of overlooked crimes are being collected. This information will help target services and funding for previously undocumented and often unrecognized crimes against women.

ADDITIONAL LAWS

Many statutory changes, addressed earlier in this chapter, have been enacted across the states to address all forms of sexual assault and rape. The following are additional reform measures:

MARITAL RAPE

Prior to the passage of these laws, rape within a marriage or cohabituating relationship was not considered rape. In the 1980s, a California legislator shocked many citizens when he asked, 'If you can't rape your wife, who can you rape?' Today, most states have reformed this exemption, making marital rape a specific offense, but exemptions still exist in some states.

PRIVILEGED COMMUNICATION FOR VICTIM COUNSELING

For many rape crisis advocates and interveners, the issue of confidential communications with rape victims has been one of their most frustrating and ongoing challenges. Without the protection of client/professional confidentiality granted to licensed mental health professionals, such as psychologists or social workers, some rape crisis workers have faced subpoenas and have even been jailed on contempt charges for refusing to divulge the substance of their conversations with rape victims. As early as 1982, the President's Task Force on Victims of Crime selected privileged communication between rape and domestic violence advocates and victims as a top priority for legislative change. It is important to note that rape crisis advocates working in criminal or juvenile justice-based agencies (law enforcement/prosecution) are not covered by this confidentiality protection due to discovery rules (their communications may contain information that is helpful to the defense).

EMERGING ISSUES RELATED TO SEXUAL ASSAULT

DRUG-RELATED RAPE

An emerging issue in the past few years has been the use of legal and illegal drugs by potential rapists who sedate their intended victims involuntarily. Such drugs are put into nonalcoholic and alcoholic beverages in a variety of social settings. Substance-related rapes present severe difficulties for survivors of rape, as well as for those trying to prevent their victimization. Many articles have appeared in the media about the threat and the susceptibility of individuals to this type of victimization.

According to the National Coalition Against Sexual Assault (NCASA), the most threatening problem is the emergence of a drug that results "in the inability of the rape survivor to remember the details of what happened as a result of the heavy sedating effect of the drug and/or alcohol, [which] heightens the difficulty of gathering information that could help prosecute the offender."

Congress passed the Drug-Induced Rape Prevention Act of 1996 to address the emerging issue of the use of sedating drugs by rapists on their victims. The act sets forth prison terms of up to 20 years for offenders convicted of using controlled substances with the intent to commit a violent crime, including rape.

New drug testing capabilities are available that may help in collecting evidence in relation to substance abuse cases (NVAA, 2000c) Hoffmann-La Roche, a major pharmaceutical company, is offering a free testing service because of its concern that one of its medicines—Rohypnol (flunitrazepam) has been misused. Currently, the medicine is not legally available within the United States, but is available in 80 countries outside the United States for the treatment of severe sleeping disorders.

While many other drugs and alcohol are used to induce potential victims, rape crisis centers, law enforcement officials, and hospital emergency rooms involved in the investigation of sexual assault cases in which drug misuse is suspected should call to access this free testing service. The testing is performed by an independent U.S. Department of Health and Human Services-certified forensic toxicology laboratory. The urine sample is tested for amphetamines, barbiturates, and benzodiazepines, as well as flunitrazepam, cocaine, marijuana, and opiates. The results of the tests are returned directly to the rape crisis center, law enforcement official, or hospital emergency room and, most importantly, the identity of the victim is kept confidential.

MANAGEMENT OF SEX OFFENDERS IN THE COMMUNITY

Approximately 234,000 offenders convicted of rape or sexual assault are currently under the care, custody, or control of corrections agencies in the United States—with most offenders in local or community corrections. Two significant initiatives have emerged recently: The implementation of sex offender community notification laws, and sex offender monitoring by community corrections agencies that recognizes the rights and needs of communities and the victims.

Sex Offender Community Notification Laws

In 1996, federal legislation mandated that all states establish a community notification program or lose 10% of their federal law enforcement funding under the Byrne Memorial State and Local Law Enforcement Assistance Funding program. As of October 1997, 47 states had passed community notification laws that require law enforcement agencies to inform local communities that convicted sex offenders are residing in their neighborhoods, or allow public access to this information.

Community notification laws allow or mandate that law enforcement, criminal justice, or corrections agencies give citizens access to relevant information about certain convicted sex offenders living in their communities. These laws are distinct from sex offender registration laws, which require convicted sex offenders who are living in the community to notify police officials of where they are living. They are also distinct from victim notification laws, which mandate that crime victims who wish to receive information about the criminal justice processing or release status of the person(s) who victimized them be provided with it.

- Provisions of community notification laws vary state to state. States differ in their methods of informing the public of a sex offender's presence in their community and in the extent of the information they provide. Some states proactively inform the community, while others make information available to citizens upon request. Those states using community notification laws have essentially established four notification categories:
    - Broad Community Notification (18 states). Releases information about sex offenders to any person or organization who requests it.
    - Organizational Notification (14 states). Informs organizations that are especially vulnerable to particular-offenders such as day care centers and schools.
    - Individual Notification (13 states). Informs victims and classes of victims of the presence of specific offenders in the community.
    - Police notification (14 states). Allows persons or organizations to obtain sex offender registry information from local law enforcement (NVAA, 2000c).

Typically, individuals and organizations get offenders' names, photos, crime descriptions, and age(s) of their victim(s). Information is often provided on how offenders target their victims as well as their modus operandi. Some notifying agencies may also provide community members with information about the nature of sexual offending, the characteristics of sex offenders, methods of self-protection or community protection, and information about what can be done when people learn that a sex offender is living in their neighborhood.

Victims of Criminal Death

9

Christine N. Edmunds, Dan L. Petersen,
and Thomas L. Underwood

T he senseless loss of life through homicide—the ultimate violation—
touches the family, friends, school mates and coworkers of approximately 40,000 victims each year (New Directions, 1998). It may
occur as a final, violent act of many years of escalating spousal, elder, or
child abuse or as a consequence of drinking and driving. It may be used
as a solution to gang-related hostilities or to silence a robbery or sexual
assault victim. It can kill dozens of victims through one terrorist act or a
series of victims by one serial killer. The motivation of the perpetrator
may vary, but the impact on the victim is the same.

The death of an individual by any means that involves intent or recklessness has severe and irreparable effects on the surviving members and
the community. The primary client served by the victim assistance practitioner is, of course, the surviving family members. This chapter provides
an overview of the types of criminal death and victim characteristics and
of some of the organizations dedicated to assisting survivors of criminal
death, we will address some of the problem areas that family members
must manage and describe some strategies for appropriate assistance by
service providers.

TYPES, PREVALENCE, AND VICTIM CHARACTERISTICS

TYPES

Various terms are used to describe the criminal loss of life. There are strict
legal terms, such as homicide and manslaughter, that are statutorily defined

and can vary across different jurisdictions. Generally, *homicide* refers to criminal death from actions that are intentional, whereas *manslaughter* stems from actions that are reckless. Sociological terms describe and provide a general description of criminal death based on either the victim characteristic or the circumstance. Some of these include the following:

- Spousal Homicide. The killing of a spouse, life partner, or other significant individual of the same or opposite sex with whom one has lived for some time and formed a stable relationship.
- Child Homicide. The killing of a person under the age of 18.
- Shaken Baby Syndrome. The violent shaking of a young child that causes permanent brain injury or death.
- Parricide, patricide, matricide, fratricide. The killing of one's parents (parricide), father (patricide), mother (matricide) or sibling (fraticide).
- Stranger Homicide. The killing of a person or persons by an individual unknown to the victim.
- Mass Murders. The murder of several victims within a few moments or hours of each other.
- Serial Killing. An offender who kills over time. They usually have at least three to four victims, and their killing is characterized by a pattern in the type of the victims selected or the method or motives used in the killings.
- Alcohol-related Fatality/Crash. A vehicular crash or pedestrian fatality involving a driver who has a positive blood-alcohol level, though not necessarily above the illegal per se or presumptive level (NVAA, 2000d). While alcohol is the most common condition related to vehicular homicide, other substances, often illegal, may result in impairment leading to recklessness and endangerment and where death results charges of vehicular homicide.

For the purposes of discussion, two general types of criminal death will be referenced in this chapter: homicide and drunk driving murder. Homicide refers to the willful and deliberate taking of a life; drunk driving murder refers to death caused by a substance-impaired automobile driver. These are not necessarily legal terms but are general definitions that are intended to guide the content.

HOMICIDE PREVALENCE AND CHARACTERISTICS

The past several decades have seen significant variations in the murder rate as well as the characteristics and patterns of murder. The homicide rate doubled from the middle of the 1960s to the late 1970s and then continued a varied high throughout the 1980s and early 1990s. Since then, the rate has declined to its lowest level in three decades, though it is still significantly higher than the low decade of the 1950s. This increase is attributed to, in part, the rise in gun violence and drug related crime committed by juveniles and young adults.

Homicide has the highest clearance rate of all violent crime, so most often the relationship of the homicide offender to the victim is known. According to the Bureau of Justice Statistics (Fox & Zawitz, 2000), of the approximately 65% of cases where an arrest was made, over half of the offenders are an intimate or acquaintance of the victim. Clearance rates for murder dropped from over 90% in 1965 to less than 70% in 1999. According to the International Association of Chiefs of Police, this is may be the result of an increase in stranger-stranger murders. Moreover, the drug trade is considered to be a major factor contributing to the increase in murders whose circumstances are unknown (New Directions, 1998).

The overwhelming majority of homicide victims are young and male. In turn, the overwhelming majority of homicide offenders are young and male. The offending rate of those 18 to 24 years of age, historically, the age range with the highest offending rates almost doubled from 1985 to 1993. The homicide offending rates of the 14 to 17 age group increased almost 150% during that same time frame (Fox & Zawitz, 2000). Juvenile gang killings are the fastest growing type of murder, increasing 371% from 1980 to 1992. Along the same line, guns have become the weapon of choice. The percent of victims in the 15 to 19 age group killed by guns increased from about 65% in 1975 to 85% in 1992 (New Directions, 1998).

Males are about three and a half times more likely than females to be a homicide victim; they are also the perpetrators of homicide in about 90% of cases. Caucasian and African American percentages of murder victims are almost equal at slightly under 50% each, with other races accounting for the remainder. Most homicides are intraracial.

DRUNK DRIVING MURDER PREVALENCE
AND CHARACTERISTICS

According to the National Highway Traffic Safety Administration (2000), alcohol-related traffic deaths constitute almost 40% of traffic fatalities. Many of the victims of these murders are children: 20% of children under age 15 killed in traffic fatalities are killed in alcohol-related fatalities; almost half of the children under the age of 14 killed in an auto fatality were passengers with drivers who had been drinking.

About three in ten of every five Americans will be involved in an alcohol-related crash at some time in their lives (NHTSA, 2000). Traffic crashes are the fifth leading cause of death in America; the leading cause of death for ages 1 to 44 years (National Center for Health Statistics, 2001). Almost half of these crashes are alcohol related.

IMPACT OF CRIMINAL DEATH ON SURVIVORS

Unlike a long illness of a loved one, sudden death leaves the survivor no time to prepare. As a result, any unresolved issues, whether personal, financial, or professional are left unresolved. In addition, the task of survivors is simply to grasp what has happened; to assimilate the reality.

The violent and senseless nature of the death may also cause survivors to experience a sense of loss beyond the loss of the victim: a loss of self, a loss of sense of control, a loss of social support, and a loss of sense of safety and security (National Crime Victim Center, 1997). Realizing that the act was deliberate or reckless in nature, survivors also realize that the death was preventable. In the search for understanding, survivors may, consciously or unconsciously, engage in victim blaming by playing the what if and if only scenarios over and over again.

The emotional impact of the loss on family survivors can be overwhelming. Consider the following family positions:

- Parents. Regardless of the victim's age, the natural order calls for parents to die before their children. This natural expectation is violated with the sudden death of a child. Parents are not prepared to deal with this unnatural event and may have tremendous difficulty coping. Furthermore, parents may reexperience the loss when they see other children reaching developmental milestones, like graduation from high school or getting married.
- Spouse. A spouse must face the grim realization that the dreams shared are no longer possible. The roles within the relationship—friends, lovers, parents—previously enjoyed are also gone. The role of wife or husband has suddenly been changed to that of widow or widower. The surviving spouse often must assume a greater role, especially if children or other dependent persons are involved.
- Siblings. Siblings move on with their lives—they go to school, move ahead in their careers, and so forth. Guilt may be associated with the living of life, especially if these events were not a part of the life-plan when the victim was killed. Siblings living at home may face a change in relationship with the surviving parents in that the parents may become overprotective or may frequently compare the victim to the sibling.
- Child. The loss of a parent is one of the most significant stressors children face. Children also face role changes, often having to assume more adult duties, such as taking care of younger siblings. Children are sometimes ignored by parents preoccupied with their own issues. The children fear adding to their parents' pain and simply withdraw. It must be noted that children experience the same psychological reactions that all survivors report. They often feel compelled to replace—in the eyes of parents—the dead sibling or family member.

FAITH ISSUES

The basic values of survivors, often an outgrowth of their religious faith or life philosophy, can be severely shaken by criminal death. Survivors will question and challenge their belief in God—questioning the reason and timing of their loved ones death. Seeking out spiritual answers, often from unorthodox sources, is not uncommon. The need for most of us under such tragic and incomprehensible events is to attempt to rationalize and recreate a world belief that makes sense of our experiences. Humans have always attempted to find meaning and structure either through science, religion or a combination of the two. When an event of such magnitude as a homicide occurs that defies some of those basic assumptions, all assumptions about faith, order, safety, goodness/evil, fairness, and meaning are at risk. Putting things back into place and redefining the world and God can be a major task for survivors. To do so they will often seek out those who they believe are more knowledgeable about such things. Often those they turn to are clergy and religious leaders. In many cases, survivors find solace and help in reestablishing meaning in their lives. However, for others it is not an easy journey.

It should be noted that on occasion, comments and philosophies of clergy and church members sometimes create problems for survivors. Well-intentioned religious advisors may exacerbate the emotional distress by offering comments that reflect a greater plan or forgiveness. At the very least, some survivors react with anger to comments that, they say, appear to suggest that the most horrible experience in their lives is something they should accept and forgive. Clergy must become knowledgeable about the psychological distress of homicide survivors and become aware of the triggering phrases and needs of homicide survivors in order to provide the help and support they need. Every aspect of one's life is shadowed by an untimely criminal death—religious and spiritual areas are not exempt.

FINANCIAL ISSUES

The impact of loss may also be financial. There may be a loss of income previously provided by the victim. Future dreams based on a projected financial income are likely to be altered. The loss of dreams should not be discounted as major source of trauma. The ability to maintain a mortgage, send children to college, retirement plans, and such may cease to exist. Financial planning is likely to be needed when homicide victim was a significant contributor to the survivor's income. Victim service providers should broach the issue and suggest the need for advice from a reputable financial planner.

Income earnings by the survivors, themselves, may also be affected. The unanticipated death of an intimate can severely affect a survivor's ability to function and perform on the job. Concentration can be difficult and health issues often become more pronounced due to stress and anxiety. Motivation is sometimes altered and survivors report that emotional outbreaks of crying or shouting frequently occur and having to explain or apologize contributes to their stress and anguish. Employers may need to be educated to the problems associated with homicide survivors. Understanding is often basic to the provision of tolerance and support. Employers should also be made aware that there will be demands on the survivor to interact with the criminal justice process that will require time away from the job. A supportive employer can be a huge benefit to a survivor but typically requires that the employer be knowledgeable and sensitive to the issues.

In addition to the income loss, there may be extensive bills for medical, funeral, mental health care, and legal expenses, further adding to the family debt as well as the family stress. Victim compensation can play a vital role helping families to deal with the financial consequences and victim service providers should be active facilitating the acquisition of all victim compensation due the survivors. Income loss and debt may alter the ability of the family to maintain a level of living once enjoyed.

VICTIM SUPPORT AND ADVOCACY ORGANIZATIONS

Several programs have been established to help survivors of homicide. Most were started by survivors themselves to provide peer counseling and support to survivors. While only a few have been selected for identification in this document, many others exist at local and regional levels. Victim service providers should be acquainted with these organizations and knowledgeable regarding the supports they can provide for their clients. Some of these programs include the following:

- Parents of Murdered Children (POMC). POMC provides a network of over 100 local chapters serving 38,000 survivors each year. POMC's goal is to allow the grief of family members to be shared with others who have been through similar experiences, thereby breaking down the isolation that many families face.
- The Stephanie Roper Committee. Created by Roberta and Vince Roper in 1982 following the brutal murder of their daughter Stephanie. The Ropers were not allowed to attend the trial and then discovered that the two convicted killers would be eligible for parole in 12 years. They turned their frustration and outrage into activism and created one of the most successful victim activism programs nationwide. With volunteers, the Stephanie Roper Committee

works on legislative reforms and operate a Court watch program that places volunteers, many of whom are victims, in courtrooms to monitor whether victims' rights are respected in Maryland.

Other support groups, such Loved Ones of Homicide Victims in Los Angeles, Save Our Sons and Daughters (SOSAD) in Detroit, and the Tender Loving Care organization in Dallas, Texas work to decrease crime victims sense of isolation, to offer support and understanding, and to provide practical information and advice.

In addition, due to the many children who have lost family members and close friends to homicide in New York City, Victim Services, the nation's largest victim assistance agency (with over 600 hundred staff members) has formed a choir composed of children who have had a family member killed.

CRITICAL ISSUES OF ASSISTANCE

Criminal justice professionals, victim assistance providers, members of allied professions, clergy, and friends who assist or come into contact with survivors of criminal death must recognize critical needs of survivors at the time of unexpected death as well as throughout the ensuing months and years of contact with the service agencies. Service providers can assist the process of life reconstruction after the devastating impact of an unexpected death of a cherished one by addressing several barriers.

DEATH NOTIFICATION

Sensitive, timely, and in-person death notification should be done by trained law enforcement, clergy, victim assistance or mental health professionals. Most families in which someone was killed say the most tragic moment in their life was the notification of the death of their loved one. Yet, too many victims receive this terrible news in insensitive ways, such as over the telephone or from the media, rather than in person. Often, families are given confusing or inaccurate information. All professionals that provide death notification, especially law enforcement, where the greatest responsibility falls, should be trained on proper death notification procedures and victim sensitivity.

When doing a death notification, care should be taken to personalize the victim by using the person's name. Impersonal terms like victim, deceased, driver, or body should not be used. Family members are likely to recoil when someone they love has been killed and another person refers to their loved one as an object by using jargon or terms that objectify rather than personalize.

Service providers should be appropriately sympathetic and not minimize any part of what happened to the victim. For example, it is inappropriate to say things such as, "It will get better with time," "You're still young," "It could have been worse," and so forth. Further, things like "I know how you feel" and "the pain will pass" should not be said. These sentiments are inappropriate because it is impossible, no matter what experiences the professional has had, for the provider to ever really know what the homicide survivor is feeling. Second, the professional who uses such language is not likely to be believed and that one statement may ruin the professional's credibility. On the other hand, it is appropriate to make a statements such as "I am sorry" and "what has happened is tragic."

It is important to understand that it is impossible to predict the family member's reactions to the death notification. Some may cry, some may lose all emotional response capability, some may become angry, and some may even take their anger out on the persons giving the notification. While the practitioner who notifies the family of the death should not allow themselves to be hurt, they should not attempt to restrain someone who is emotionally upset unless danger to themselves or others is clear and imminent. A wide range of reactions and on occasion even incongruent emotional and behavioral reactions should be expected.

The preferred process (e.g., California Youth Authority, Office of Prevention and Victim Services, 2001) is to have a notification team. Death notification should always be done in pairs by trained individuals. On occasion, that team can be expanded to three, but the numbers of the team should not overwhelm the members of the family. Ideally, a uniformed officer and a victim service professional trained in crisis intervention and death notification would constitute the preferred team. The team should have as much accurate information as possible before making the notification; however, that does not mean that the team should delay the notification allowing the survivors to be informed by insensitive or poorly informed others.

In summary, death notification should always be done in the following ways.

- In person.
- In time—and with certainty.
- In pairs.
- In plain language.
- With compassion.

These are some guidelines that can help in the process but specialized training in this area is essential.

TIME FOR GRIEVING

The dynamics of criminal death need to be understood by focusing on the characteristics of grief and trauma. It is important to remember that

- Grief is not abnormal but is a healthy reaction to loss.
- Grief can be instrumental in the process of letting go.
- The grieving process is the mechanism through which the survivor copes with various reactions—shock, major loss, helplessness, fear, rage, and even murderous impulses.
- Grieving allows the survivor to deal with the reality of loss and to say an appropriate goodbye to the loved one.
- Grief can be viewed as the path one takes on the journey to recovery.
- For homicide survivors, it is important to recognize that very often the grieving process is interrupted and delayed by elements and events of the criminal justice system. Survivors sometimes put their grief on hold to focus on the arduous task of seeing that justice is served.

THE NEED TO SAY GOODBYE

Survivors of homicide should not have to fight a battle to view the body of their loved one or photographs. Rather, as POMC and MADD advocate, supportive professionals should prepare them for what they will experience and then let survivors make an informed choice. The inability to view the loved one's body appears to make it much more difficult on the survivors to accept the loved one's death. It is for this reason that experts (Redmond, 1989) encourage officials to permit the viewing process to occur. However, the victim assistance practitioner should offer viewing options to the survivors. Where the homicide resulted in severe damage to the victim's body, viewing some portion of the body that is not damaged, may be a more appropriate option. Simply viewing the loved one's hair or a hand may be sufficient. It may also be helpful to explain to the survivors that the last image they see of their loved one could be an image that will stay with them forever. Consideration of how much of the body they wish to see is their choice, but it should be an informed choice weighing all options. Often at the time of viewing the deceased the survivors will be in crisis and victim service providers can not expect survivors to think through all the options and ramifications. Regardless of the options presented, the decision must rest with the survivors.

POLICE

Frequently, the survivors of a homicide do not understand the behavior of police. While police can be extremely sensitive and provide a level of safety that no other group can, police often seem cold and distant to the survivors. Often times, the reason for what appears to be a lack of understanding can be understood if the victim service professional can explain the police role and perspective. As was indicated in the beginning of this chapter, most homicides are committed by a family member or someone close to the victim. Police are required to consider everyone as a suspect until evidence and information gathering suggest otherwise. Police also operate under regulations that severely limit the amount of information they can share with the survivors. This does not mean that police cannot be educated to be more sensitive to survivors, but their role is different and does to some extent explain the need to have a victim service provider involved in homicides as a first responder.

As a case progresses a victim services provider can assist the survivors considerably in several ways. They can explain the investigative process and help assure the survivors when an active case is being pursued by the police. They can interface with the police to gather information and keep the survivors informed. They can also help prevent survivors from antagonizing police through too frequent contacts or by harming an investigation by attempting in an ongoing investigation to gather their own evidence and possibly interfere with the investigation. The last thing either the police or the survivors want is to have a weakened case resulting from interference brought on by either frustration or ignorance on the part of the survivors who act with good intentions but in ignorance.

The police are also likely in some homicides to provide protection to surviving family members and friends. This is particularly likely when the perpetrator is still at large and survivors are witnesses to the crime or carry information essential to the perpetrator's conviction/apprehension. Providing this kind of protection is not necessarily a common practice for police assigned the duty. The victim service professional can play a key role here also. They can interpret for the police the bereavement process and crisis behavior the survivors may be experiencing. Helping the police officers understand the victim's perspective and needs can be beneficial to all involved.

Finally, while homicides have a high clearance rate as previously mentioned, some cases result in investigations that become a protracted and frustrating process for the survivors. These cases are sometimes referred to as *cold cases*. Years can pass with little or no change in the conditions of the case. For those survivors of a homicide involved with cold cases there is no resolution, no day in court, and often no relief. Victim service providers should be aware of the emotional struggle these survivors face. With these homicides, the family may for decades struggle with the need to know what happened, why, and who committed the crime. At the same time, there is almost always a need to see justice in the case. These cognitions and feelings translate into a need to have the perpetrator found and the system enact retribution for the crime. It also involves the process of attempting to reconstruct from damage a meaningful world. To do so, it is often imperative to the survivors to have both knowledge and justice.

Victim service providers can be active in these protracted investigative processes. The role may be as intermediary between family and investigators explaining to both parties the efforts, needs and emotional commitment of the other. In some cases, the victim service providers contacts with investigators may add the motivation to maintain the vigilance or perseverance necessary to someday arrive at closure in one form or another.

MEDIA INTRUSION

Too often, the media invades the survivors' privacy, especially in multiple victim homicides or high profile cases, shoving cameras and microphones into victims' faces as they await news about their loved ones or case developments, such as the outcome of a jury trial. As discussed under the portion of this section that addresses death notification, the name of the deceased must never be released by the media before immediate survivors are notified.

> I had just finished grocery shopping when I heard the chilling report of a police officer shoot-out on the car radio. The reporter was the one who informed me that it was my husband that had been killed. My neighbors found me crying hysterically, parked in the middle of the road several blocks from home.
>   —A police widow from Texas

While some members of the media family engage in victim centered ethical conduct, there are many that do not (Carter, 1999). Survivors may and often do need help with the media. One suggestion is for the family to choose someone to run interference with the media for them. Having a media representative can allow the survivors to have access to the media when needed but also to protect themselves from what can be considered harassment and a violation of privacy.

Another recommendation is for victim service providers to nurture and educate the media professionals in their community prior to crisis situations. By developing a relationship that fosters ethical and sensitive media contact through education on victim issues, the victim service provider takes a significant step toward reducing continued victimization of the survivors. The basic principles underlying the media practice should be safety, privacy, and respect. A reporter who is sensitive to the homicide survivors can actually be an ally to help the family and friends present their view and perspective.

REFERRALS AND RESOURCES

Victim assistance practitioners should provide information and support necessary to address the financial issues previously discussed, that is, unexpected expenses and loss of income. Most crime victim compensation programs have conditions on allowable costs, including sublimits on the amount of award allowable for funeral costs. This leaves many survivors with unexpected and additional debt during this vulnerable stage. Other resources of financial assistance may need to be considered.

Survivors should have access to supportive counseling, including individual sessions and peer support groups for survivors. Crime victim compensation, at one time, did not cover survivor of homicide counseling expenses. Today, unless circumstances prevent their qualification, all programs provide payment for counseling services and all survivors should be encouraged to apply for compensation.

The challenge is for victim services professionals, as discussed in the chapter titled "The Impact of Stress," to identify competent mental health counselors in their jurisdiction. While government-based victim advocates are not allowed to recommend specific counselors, a one-page handout listing competent counselors in the community/county is allowable. It is also allowable to list information that is public knowledge such as which therapists have had training in trauma counseling or who have formally acquired special expertise that is beneficial to crime victims. Unfortunately, in many communities across the nation, especially rural jurisdictions with large geographic distances to cover, such supportive services may not exist. Peer groups may be hard to establish with the distances required for participants to attend. At minimum, publications developed by POMC and MADD should be distributed to survivors.

BARRIERS TO FULL PARTICIPATION
IN THE CRIMINAL JUSTICE SYSTEM

Early victims' rights laws did not recognize surviving family members of homicide victims, extending rights only to the primary or direct victim and not to covictims or survivors of homicide. Throughout the 1980s, victims' rights laws were amended and new ones were enacted, to legislate survivors as true victims with full rights.

Survivors should have full involvement in the criminal investigation, prosecution and final disposition of the perpetrator, including notification and input into sentencing and parole decisions. The myriad problems facing survivors by the justice system are heightened by the cold reality that for survivors, the harm against the victim cannot be addressed through counseling or reconstructive measures. Thus, for the survivor, there is an emphasis on justice being served through holding the offender accountable and having input into the decision-making process of the justice system.

While the critical points of victim participation are discussed in the chapter titled "Victim Advocacy and Public Policy," certain policies, protocols, and legislative rights are critical to survivors, including these:

- Criminal justice agencies should develop protocol for responding to homicide cases that begin with law enforcement's on-scene response, through death notification, investigation, arrest, charging, hearings, trial, sentencing, appeals, incarceration, change of offender status and release.
- Survivors should have the right to attend the trial and to remain in the courtroom throughout all proceedings.
- In cases where there is an appeal, victims should receive notification and be kept informed of the status of the case regardless of the length of the appeal.
- Clemency hearing—the final insult—with the victim thinking that the criminal justice process is final, the incarcerated offender applies for clemency.

CHILD DEATH REVIEW TEAMS

Children, especially the very young, are subject to a host of circumstances that put them at risk for premature death. Children of 1 to 4 years die from nonvehicle related accidents more than from any other cause. In some cases, the violence is direct and brutal. In other cases, it is more difficult to detect. Currently, it is hypothesized that some portion of deaths attributed to sudden infant death syndrome (SIDS) may be due to suffocation or other inflicted harm that is intentional. In other cases, such mental disorders such as Munchausen by Proxy (aka factitious disorder by proxy, [DSM-IV]) may result in child endangerment and even death. With the Munchausen by proxy disorder, there is an intentional production or feigning of physical symptoms in another person (child or person under their care) for the purposes of directly enhancing the caretaker's role.

Child death review teams now exist in 45 states. These teams are charged with examining the circumstances surrounding certain fatalities known or suspected to be the result of child abuse or neglect. The goal is to identify indicators or risk factors to signal earlier intervention in hopes of preventing future deaths (New Directions, 1998).

SUPPORT STRATEGIES FOR SURVIVORS

While nothing the victim assistance practitioner can do will alleviate the tremendous loss of a homicide or drunk driving victim, survivor sensitive strategies include these:

- Learning as much about the case as possible before speaking with the family.
- Tactfully and sensitively alerting the family to facts of case, even unflattering facts.
- Preparing the family for the media report of the facts.
- Determine the survivor's need for contact—some will require constant attention, while others will want minimal intervention.
- Personalizing the deceased by asking the family to tell stories, show pictures, and so forth.
- Protecting survivors from unwanted media attention.
- Assisting in funeral arrangements or other family notification responsibilities if needed.
- Assisting in filing for crime victims compensation, Social Security survivor benefits, insurance, and so forth, if needed.
- Providing information and encourage participation in mental health services and support groups.
- Providing continuous information about the investigation or criminal justice process.
- Recognizing that each family member has individual needs, work with all family members—including grandparents, siblings (if age appropriate), and extended family members—to determine their need for information and support.
- Reviewing, as necessary, autopsy and/or murder scene photographs to help the family assess suitability to remain in courtroom during their viewing.
- Consider using an outside family friend or distant relative to identify the victim in any court proceedings if using an immediate family member will disqualify them from remaining in the courtroom during trial.
- Assisting in preparing victim impact statement as appropriate.
- Alerting prosecutor or law enforcement of survivor's concern for safety or other emotional or physical concerns.
- Informing survivors of their rights to file civil law suits against the offender to third parties, where applicable.
- With survivor permission, contacting or sending materials to employers explaining the emotional ramifications of criminal death on survivors so that allowances can be made for court or for emotional needs.

As a final comment to the above list, victim service providers should be prepared to provide long-term assistance in cases involving death penalty. Homicide cases can easily last years in the court system before any sort of resolution is reached. Even following a judicial verdict of guilty, appeals through the criminal justice process can prolong the process. Supports to homicide survivors must be viewed as a protracted process that will result in a long term relationship between the survivors and the victim service providers.

EFFORTS TO REDUCE HOMICIDE

Considering the overall statistical risk of homicide and drunk driving murder, the chances of being a victim of criminal death is relatively rare. However, the taking of life is considered such an insult to society that any loss is too much.

Prevention of homicide should be an ultimate goal of society. Prevention programs should be developed for at risk populations. Particular attention should be focused on young black males. In addition, prevention programs must be located where there are high levels of homicides, such as urban cities and counties.

Violence Within Family Systems

10

Nancie D. Palmer and Christine N. Edmunds

Family or domestic violence is a multifaceted phenomenon that includes acts toward significant others in cohabitation relationships, children, and the elderly. These abusive acts may be physical, emotional, neglectful, or sexual in nature. Family violence has existed for many centuries but has only recently come to the consciousness of the United States. This chapter addresses the various types of family violence, the demographic factors associated with relationship violence, and theories that help explain the complicated dynamics of family violence. Public policy measures developed to address domestic violence, protocols for criminal justice system response, and initiatives of community agencies and health providers are examined.

DEFINITIONS AND PREVALENCE

Family violence is a complex issue with no easy answers for intervention and prevention. Even to begin to define family violence can pose problems. Though most family violence literature is in reference to women and children, it must be acknowledged that family violence occurs to all members of a family, including males. Recognizing statistical prevalence and overall impact, most of the discussion in this chapter is focused on women and children.

The legal definition of domestic violence varies according to state and federal law, and also among specific disciplines—such as victim advocates, mental health and medical professionals, and criminal justice practitioners. All practitioners who serve victims of crime need to be well versed in legal criminal and civil legal definitions of family violence in their respective states.

Definition

Family violence is physical, emotional, and financial injury, inflicted by one person onto an intimate, that exceeds normative or legal bounds. Generally, family violence is defined as follows:

> Any assault, battery, sexual assault, sexual battery, or any criminal offense resulting in personal injury or death of one family or household member by another, who is or was residing in the same single dwelling unit. "Family or household member" means spouse, former spouse, persons related by blood or by marriage, persons who are presently residing together, as if a family, or who have resided together in the past, as if a family, and persons who have a child in common regardless of whether they have been married or have resided together at any time. (Office of the Attorney General, Florida, 1993)

Overall Incidence

Family violence cuts across many demographic lines. Consider the following statistics on family violence:

- Gender. As defined by rape, physical assault, and stalking, women are more likely to be victimized by an intimate partner than men. The risk of lifetime victimization for women is over 25%; the risk for men is almost 8% (Tjaden & Thoennes, 2000).
- Race. While intimate violence affects persons from all races, non-white women and men report significantly victimization than white women and men. However, data on victimization of distinct categories, persons of Asian/Pacific Islander report significantly lower victimization.
- Age. Women between the ages of 16 to 24 are the most vulnerable to intimate violence. Overall per capita rate of intimate partner violence against women is about six per 1,000, but among females age 16 to 24, it is over 15 per 1,000 (Rennison, 2001).
- Marital Status. Separated females experience intimate partner violence at rates significantly higher than women in any other marital category followed by divorced women (Rennison, 2001).
- Income. Generally, the lower the annual household income, the higher the rate of intimate partner violence (Rennison, 2001).

WHO ARE THE VICTIMS OF FAMILY VIOLENCE?

Partners

According to the National Crime Victimization Survey, over half of all crimes are committed by non-strangers; of these, almost 20% are committed by an intimate (Rennison, 2000). Tjaden and Thoennes (2000) research of the National Violence Against Women Survey supported prior research (Yllo & Straus, 1981) that the risk for violence by intimates is more likely in relationships between unmarried cohabiting couples than married couples.

GENDER AND FAMILY VIOLENCE

Intimate violence is primarily a crime against women. About two-thirds of crimes committed against women are committed by nonstrangers; of these, about a third are committed by an intimate (Rennison, 2001). Females are victims of three out of every four murders committed by intimates; about 85% of the victims of nonlethal intimate violence are female (Rennison & Welchans, 2000). Women are significantly more likely than men to report being raped, physically assaulted. or stalked by an intimate partner (Tjaden & Thonnes, 2000; Rennison & Welchans, 2000). Women are also significantly more likely to sustain injuries than men (Tjaden & Thonnes, 2000; Rennison & Welchans, 2000.

Tjaden and Thonnes (2000) found that "same-sex cohabitant reported significantly more intimate partner violence than did opposite-sex cohabitant" (p. 30) in their lifetime. However, women in the same-sex relationships reported by a margin of almost three times that they had been victimized by a male partner, not a female partner.

CHILDREN

Ongoing research studies continue to reveal new information about the intergenerational cycle of violence. A link between early victimization and later involvement in violent crime has been identified, although additional research is needed to understand fully why some abused or neglected children become violent, while the majority do not.

According to the National Crime Victimization Survey, children under the age of 12 reside in 43% of the households where intimate partner violence occurs (Rennison & Welchans, 2000). Statistics on the actual number of children who witness violence in their homes is somewhat lacking, but it is estimated that at least 3 million children witness domestic violence each year (New Directions, 1998). Research is also showing that witnessing violence in the home and community adversely impacts a child's mental health and development, including an increased likelihood in some children to become directly involved in violence, whether as victims or perpetrators, as they mature.

ELDERLY

For all women over the age of twelve, those over the age of fifty face the least risk of violence by an intimate. Of those victimizations by an intimate that occur, close to 70% are by spouse (Rennison, 2001). While this age group is generally more likely than others to report crimes, they are less likely to report crime committed by family members and spouses. Many experts believe that only one in fourteen incidents of domestic elder abuse comes to the attention of the authorities (New Directions, 1998).

Like other forms of family violence, assault, intimidation, and exploitation of elders occurs in the secrecy of the home. Estimates of elder abuse rates vary from 4% to 20% (NVAA, 1999). Given that this vulnerable population is often invisible, statistics are at best inaccurate. According to a study by the National Center on Elder Abuse and the American Public Human Services Association (1998) it is estimated that 90% of elder abuse and neglect involved family members. In addition to all forms of family violence described in this chapter, an additional dynamic concerns fiduciary or financial exploitation, involving retirement or social security checks or other survival benefits may be controlled by the perpetrator, or misdirected. Fiduciary abuse may also include loss or control of property. As elders age, additional stress may be experienced by the family system, thus their vulnerability may further increase. Given the graying of the American population, it is projected that violence including exploitation of elders will likely increase.

FORMS OF FAMILY VIOLENCE

Violence is "different from any human interaction" (Summit et al., 1998, p. 46). When human beings are violent (psychological/emotional/physical), we come "face to face with [our] human vulnerability in the natural world" and realize the "capacity for evil in human nature" (Herman, 1997, p. 7). Recall in the chapter on sexual assault that human beings have fears that are universal:

- Fear of annihilation/threat to life.
- Fear of abandonment.
- Fear of disintegration with loss of identity.
- Fear of fusion with loss of identity or of being consumed.

To be traumatized and alone is the most excruciating and terrifying of all human experiences, because it is the realization of one's most universal human fears. Family violence brings together these two most compelling dimensions, that is, trauma and being alone, for such experiences are most often the secret behind closed doors. Although violence is expressed in innumerable forms (there is no universal agreement as to definition), it may be useful to identify general categories of violence and how each is generally expressed and interconnected with our biological self including attachment.

There are three general types of family violence:

- Physical Violence.
- Sexual Violence.
- Psychological or emotional violence.

PHYSICAL VIOLENCE

Battering is the greatest single cause of injury among women in the United States, accounting for more emergency room visits than auto accidents, muggings, and rapes combined. For crimes committed by intimates, over 28% of women and almost 22% of men who have been physically assaulted by an intimate seek medical attention; 31% of rape victims do so (Tjaden & Thoennes, 2000).

Power escalating into physical pain, breaking the most exquisite of human barriers, the human skin. "The skin, like a cloak, covers us all over, the oldest and the most sensitive of our organs, our first medium of communication, and our most efficient of protectors" (Montagu, 1971, p. 1).

The nature of physical violence is most often described in acts of violence that involve touching the human skin, touches that threaten and injure the body's integrity (see list). What is not recognized is that our most primary and most significant conduit of communication, the skin, that is intact and functioning at birth, is traumatized both physically and psychologically. In other words, physical violence is always accompanied by emotional/violence, and physical contact threatens one's very life, thus making it the weapon of choice for those who use force to get what they want. Violence is often described as being about power and control, which indeed it is. However, violence is so much more and it is necessary to understand the physical and emotional choreography to better understand the most frequent and fundamental question that most influences responders' reactions to family violence, namely, "Why does she or he stay?" So influential is this question that a separate section is devoted to this major issue.

Physical violence within the family includes all forms of physical touching that harms, conveys a threat to harm, and/or intent to harm another person. This definition includes children and adults in a family, intimates living together, or extended family, and kinship systems. Family violence includes physical, sexual and emotional abuse by siblings. "Although studied for over 30 years, an absence of information regarding its characteristics remains" (Wallace, 2002, p. 113). Absent from discussions on family violence is violence in what may be described as other forms of family constellations, such as same sex partnerships that may include children, and communal or multiple family arrangements. Separate sections will be devoted to these frequently overlooked populations.

Physical abuse is usually recurrent, and it escalates both in frequency and severity. It may include the following (NVAA, 1999):

- Pushing, shoving, slapping, punching, kicking, or choking the victim.
- Assaulting the victim with a weapon.
- Holding, tying down, or restraining the victim.
- Leaving the victim in a dangerous place.
- Refusing to help when the victim is sick or injured.
- Burning (water, i.e., immersion burns) holding a hot object against the skin.
- Shaking a child or adult (can be fatal).
- The inability or refusal to provide care to an infant or child or disabled, injured adult. (Children may be diagnosed with failure to thrive, which can be fatal).
- Tickling, when prolonged and intended to inflict suffering, distress, or pain.
- Physical neglect that results in harm, such as leaving an infant or child unattended in potentially dangerous circumstances—bathtub, kitchen, and other.
- Intentional infliction of exposure to deadly disease, such as HIV, AIDS, or other STDs or communicable infections (see also sexual violence).

It is important to note that attempting to place types of physical violence on a continuum of severity fails to recognize that it is the use of force, not the degree of damage inflicted, that is so harmful and threatening to one's body and psychic integrity.

HOMICIDE: THE ULTIMATE PHYSICAL VIOLATION FROM DOMESTIC VIOLENCE

Over 30% of female murder victims are slain by an intimate partner. Only about 4% of male murder victims are slain by an intimate partner (Rennison, 2000).

EMOTIONAL OR PSYCHOLOGICAL ABUSE

Expressions of emotional or psychological violence are intended by the perpetrator to instill fear, and make real the threat of annihilation, abandonment, disintegration, or fusion. In essence, the very universal fears that all humans have are made real.

Emotional or psychological abuse may precede or accompany physical violence as a means of controlling through fear and degradation. It may include the following (NVAA, 1999):

- Threats of harm.
- Physical and social isolation.
- Extreme jealousy and possessiveness.
- Deprivation of resources to meet basic needs.
- Intimidation.
- Degradation and humiliation.
- Name calling and constant criticizing, insulting, and belittling the victim.
- False accusations, blaming the victim for everything.
- Ignoring, dismissing, or ridiculing the victim's needs.
- Lying, breaking promises, and destroying the victim's trust.
- Driving fast and recklessly to frighten and intimidate the victim.
- Forced control of body functions, particularly excretory functions.
- Forced violation of one's moral principles.
- Systematic, repetitive infliction of trauma, designed to disempower, disconnect, a person from primary attachments to others and instill terror and helplessness.
- Systematic, repetitive infliction of trauma, designed to destroy the victim's sense of self in relation to others.
- Systematic yet seemingly capricious granting of "favors" intended to instill gratitude and create a willing victim.
- Systematic, repetitive disruption of sleep.
- Threatening to "out" (disclose) a person's sexual orientation.
- Threatening to deport an illegal resident.

SEXUAL ABUSE

Sexual abuse in violent relationships is often the most difficult aspect of abuse for individuals to discuss. It may include any form of forced sex or sexual degradation conducted by partners, siblings, and it is nongender specific. It includes

- Trying to make the victim perform sexual acts against his or her will.
- Pursuing sexual activity when the victim is not fully conscious, or is not asked, or is afraid to say no.
- Physically hurting the victim during sex or assaulting her or his genitals.
- Coercing the victim to have sex without protection against pregnancy or sexually transmittable diseases.
- Criticizing the victim and calling him or her sexually degrading names.
- Using sex and coercion together, for example, rituals of torture.
- Committing incest (see chapter on sexual assault). Almost half of battered women reported they had been repeatedly sexually victimized as a child (Walker, 1987, p. 152).

CAPTIVITY

"A single traumatic event can occur almost anywhere. Prolonged, repeated trauma, by contrast, occurs only in circumstances of captivity" (Herman, 1997, p. 74). Captivity means that a victim is under the control of the perpetrator and unable to flee. Even if doors are opened or rescuers respond, a victim may stay in the "special" relationship (Herman, 1997) of her or his captor. Why is this the case?

The analogy of a glass room may best explain captivity. Imagine person A inside a glass room and imagine that people on the outside could not see the glass walls, but they could see the person and another person, B, inside the room. Now imagine that inside the room, person B lights a fire that begins to smoke. A is frightened and alarmed. Outsiders see the smoke and become alarmed as well. They want A to flee, but when A tries to escape, A severely injures herself or himself by running into the glass walls. A can't get out from the inside. Outsiders become increasingly distressed and wonder why A doesn't run out of the room to escape the dangerous smoke and the fire. Outsiders become very confused— they don't see the glass barriers, they only see you, the smoke, and the fire. Responding outsiders become increasingly frustrated that A won't help himself or herself get from the inside to the outside. Outsiders may secretly become alarmed at their own vulnerability, that is what if the fire spreads, or the fire leaps on to something or someone else? In the end, the outsiders give up trying to help and focus on themselves. A becomes paralyzed from the smoke and fire inside the room and feels more isolated, alone, and terrified than ever when the crowd leaves in frustration. A is doomed.

The most fundamental idea to hold when responding to persons in distress or who are injured inside the family, is to understand, that you are always on the outside. "In situations of captivity, the perpetrator becomes the most powerful person in the life of the victim, and the psychology of the victim is shaped by the actions and beliefs of the perpetrator" (Herman, 1997, p. 75). The methods of controlling another human being are "remarkably" consistent across political, cultures, or domestic situations. Such methods are calculated and deliberate in their approach (Amnesty International, 1973 *Report on Torture,* in Herman, 1997; and Walker, 2000, pp. 34–35). A key feature in domestic battery is that barriers are most often unseen. Like the glass-walled room, both insiders and outsiders are unable to appreciate the forces and barriers at work. A person is held captive through coercive control, (physical and emotional) intimidation, enticements, and entrapment. How is this achieved?

Most beguiling is the perpetrator, who appears to be normal. That is, normalcy is the facade of the perpetrator (De Becker, 1997). The camouflage is conventional and in keeping with social norms. Many victims describe a perpetrator as nice, even gentle and loving. Outsiders describe the perpetrator in similar terms, ("He was a nice guy"). The stealth at which a perpetrator of family violence moves in deliberate fashion may be likened to the building of glass walls, unseen, yet real. Violence is the fire that creates the glass. Intermittent punishment and enticement keep the walls not only in place but silently closes the victim off from the outside world. The systematic and repetitive approach is designed to

- Disempower (create a sense that to resist is futile, even dangerous).
- Disconnect (prevent the continuation of attachments, particularly with significant persons, such as family, friends, even one's own children).
- Instill terror and fear: (people inherently want to avoid pain) (De Becker, 1997).

Bring a victim into total surrender and control of the perpetrator.

THE CHOREOGRAPHY OF CAPTIVITY

All human beings innately desire the avoidance of pain. Physical and emotional pain, and fear of pain, with the accompanying terror, is increased by inconsistent and unpredictable outbursts of violence and/or coercion through physical force. The very fear of annihilation is realized. Violence is used to punish the victim for non-compliance, often of capricious and petty rules (Walker, 1987, 2000; Herman, 1997). Punishment, in behavioral terms, has a positive effect, that is, the victim complies, the perpetrator is rewarded, and likewise the victim is rewarded through being spared further harm or one's life. Violence is used because it convinces the victim that the perpetrator is omnipotent and that resistance is futile, even dangerous: that the victim's life depends on winning the perpetrator's indulgence. It also destroys the victim's sense of autonomy (Herman, 1997; Wallace, 2002).

"Stress and trauma can wreck havoc with physiology, for it evokes the flight or flight response which entails massive physiological arousal associated with sympathetic nervous system activation" (Allen, 1995, p. 46). Helpless to escape situation of danger, may evoke not only terror and rage, but also, paradoxically, a state of detached calm, which in terror, rage, and pain, dissolves" (Herman, 1997, p. 42). Perceptions may be numbed or distorted, a kind of anesthesia, or loss of body sensations (Allen, 1995; Herman, 1997; Hunter, 1990). The state of calm is indicative of an altered state of consciousness as well as a numbing of the arousal system. Dissociation takes many forms and in degree (Shirar, 1996; Putnam, 1997; Gil, 1996). Dissociation disconnects a person's conscious processes from awareness. "Traumatic reactions occur when action is of no avail (neither resistance or escape is possible), the human system of self-defense becomes overwhelmed and disorganized. Each component of the ordinary response to danger, having lost its utility, tends to persist in an altered and exaggerated state long after the actual danger is over" (Herman, 1997, p. 34). [It is often this state of numbing that is mistaken by responders as indicative of the victims lack of harm rather than viewing it as diagnostic of trauma].

Trauma and the terror of further pain is heightened by compromising the victim's physiological system, through long period of sleep deprivation. This may be achieved by the perpetrator through violence, jealous interrogation, sexual assault, the prolonged efforts to prevent a victim from gaining sufficient sleep. Sleep deprivation effects a person's ability to withstand stress, make judgments, manage stimulation, and more.

More confusing to victims is the perpetrator's use of intermittent reward, that is, the granting of small favors and comforts, such as a meal, a bath, sleep. This aspect of perpetrator's behavior undermines the psychological resistance of the victim more effectively than unremitting fear (Herman, 1997). The ultimate goal of the perpetrator is total surrender of the victim. Yet, the punishment, terror, intermittent reward, isolation, and physical assaults, may not succeed. Total surrender, that is an utterly compliant victim, is achieved through the most destructive of all coercive techniques designed force a victim to violate her or his own moral principles and betray their most primary human attachments. Examples include allowing one's child to be assaulted or sexually assaulting one's child (this may be further degrading and humiliating when forced to perform sexual acts in front of one's children or other, including having photos and videotapes produced in the process). When forced control is so complete that victims' bodily functions are dominated, particularly when that control leads to the victims defecating on themselves or others, victims begin to loathe themselves, even perceiving themselves as nonhuman in order to survive unbearable pain. They give up their inner sense of self and their world view. The result is a shutting down of feelings, thoughts, initiative, judgement, and in its most extreme form, losing the will to survive, to live (Herman, 1997). The cognitive, emotional, physical aspects of a victim, may be forever altered (Van der Kolk et al., 1996).

Responders, however, must recognize the glass walls for what they are. They must understand the overwhelming effects of trauma and continue to create avenues of escape for victims of family violence rather than judge or maintain avenues that perpetuate the myths that surround victims. Most of all, it is imperative that response systems not expect victims to act like nonvictims.

Recall from the chapter on sexual assault that two factors are most often present in family violence:

1. Violence will most likely be in the home or familiar surroundings.
2. Violence will most likely be protracted.

These two phenomenon can only occur in captivity.

Paradoxically, the power of being alone and traumatized underscores the drive for attachment, which, when impaired, creates within the person a greater difficulty in forming positive social relationships that are a cornerstone of nonviolent relationships. In the chapter on sexual assault, the fundamental premise of attachment theory was presented, namely, "The presence of a biologically rooted and species-characteristic attachment behavioral system that brings a child close to its caretaker" (Melody, 1997, p. 3). This attachment occurs over time through a prolonged period of sensitivity (Melody, 1997; Allen, 1995). Disruption of attachment or nonattachment through inconsistency, absence, violence, substance abuse, for example, may impact an infant/child's ability to experience and express a deepening empathy for other human beings and for themselves. The result frequently is violence used as a means of securing a love object that will remain attached over time. Violence is used by human beings because it works, thus achieving the comforting thought (an illusion) that the victim is not alone. In violent relationships, all parties, particularly adult partners or spouses, become intertwined in a dance with deadly potential through the use of power and force in what is most often captivity.

Just as the child sexual abuse accommodation syndrome was included to facilitate understanding of how the criminal justice and other social institutions respond to children, this provides a level of understanding of the frequently and fundamental question: Why does she or he stay? The prevailing beliefs associated with this question, tremendously influence system response, because the expectation is very normal behavior (i.e., nonvictim) to circumstances that are very abnormal (Summit et al., 1998, pp. 45–46). In other words, much like child victims of sexual assault, adults who experience family violence are placed in the position of being expected to act like nonvictims. It is imperative, then, to understand the inner world of victims of family violence (this chapter focuses primarily on adults, as children were discussed in prior chapters).

THE CYCLE OF VIOLENCE REVISITED:

A new era of understanding the phenomenon of domestic or family violence, was initiated in 1978 by Lenore Walker in her book, *The Battered Woman*. Walker identified what has become well-known as the cycle-of-violence theory. This model identified three distinct phases that occur (varying in duration and intensity) in a battering relationship. These phases were

- The Tension Building Phase. Perpetrator becomes more prone to react negatively to frustration, "little episodes" of violence begin to escalate. Tension increases.
- The Acute Battering Phase. Perpetrator uses various methods of violence to gain control of the victim (children and adults). Violent episodes are perceived by victims and responders as uncontrolled. Initially, Walker described this as the shortest phase, however it is much more systematic (i.e., controlled) and prolonged.
- Honeymoon: Calm, Loving, Respite Phase. Perpetrator may be characterized as kind, loving, and contrite. The perpetrator may grant favors, or romance the victim into forgiveness. Recent research indicates that this phase may disappear completely as perpetrators escalate their use of violence in the relationship.

Since this early work, Walker (2000) continues to support the existence of this theory. "Results strongly suggest further investigation into the psychological costs and rewards of these relationships" (p. 128).

OTHER THEORIES RELATING TO FAMILY VIOLENCE

Attempts to understand battering/violent relationships have included other theories such as

- Learned helplessness. Over time a victim learns that no matter what she or he does, violence will happen through another who has the power.
- Power and control. Couples have great differential of power (i.e., regarding physical abilities, financial, emotional, social resources).
- Stockholm syndrome, or traumatic bonding. Victims are captives of their perpetrators, and in the process become attached to them.

While such theories facilitate understanding and hopefully compassion for victims, the prevailing beliefs of many responders (and systems) continue to approach victims in a manner that negates their victimization. This issue is fundamental, because it influences the behavior of outsiders to the result of behavior of persons inside the family system and fails to recognize the intricate psychological processes that a victim experiences. The inner life of victims is best understood in relation to the concept of captivity. This model of understanding not only incorporates previous models, such as learned helplessness and the stockholm syndrome—it moves us beyond to a more sophisticated level of awareness. At the writing of this chapter, new research continues to further understanding of these complex and intriguing relationships (see, for example, Walker, 2000, pp. 141–53).

FACTORS ASSOCIATED WITH FAMILY VIOLENCE

Several factors can contribute to family violence:

- When the social resources of the family are inadequate to cope with the problems the family faces.
- When families are unable to deal effectively with the family's problems.
- When family members exhibit other severe personal disabilities (alcohol, mental illness, etc.).

DRUGS, ALCOHOL AND FAMILY VIOLENCE

According to a study by the National Institute of Justice (Brookoff, 1997), almost all assailants had used drugs or alcohol during the day of the assault and two-thirds had used a dangerous combination of cocaine and alcohol. Furthermore, the vast majority of those assaulted were repeat victims of the current assailants. Two-thirds of the perpetrators were on probation or parole at the time of the assault and the majority used or displayed a weapon.

Based on these findings, researchers recommended that future responses to domestic violence should include testing assailants at the time of arrest for alcohol or other drug intoxication and detoxifying arrested drug or alcohol-dependent assailants prior to release from jail. Further, it was recommended that domestic assault victims be allowed to swear out arrest warrants at the assault scene.

WHY DOES SHE STAY?

This is the frequently asked question pertaining to victims trapped in domestic violence relationships. In addition to the theories presented previously, several additional factors contribute to a victims' reluctance to leave the relationship and are briefly discussed.

Fear

Battered women cite fear as the most commonly expressed reason for staying in an abusive relationship. They are afraid the batterer will come after them if they leave. The abuser may not only threaten the spouse but also her children or other family members. Since she has lived with his violence, she believes the threats and rightfully fears for her family's safety.

The rate of reporting domestic violence by females to law enforcement ranges from about 27% (Tjaden & Thoennes, 2000) to 53% (Rennison &

Welchans, 2000). The rates for males range from about 14% (Tjaden & Thoennes, 2000) to 46% (Rennison & Welchans, 2000). Only 17% of rapes victims reported (Tjaden & Thoennes, 2000). The most common reasons given for not reporting were fear of reprisal, that the incident was considered a private matter, or they felt the police would not be able to do anything about the victimization.

Lack of Self-Confidence

Many abused women feel trapped and cannot envision a way out of their situation. A feeling of being completely alone with no one to turn to is common. The abuser takes on bigger than life proportions and becomes all powerful.

Guilt Feelings of Failure

Many women have been raised to believe it is their responsibility to make the marriage or relationship work and leaving the abusive situation would be an admission of failure. Additionally, some women believe that they caused or deserve the punishment.

Lack of Support System

When a victim of domestic violence leaves the relationship, many times she is isolated, scared, and has no place to go. Over time, the abuser has made sure she has no outside support system by cutting off her relationships with family, friends, and coworkers.

Adherence to Traditional Beliefs

For some domestic violence victims, pressure is felt internally that regardless of the degree of violence, divorce is not an acceptable alternative.

Economic Dependence

Victims may not have access to any funds to pay for food or shelter for themselves or their children. Lack of funds and long waiting lists on affordable housing may require a victim to chose between staying in the relationship or living on the streets.

A number of studies have concluded that domestic violence contributes to homelessness, particularly among families with children. Recently, 44% of cities surveyed by the U.S. Conference of Mayors responded that domestic violence is the primary cause of homelessness (NVAA, 1999). Similarly, children who are desperate to leave violent home environments run away from home, living on the streets or seeking temporary shelter relief.

Abusers who are extremely domineering and controlling frequently keep or destroy documentation (such as birth certificates and immunization records) as part of their control of the family, thus preventing or seriously delaying the family from receiving welfare benefits or housing assistance.

Fear of Loss of Children

Over time, victims believe the threats of their abusers that if they leave the abusive relationship, the batterer will get the children. This is reinforced when victims do not have financial independence.

CHARACTERISTICS OF CHILDREN LIVING IN VIOLENT FAMILY SITUATIONS

Today across the nation, seven out of ten persons who enter domestic violence shelters are children (NVAA, 1999). In a study published in 1998, the Centers for Disease Control found that violence against mothers by their intimate partners may also pose a concurrent risk of abuse to the victim's children.

Children are often incorporated into patterns of abuse. The batterer may also do the following:

- Physically or sexually abuse their children.
- Neglect children emotionally or financially.
- Threaten to harm the children.
- Use the children as pawns in episodes involving partner neglect or abuse.
- Attempt to get children to take sides in partner disputes.
- Degrade and humiliate their partners in front of the children.
- Threaten to or actually cut off financial support for children in the event that the partner leaves the battering environment.

Characteristics of children living in domestic violence situations include

- Extreme passivity.
- Extreme aggressiveness.
- Parentification.
- Lags in development.
- Lack of boundaries.
- Changes in psychosocial functioning.

The effects on children who witness family violence or who, in some cases, are themselves victims, may include:

- Children learn from an important role model (the parent) that violence toward a loved one is acceptable.
- Children exhibit fear and emotional symptoms such as psychosomatic complaints (physical complaints created by psychological stress), school phobias, enuresis (bed wetting), and insomnia. Young children may try to stop the violence, thus putting themselves at risk for unintended harm or may respond with immobilized shocked staring, running away and hiding, or bed wetting and nightmares.
- After age 5 or 6, children show strong indications of identifying with the aggressor and losing respect for the victim.
- Many abused and neglected children suffer low self-esteem, sadness, depression, stress disorders, poor impulse control, and feelings of powerlessness, and they are at high risk for alcohol and drug use, sexual acting out, running away, isolation, loneliness, fear, and suicide.
- Sons become aggressive, '"act out, become disobedient, and behave defiantly and destructively," whereas daughters become "withdrawn, clingy, dependent."
- Some adolescent boys assault their mothers and siblings. Older children, especially girls, take on the burden of protecting their younger siblings during the father's beatings. They feel constrained from leaving home.

THE NATION'S RESPONSE TO FAMILY VIOLENCE

A network of more than 2,000 programs has been established to support domestic violence victims. In addition, many domestic violence programs have recently expanded their services to meet the special needs of elderly battered victims, and children who witness violence in their homes.

DOMESTIC VIOLENCE AND THE CRIMINAL JUSTICE SYSTEM

Domestic violence has been called a hidden crime because until the recent past it was often not reported by the victim or treated as criminal behavior by the justice system. The 1982 President's Task Force on Victims of Crime recognized the lack of serious attention given to victims of domestic violence, stating in its report that the cries of family violence victims can no longer go unheeded. Since that time, significant changes have occurred in the nation's response to domestic violence.

Key points for justice system response include

- Initial Contact.
- Police Response/Arrest.
- Pretrial Release.

- Orders of Protection.
- Docketing.
- Dispositions.
- Monitoring of Offenders.

Orders of protection—also called restraining orders—are court orders that forbid the abuser from doing certain things to victims, having contact with victims, and/or compelling abusers to comply with certain requirements. While orders of protection can be issued at any time, it is helpful for victims to seek restraining orders as soon as possible after a domestic violence crime has occurred. Each jurisdiction has different policies and procedures for issuing and monitoring orders of protection.

MODEL DOMESTIC VIOLENCE CODE

The Model Domestic Violence Code was drafted through the National Council of Juvenile and Family and Court Judges and introduced to the National Conference of State Legislatures in 1994. Since then, it has been enacted in whole, or in part, by some jurisdictions.

Its key provisions seek to upgrade interventions and limit discretion of individuals within the criminal justice system to make it more responsive to the safety needs of victims. Specifically, the Model Code requires the following:

- Mandatory arrest.
- Mandatory no-contact orders.
- Restrictions on home detention and deferred prosecutions for batterer.
- Restrictions on plea bargaining domestic violence cases.
- Standards for certification of domestic violence treatment programs.

VIOLENCE AGAINST WOMEN ACT (VAWA) OF 1994

Passage of the Violence Against Women Act (VAWA) of 1994 secured additional federal funding for domestic violence programs and a new base of funding for criminal justice interventions and important research to address violence against women. Programs under VAWA are managed by the Violence Against Women Grants Office of the U.S. Department of Justice. The Act also established federal criminal and civil remedies for battered women and created protections for immigrant women who are battered. Additionally, VAWA supported the creation of the National Domestic Violence Hotline in 1996 to provide crisis intervention information and assistance to victims of domestic violence. In its first year of operation, the hotline responded to more than 73,000 calls for assistance from around the country (New Directions, 1998).

HEALTH SYSTEM INTERVENTIONS AND INITIATIVES

Medical research has confirmed the prevalence of domestic violence among patients and the ways in which medical personnel have traditionally overlooked the problem. According to one study, 30% women who seek emergency medical treatment at hospitals were there as a result of injuries caused by battering (Abbott, J. et al., 1995). In a survey by the American Medical Association, 92% of women that were physically abused by their partners did not discuss these incidents with their physicians, and 57% did not discuss the incidents with anyone. (ibid). Further, less than 10% of primary care physicians routinely screened for domestic violence during regular office visits (Rodriguez et al., 1999).

Numerous national health organizations joined together to work to reduce the prevalence of domestic violence. Task forces have been formed across the country to create policies and practices to improve the health care system response, for example:

- The AMA has spearheaded numerous efforts to develop screening protocol for medical professionals to recognize the common injuries and signs of abuse experienced by victims of domestic violence, as well as intervention protocol for a comprehensive multidisciplinary response to victims of domestic violence.
- The National Health Initiative on Domestic Violence, in conjunction with the Family Violence Prevention Fund and the Pennsylvania Coalition Against Domestic Violence, is developing, evaluating, and disseminating standardized protocols and training programs to help hospitals throughout the country improve their emergency departments' response to domestic violence.

ADVOCACY FOR VICTIMS OF FAMILY VIOLENCE

There are thousands of staff and volunteers in communities across America who assist, support, and serve victims of domestic violence. Often these professionals provide a lifeline to women and children who desperately need assistance and direction but are confused by the dynamics of their victimization, the thought of leaving a violent environment, and, in some cases, entering into the criminal justice system.

INTERVENTION STRATEGIES

There are myriad responses to victims of domestic violence. At minimum, these four areas should be addressed:

- Empowerment. Empower women with the ability to make significant changes and solve problems.
- Establish Independence. Increase a victim's ability to make a successful transition from a battering environment to independence.
- Community Resources. Connect the victim—both in the short term and in the long term—with community resources that provide support, encouragement, and assistance.
- Criminal Justice Support. Provide information and support throughout the criminal justice system and beyond.

For victim services programs that respond to domestic violence victims, the multiple responsibilities associated with assisting victims are outlined below (NVAA, 1999):

- Responding to crisis calls from victims through 24-hour hotlines.
- Accompanying or following law enforcement officials who respond to domestic violence incidents.
- Providing safety and shelter to battered women and their children.
- Providing follow-on services to increase the number of victims who file charges or seek protection through the civil or criminal courts.
- Advising victims about their legal rights throughout the criminal justice system.
- Advising victims about information and resources relevant to protection and security, divorce, custody, and visitation.
- Helping victims develop safety plans.
- Providing information and assistance to victims who leave battering environments, including temporary and long-term housing, employment training (or retraining) and placement, and child care.
- Providing assistance in financial matters, including child support, restitution, victim compensation, and financial planning.
- Upon request, acting as liaison between the victim and the criminal justice system.
- Providing peer counseling.
- Providing support groups.
- Providing information and referrals to community resource agencies, including public assistance, child protective agencies, public and mental health agencies, social services, and schools.
- Providing training to law enforcement, criminal justice, social service, mental health, and other allied professionals about the dynamics of domestic violence and the specific rights and needs of domestic violence victims.
- Working to establish or strengthen a coordinated community response to domestic violence and its victims.

- Generating greatly needed public awareness about domestic violence and its effects on victims, witnesses, communities, and society in general.
- Working to effect changes in laws, agency policies, protocols, and programs that enhance rights and services for victims of domestic violence.

DEVELOPING A SAFETY PLAN

If and when an abused woman is able to leave her battering environment, it is essential that she has a safety plan to increase her opportunity for a successful departure. Advance planning is crucial. Concerns and actions to be addressed include the following:

- Does she have family and friends with whom she can stay?
- Would she find a protective or restraining order helpful?
- Can a victim advocate safely contact her at home? What should the advocate do if the batterer answers the phone?
- Does she know how to contact emergency assistance (i.e., 911)?
- If she believes the violence might begin or escalate, can she leave for a few days?
- Does she know how to contact the shelter? (If she doesn't, provide her with information for future use.)
- Does she have a neighbor she can contact or with whom she can work out a signal for assistance when violence erupts or appears inevitable?
- If she has a car, can she hide a set of keys?
- Can she pack an extra set of clothes for herself and the children, and store them—along with an extra set of house and car keys—with a neighbor or friend?
- Can she leave extra cash, checkbook, or savings account book hidden or with a friend for emergency access?
- Can she collect and store originals or copies of important records such as birth certificates, social security cards, driver's license, financial records (such as banking and other financial accounts, mortgage or rent receipts, the title to the car, etc.) and medical records (for herself and her children)?
- Does she have a concrete plan for where she should go and how she can get there regardless of when she leaves?
- Does she have a disability that requires assistance or a specialized safety plan?
- Does she want access to counseling for her children or herself?

SUMMARY

The topic of family violence must be examined across the age spectrum as emphasized throughout this chapter. The impact of family violence is felt intergenerationally, and as this chapter discussed, research is just beginning to identify the long-term effects of children witnessing violence in their home. It is no longer acceptable to link discussion to only partner or spousal assault. Rather, the implication of violence against all intimates, whether children, the elderly, or within same-sex partnerships must be examined and responded to. Emerging theories, such as captivity, help explain the dynamics of the abusive relationship and its long-term ramifications to the victims. It is obvious that only a coordinated communitywide response to family violence will be effective in addressing this critical problem in the future.

Victims of Hate and Bias Crimes

11

Richard B. Ellis

T he American public is frequently reminded of the differences in our society; differences of race, religion, sexual orientation, ethnicity, or national origin. Unfortunately, the national and local events that drive these differences home are often characterized by violence.

By definition, hate and bias crimes are directed toward persons who are a minority. What does this term mean in America? How does one know whether an illegal act is hate and bias crime? Understanding these concepts will help in the understanding of the impact of hate and bias crime on the victim and the community.

BEING A MINORITY

STATUS

In the United States, for one to understand victimization that is based on a bias against a group, it is essential that the issue of minority status be discussed. Minority status is defined by five characteristics: unequal treatment, physical and cultural traits, involuntary membership, in-group marriage, and awareness of subordinate position in society (Alport, 1979).

Unequal Treatment

This concept refers to the characteristic that within a society one group will be the dominant with all others being subordinate. It is the nature of this social structure that the subordinate group receives less than equal treatment (Alport, 1979). For example in America the dominant group is white, heterosexual, protestant males. This group has control of the power in the United States, and therefore the cards are stacked in their favor.

Opportunities in education, business, politics, and economics have been more accessible to the dominant group. The young, the aged, the disabled, and other distinct groups do not have the same level of opportunities.

Physical and Cultural Traits

These are either appearance, such as skin color, texture of hair, shape of face, and so forth or cultural characteristics such as distinctive type of clothing, visible behavior patterns, and celebrating holidays that are different than those in the dominant culture or not celebrating the holidays of the dominant culture (Alport, 1979).

Involuntary Membership

Minority status is typically a nonchoice. One is born into racial, ethnic, religious, or gender groups. Further, people do not choose to be blind, deaf, or to require a wheelchair for mobility (Alport, 1979).

In-Group Marriages

Many subordinate groups will practice in-group marriage as a way of protecting the culture and themselves from the dominant group (Alport, 1979). In some cultures, out-of-group marriage is forbidden to the extent that when members of the group marry outside the group, they are shunned by the group (i.e., In Orthodox Jewish families if a member of the family marries a nonJew he or she is treated as if dead. The family will have no continued contact with the person and they will participate in a ritualistic mourning ceremony for the member who married outside the group).

Awareness of Subordinate Position

People in a minority status within a society are always aware of the subordinate role they hold within the system. This is typically reinforced by the fact that the minority group has more knowledge of the behavior, beliefs, and values of the dominant group than the dominant group has of the minority (Alport, 1979). Most people of the dominant group, for example, are not aware of the impediments faced by persons with disabilities or persons belonging to nondenominate cultures

TYPES OF MINORITY GROUPS

Racial

Based solely on skin color: for example, African Americans. In the United States, one is considered African American even if only one parent is

African American (Alport, 1979). In other countries—for example, Brazil—race will have many different categories based on the combinations of racial characteristics.

Ethnic

Based on cultural social classification. For example, to be Jewish is to have an ethnic identity rather than just a religious one due to the cultural significance of a variety of social characteristics. Being Jewish entails more than a religion; it is an identity with certain rituals, art forms, literature, and set of values (Alport, 1979).

Religious

Clearly there are many religions that are different than the dominant religion category of Protestant. This may vary, though, according to geographic areas. For example, in Utah, Mormons would not be the minority religious group. Religious minorities are typically identified by their behavior rather than their appearance (Alport, 1979).

Gender/Sexual Orientation

This includes women, gays, lesbians, and bisexual, and transgendered individuals. Again, these groups are different from the dominant group.

Disability

Persons with some form of physical or mental disability are, by definition, of a different ability of those in the dominant group.

Age

Though within every type of the above mentioned groups there are young and elderly persons, as groups, they are different from the dominant age group and are often treated differently.

REACTION TO MINORITIES

Within any society where minority status is identified, there can be a number of reactions on the part of the dominant group. These reactions can range from individual attitudes toward the minority to organized exclusion. At the individual level one encounters prejudice. Prejudice is a negative attitude toward an entire category of people. The two important components in this definition are attitude and entire category. Prejudice involves attitudes, thoughts, and beliefs, not action. Frequently prejudice is expressed through the use of ethnic slurs (e.g., honkie, gook, wetback) or speaking about members of a particular group in a condescending way (e.g., "Jose does well in school for a Chicano", or referring to a middle-aged woman as "one of the girls"). Prejudice beliefs lead to categorical rejection. Prejudice is not disliking someone you meet because you find his or her behavior objectionable—it is disliking or forming negative opinions about an entire racial or ethic group (Alport, 1979).

The next reaction toward a minority group involves action rather than mere attitude. Discrimination involves behavior that exclude all members of a group from certain rights, opportunities, or privileges (Alport, 1979). Like prejudice, it must be categorical. However, if an individual refuses to hire as a typist an Italian American who is illiterate, it is not discrimination. If an individual refuses to hire any Italian American because she or he thinks they are incompetent and does not make an effort to see if the applicant is qualified, it is discrimination.

The third reaction toward a minority group is elimination or genocide. This occurs when organized actions are taken to eliminate the group's existence (Alport, 1979). Like prejudice and discrimination, genocide must be categorical. There must be a designed attempt to eliminate all members of the minority group (Alport, 1979). The Pogroms of Nazi Germany and the ethnic cleansing in Bosnia are both examples of genocide.

HATE CRIME: DEFINITION, INDICATORS, PREVALENCE

The Federal Hate Crimes Act of 1990 defines bias crimes as crimes motivated by hatred against a victim based on his or her race, religion, sexual orientation, ethnicity, or national origin. Prior to 1990, no comprehensive source of bias crime incidence data existed in the United States, due in part to differences in defining, reporting, and compiling incidents of bias crime in different states. In an effort to remedy this lack of reporting, the federal government enacted the Hate Crimes Statistics Act in 1990; state compliance is voluntary, however "during 1998 a total of 7,755 bias motivated criminal incidents were reported to the FBI by 10,730 law enforcement agencies in 46 states and the District of Columbia" (Hate Crimes Statistics, 1998, 1999).

Currently, state law enforcement agencies and police departments collect and document bias crime in different ways. The FBI reports significant underreporting due to poor practices of data collection, documentation, and reporting, as well as to lack of compliance among states. Advocacy groups have done exemplary work in documenting bias crimes and incidents, (e.g., Anti-Defamation League, the National Urban

League, National Gay and Lesbian Task Force, the American-Arab Anti-Discrimination Committee, the Committee Against Anti-Asian Violence, the Asian Law Caucus, the Japanese American Citizens League, and the National Institute Against Prejudice and Violence).

Although some data problems do exist and it is currently impossible to say with certainty what the incidence of bias crime is nationally, it is important to remember that these crimes have a significant impact in several areas: on the victim, the community, our democratic society, civil rights, and protection. These crimes threaten the well being of our society. Although these attacks may vary widely in severity, their impact on the broader community is profound.

BIAS CRIME INDICATORS

When law enforcement officials are investigating a crime, there are clues they can look for in determining if a case should be investigated as a bias crime. These clues are called bias crime indicators. These indicators suggest a possibility, not a legal certainty, that a bias crime has taken place.

The first indicator would be if the racial, religious, ethic/national origin, or sexual orientation of a victim differs from that of the offender. A second would be if the victim is a member of a group that is overwhelmingly outnumbered by members of another group in the area where the incident occurred.

A third indicator that the crime was bias motivated would be if the victim was involved in activities that promoted his or her group. Investigators would also try to determine if the incident coincided with a holiday or date of particular significance to the victim's group. If the victim is not a member of the targeted group but is a member of an advocacy group that supports the victim's group, or the victim was in the company of a member of the targeted group one could view the crime as one motivated by bias.

One thing that investigators will try to determine is whether historical animosity exists between the victim's group and the suspect's group. Any history of animosity can be a clear indication of a bias crime. Bias crime tends to follow a historical pattern.

At the scene of the crime, investigators will look for bias related comments, written statements or gestures that were made by the offender. They will also try to identify any bias related drawings, markings, symbols, or graffiti that may have been left at the scene of the incident. In addition, they will look for objects or items that represent the work of organized hate groups that may have been left behind, such as white hoods or burning crosses. In many cases an organized hate group may claim responsibility for the incident.

If the victim was visiting a location where other hate crimes had been committed against members of the victims group, the crime may be motivated by bias. In addition, if several incidents occurred in the same area and the victims were members of the same group, one could suspect a bias motivated offense.

Investigators will also attempt to determine if the victim received previous harassing mail or phone calls or has been the victim of verbal abuse based on his or her affiliation with a targeted group. Additionally, one would want to know if the victim or witness perceived that the incident was motivated by bias.

The suspect's motivation will also be investigated to determine if the offense was a bias crime. Initially investigators will try to determine if the suspect was previously involved in a similar incident or is a member of or associates with members of organized hate groups. Also consideration would want to be given to whether the victim was perceived, by the offender, as violating or breaking traditional conventions or working in nontraditional employment.

Another characteristic of bias motivated crime is the location of the offense. If the victim was in an area commonly associated with or frequented by a particular citizenship, race, religion, ethnic group, sexual orientation, or gender (e.g., a gay bar) either when the crime occurred or shortly before, one may assume a bias motivation. Last, if no clear economic or other motive for the incident exists, the motivation could be considered to be bias or hate.

EXTENT OF HATE AND BIAS CRIME

The FBI's hate crime statistics program reported 7,755 hate crime incidents in 1998. In 1999, the number rose to 7,876 (Hate Crimes Statistics, 1998, 1999). The incidents reported in 1998 represented 4,321 crimes motivated by racial bias; 1,390 by religious bias, 1,260 by sexual orientation bias; 754 by ethnicity/national orientation bias, and 5 by multiple biases. These incidents involved 9,722 victims and 7,489 known offenders. Seventy percent of the incidents involved only one victim, while 97% involved a single offense (Hate Crimes Statistics, 1998).

The 7,876 hate motivated crimes reported in 1999 represent 9,301 offenses, 9,802 victims and 7,271 offenders. Of the total reported 4,295 were motivated by racial bias, 1,411 by religious bias, 1,317 by sexual orientation bias, 829 by ethnicity/nationality bias, 19 by disability bias, and 5 by multiple biases (Hate Crimes Statistics, 1999).

Eight of every ten of the 9,722 reported hate crimes were against individuals; the remaining were against businesses, religious organizations or various other targets. Thirteen persons were murdered in 1998 in hate motivated incidents. Racial biased motivated 8 of the murders; sexual orientation bias resulted in 4 murders, and ethnicity/nationality accounted for a single murder (Hate Crimes Statistics, 1998).

During 1998, 14% of state agencies had specially trained personnel assigned to address hate crimes. Thirty-three percent had incorporated special policies or procedures that address hate crime, while 49% of State agencies had no special policies or procedures governing hate crimes (Reaves & Goldberg, 1999).

In 1998, 31% of reported hate crimes, occurred in or on residential properties. Incidents perpetrated on highways, road, alleys or streets accounted for 20% of reported hate crimes. Nine percent of the reported hate crimes occurred at schools or colleges (Hate Crime Statistics, 1998).

IMPACT OF HATE AND BIAS CRIME

Hate and bias crimes have certain unique features that impose a serious impact on the victim. Since hate crimes are motivated by a perception that the victim is less of a person than the perpetrator, bias crime is more likely to be seriously injurious or lethal than any other personal injury crime. What may have begun as an assault will result in a death. With hate crimes, there is a diffusion of responsibility so that no one person is held personally accountable. This leaves the victim with no one individual to hold accountable for the offense.

Since many hate crimes are committed by groups, it is important to understand the group mentality. The group seems to generate courage, particularly among those who fit the description of cowardly. Therefore, the crime may be more serious than any crime that might be committed by the individual. Groups tend to exacerbate the viciousness of the crimes. The most egregious type of victim trauma of all hate crimes results in mass murders and/or assaults. Hatred has been thought to be one of the primary motives in a number of mass crimes.

In 1989, 300 children were playing when Patrick Purdy walked onto the Stockton, California playground and fired 66 rounds in their midst. Five children died and 29 children and 1 teacher were wounded in less than two minutes. Many have thought it was Purdy's racial hatred that caused him to attack the school, where close to 70% of the student body were of South Asian origin (Purdy's victims were in this group).

On December 6, 1989, a young man walked into the engineering school at Ecole Polytechnique in Montreal, Canada and started firing an automatic weapon. After separating male students from females, he fired on the women, killing 14 and wounding 13 others before killing himself. As the shooting occurred, he expressed out loud his hatred for women.

Bias crime has also emerged in response to the AIDS epidemic. According to the Presidential Commission on the Human Immunodeficiency Epidemic, there is "increasing violence against those perceived to carry

HIV," and that for them, "so-called hate crimes are a serious problem." This may account for the increase in crimes committed against those perceived to be gay.

A large number of bias crimes seem to be aimed at individuals who are not only members of an identified group but who are perceived as infringing on another group's sovereignty. Northeastern professor Jack McDevitt analyzed 452 cases of bias crime that occurred in Boston from 1983 to 1987 and found that 57% of the crimes were attacks on persons walking, driving through, or working in a neighborhood or on a family moving into the area perceived to belong to persons different from the victims (McDevitt & Levin, 1993).

VICTIM IMPACT

Victims of bias crimes have been hated and attacked for being different and for being misunderstood. Since the basis for their attack is their identity, they may suffer a deep personal crisis that is different from the suffering of victims of other crimes. Victims of bias crimes are targeted due to a core characteristic of their identity that is immutable. This may lead to increased vulnerability.

When a bias crime is committed against a member of a minority group, the victim frequently perceives the offender as representative of the dominant group in society who may frequently stereotype the victim's culture. This makes the victim less likely to trust any member of the dominant group, making it more difficult for those individuals expected to assist the victim.

If their membership in a targeted group is readily visible, victims of bias crimes may feel particularly vulnerable to a repeat attack. This heightened sense of vulnerability may result in the feeling of hopelessness. Victims may become afraid to associate with other members of the targeted group, or may fear seeking needed services, believing that these actions increase their vulnerability.

Victims of bias crime may become confused regarding how to behave. As a result of the victimization, bias crime victims may respond by more strongly identifying with their group—or, conversely, by attempting to disassociate themselves or deny a significant aspect of their identity. This may result in victims questioning their assumptions. Assumptions about their life/worldview may be shattered. For bias crime victims who are minorities, this may be particularly devastating, because their worldview may have been very different than the dominant culture's worldview. The victim's perception may have been one that he or she was an accepted member of society. The impact of the crime may force victims to reconsider their position in the community.

Many victims of bias crime have a great deal of difficulty understanding the crime. It may be very difficult for the bias crime victim to resolve that the crime was motivated by hatred, as opposed to another motive, such as economic.

COMMUNITY IMPACT

When individuals are targets of hate because of their race, religion, ethnicity, gender, or sexual orientation, their victimization is projected outward to all members of the wider community. Other members of the same group may also feel victimized. They become aware of their own vulnerability. This may result in members of the same group as the victim distancing themselves from the victim. This leaves the victim feeling alone and without support. Additionally, members of other commonly targeted groups are reminded of their vulnerability to similar attacks.

Places of worship are often targeted by bias crime offenders for acts of vandalism, these attacks on sacred spiritual symbols may harm victims more than other acts of vandalism. They also harm other members of the community. The intent of the crime may have been toward a single member of that religious group; however, every member will feel violated.

RESPONSES TO HATE AND BIAS CRIME

A number of civil remedies are available to victims of hate and bias crime. Regulatory agencies and the courts routinely deal with claims of discrimination in housing, employment, and the like on the basis of race, ethnicity, religion, gender, and other characteristics (but not sexual orientation), in spite of the U.S. Supreme Court rulings making these claims more difficult to sustain. Although criminal actions can be taken under federal law, most criminal charges are filed under state law.

Nearly half the states have passed hate crime reporting acts in addition to the Federal Hate Crimes Statistics Act of 1990. Most states have institutional vandalism laws that include a number of hate crimes because they cover defacement, destruction or damage directed toward churches, cemeteries, schools, and other facilities often identified with particular groups.

Enhancement of penalties for crimes identified as hate motivated have been adopted by over two thirds of the states. These enhancements take two forms. First is simply to add to the existing penalty for a crime when the court determines hate motivation. Second, existing crimes are listed as one class or grade higher in the penal code when hate motivations present.

One of the problems in responding to hate motivated crime is the disagreement among officials as to what to include in the statutes. Racial, religious and ethnic hatred are routinely covered, but there is less agreement about those same crimes committed as a reaction to sexual orientation, gender, age, or disability.

In addition to punishment oriented responses to hate crime, some locales are initiating extensive education, prevention, investigation and victims' services programs. In 1997, under the direction of Attorney General Janet Reno, the Department of Justice convened a working group of prosecutors, law enforcement personnel, victim's services providers, and training experts. The Attorney General's charge to this group was to develop four training curricula on hate crimes,each designed for a different level of law enforcement. In November of that same year, President Clinton announced the initiation of the training curriculum at the White House Conference on Hate Crimes. The national trainers program began in Fall 1998. Each curriculum provides trainers at the local level with lesson plans and training material for an eight-hour course covering topics such as history, identification, legal issues, investigative techniques, victim trauma, and case studies related to hate and bias crime. In total, 78 teams representing all 50 states and the District of Columbia were trained (Bureau of Justice Assistance, 2000).

When providing assistance to hate crime victims, service providers should be sensitive to the cultural dynamics of the victim. Most literature on trauma and appropriate interventions is based on theoretical and philosophical paradigms drawn from a white, Anglo-Saxon, Judeo-Christian perspective in the United States. However, it is clear that people with different cultural backgrounds may perceive trauma and treatment differently. All ethnically focused clinical, sociological, anthropological, and experimental studies converge to one central conclusion regarding ethnic America: Ethnic identification is an irreducible entity to how persons organize experience and understand the unique cultural prism they use in perceiving and evaluating reality. Ethnicity is thus central to how the patient or client seeks assistance (help seeking behavior), what he or she defines as a problem, what he or she understands as the cause of psychological difficulties, and the unique, subjective experience of traumatic stress symptoms. "Ethnicity also shapes how the client views his or her symptoms, and the degree of hopefulness or pessimism toward recovery. Ethnic identification, additionally, determines the patient's attitudes toward his or her pain, expectations of the treatment, and what the client perceives as the best method of addressing the presenting difficulties" (Parsons, 1985).

Several different schemes can provide insight into how different cultures may need different types of intervention. When intervening with individuals of different cultures, the professional should keep in mind three schemes that focus an individual's worldview. The first is known as the axis of control, which is the degree to which individuals feel personal control of their lives, and the degree to which they may feel personal responsibility for what happens to them or their community. Second is the axis of conflict, which describes how people tend to react to conflict in their lives and the goals they seek in resolving that conflict. Third is known as the axis of life, which illustrates the different perspectives on life and death issues and whether individuals seek to resolve their concerns about life and death through communing with nature, God, or technology. Each perspective described suggests differences in attitudes, philosophies, and values when providing outreach and service to different cultural groups.

CULTURAL ASSESSMENTS

When intervening with individuals of a different cultural, it is most helpful to complete a cultural assessment. The purpose of a cultural assessment is to determine to what extent the individual is grounded in his or her culture. Do not assume that just because a consumer of your service appears to be of a certain culture that he/she is grounded in that culture. The analysis can be based on any dominant and uniting characteristic of a population. For instance, if victim services were being planned in a community in a rural area that has a large population of Vietnamese, it would be important to think of the frame of reference of the Vietnamese population. The rural Vietnamese victim may differ from a Vietnamese victim located in a large, industrialized urban area. It would be critical to think about the integration into the Vietnamese culture, or lack thereof, of any particular group or individual, within the communities.

For the purposes of illustration, the following is a checklist for helping services providers determine the level of ethnic identification that a victim may have:

- Determine the extent that ethnic language is spoken in the home.
- Determine how well English (or the dominant language or dialect in a country) is spoken.
- Determine the stresses of migration on the ethnic group as a whole and how long the individual or community has been in the United States.
- Determine the community of residence and the opportunities the individual has for linking with people of similar ethnic origin.
- Determine the educational attainment and socioeconomic status of the individual and the community.
- Determine the degree of religious faith of the individual or the community and whether that faith reflects the religion of the ethnic group.
- Determine the presence of intermarriage in the community—by individuals, within families, or within the community as a whole.

CULTURAL COMPETENCE

One long held theory has been that it is best if members of the same culture, racial, or ethnic group assist each other: for example, Hispanic/Latino victims, in this view, would best be served by a Hispanic/Latino counselor. While this may be a goal in some cases, it may not be practical given the shortage of helpers from different cultures in the communities where they are most needed. James Green offers the following definitions of ethnic competence that can be utilized to explain a more generic definition of cultural competence.

Ethnic competence should be understood as an awareness of one's own cultural limitations. The ability to understand another cultural is limited by the degree of awareness one has of that culture. Ethnic competence can only be developed if one is attuned to cultural differences, and has a client-centered systematic learning style. The helper must believe that all cross-cultural encounters are a potential learning experience. Ethnic competence comes from utilizing cultural resources. To do this, the helper must know the resources available to the client and how they may best be used. Resources here mean not only community agencies but also institutions, individuals, and customs indigenous to the client's community. Essential to developing ethnic competence is acknowledging cultural integrity. The helper must believe that all cultural traditions and communities are by definition rich, complex, and varied (Green, 1982).

RECOMMENDATIONS FOR CROSS-CULTURAL SERVICE DELIVERY

In preparation for providing cross cultural victim assistance, the helper should take advantage of as many cross-cultural educational opportunities as possible. This could include formal education opportunities as well as informal. The counselor may want to attend cultural specific entertainment, festivals or religious activities. Consider the following possibility: Most people who think of themselves as members of a dominant cultural group spend less time learning about minority groups than do the minority groups spend learning about dominant groups. Minorities need to learn about dominant cultural values in order to survive.

Be aware of institutional and latent cultural bigotry. Such bigotry includes racism, sexism, homophobia, and so forth. While it is easy to identify obvious indicators of bigotry, subtle signs of discrimination, ignorance and prejudice may be more difficult to observe:

- Language often carries inherent messages of prejudice ("Jew him down").
- Stereotypes also often are indicators of prejudice ("the Frito Bandito").

- Educational programs can carry implicit biases in favor of the dominant cultural (Western European laden content).
- Symbols, traditions, and behaviors may be implicitly discriminatory (Christmas decorations in the work place).

It is wise for service providers to think about the difference between bigoted words, phrases, or humor and what constitutes nonbigoted or discriminatory speech.

Racism is one of the most important factors in cultural experiences. Some have suggested that the more people of one race are exposed to people of other races, the less likely either race will be racist. However, others suggest that if people lack any exposure to a different race they may also be nonracist.

People become racist when exposed to negative experiences or stereotypes about other races. When those experiences or stereotypes are reinforced by media, friends, and family, language or formal education, racism becomes entrenched.

Victim Advocacy and Public Policy   **12**

Christine N. Edmunds and Thomas L. Underwood

> *Victims are regarded as obscure or unimportant, even invisible. The suffering and plight of victims, until recently, have been neglected in the minds and actions of legislators and chief executives of government, and even by those government agencies set up to support, protect, and defend victims.*
> —*Sank and Sank Firschein, 1991, p. 19.*

> *Tremendous strides have been made to enact victims' rights laws and to deliver services to victims in the United States. Few movements in the history of this nation have achieved such success in igniting the kind of legislative response that victim rights activists have fostered.*
> —*U.S. Department of Justice, Office for Victims of Crime New Directions from the Field: Victims' Rights and Services for the 21st Century, 1998, p. ix.*

These statements reflect the turbulent yet progressive nature of advancements made by and on behalf of crime victims. Why are crime victims a part of the public consciousness and how is that reflected in public policy? The progression of victims' rights and services over the past several decades has been realized through advocacy efforts of victim groups that, in turn, has prompted legislation and administrative policy that are responsive to victims.

This chapter discusses how some of the major victim advocacy organizations have shaped the victims' movement. The origin of public policy initiatives on the federal, state, and local levels is presented along with the major policy issues that pertain to victims.

VICTIM ADVOCACY

Individuals harmed by crime represent the entire spectrum of the human race. While statistics can direct attention to characteristics of age, race, and other features, there is not any one group who is excluded from the status of crime victim. They "comprise an unstigmitized class that cuts across all other social categories and includes many persons with substantial social, economic, and political power" (Wertheimer, 1991, p. 411).

Feeling alone and isolated, a person victimized by crime often reaches out to those most like themselves. Since crime knows no boundaries, those most like themselves are other crime victims. Many victim advocacy groups started primarily as support services and, either independently or in coalition with other like groups, became an organized voice for social change, giving "victims who otherwise would feel powerless, guilty, and enraged . . . a sense of control over their lives" (Karmen, 1996, p. 30). Advocacy efforts may include lobbying for rights and services, public demonstrations, and public and professional education through written information and programs. Advocacy groups generate broad support by a diversity of individuals and groups. Unlike many other social issues, crime victimization is a cause that solidifies diversity. "Virtually everyone agrees that victims should be treated with dignity and that the justice system should be sensitive to their needs" (Kennedy & Sacco, 1998, p. 54). In spite of this solidarity for the broad cause of crime victims, there are differences and conflicts among various advocacy groups. These differences reflect philosophies regarding the victim groups they represent (e.g., battered women, homicide survivors, children), the political agenda promoted by the group (e.g., enhanced services, increased punishments), the primary activities undertaken by the group (e.g., lobbying, education, support), and competition for limited funds between the groups.

THE CRIME VICTIMS' FIELD TODAY

Since the first victim assistance programs were established in 1972, the "victim assistance movement has grown into a full-fledged advocacy and service field dedicated to meeting the physical, financial, and psychological needs of victims and their families" (New Directions, 1998, p. 153). Today, according to the U.S. Department of Justice, Office for Victims of Crime, based on figures provided from national crime victim organizations, 10,000 programs provide support and assistance to victims in the aftermath of crime (New Directions, 1998).

Victim assistance programs have become part of the nation's criminal and juvenile justice infrastructure and now exist in literally hundreds of law enforcement agencies, prosecutors offices, and correctional agencies.

Victim assistance agencies in the private nonprofit sector have also grown tremendously over the past two decades. For example (New Directions, 1998):

- The National Coalition Against Domestic Violence states that over 2,000 programs provide assistance to battered women. Over 1,000 of these programs provide shelter.
- According to the National Coalition Against Sexual Assault, there are 2,000 rape crisis centers nationwide.
- More than 200 chapters of the advocacy and support group Parents of Murdered Children have been established.
- Mothers Against Drunk Driving today has over 500 chapters nationwide.
- Multidisciplinary childrens; advocacy centers, many of which are community or hospital-based, have been created to help abused children in more than 350 jurisdictions.
- Triad programs, a partnership with law enforcement agencies and victims, now assist elderly crime victims in more than 525 communities.

Numerous national organizations assist and advocate on behalf of crime victims, providing essential support for the expanding network of Victim Assistance programs across the country (New Directions, 1998). These are extraordinary accomplishments for a movement that started modestly only three decades ago.

Some of the significant advocacy groups in victims assistance provided a description of their purpose and services for the 1998 publication, *New Directions from the Field: Victims' Rights and Services for the 21st Century*, issued by the Office for Victims of Crime.

National Organization of Victims Assistance (NOVA)

The National Organization for Victim Assistance, founded in 1975, is the worlds oldest broad-based victim rights group. A nonprofit, membership organization, NOVA is guided by four purposes: to be of service to its members; to be an advocate for victim rights and services in federal, state, and local legislatures and executive agencies; to be a training and educational resource to victim assistance and allied professionals; and to be of direct service to victims who call the NOVA offices or who are involved in a large-scale disaster to which a NOVA crisis team responds.

National Center for Victims of Crime (NCVC)

The National Center for Victims of Crime, founded in 1985, (formerly the National Victim Center), is a resource and advocacy center for victims of crime. The Center serves as a national advocate to establish and protect legal rights for victims and to secure the resources they need to recover from the trauma of crime. NCVC programs emphasize public education, public policy through legislative advocacy, and resource development for victims. NCVC provides technical assistance to victim service providers, criminal justice, and allied professionals and supports the creation of model programs and materials including the nations most comprehensive library collection on victim-related issues.

National Coalition Against Domestic Violence (NCADV)

The National Coalition Against Domestic Violence, founded in 1978, represents more than 2,000 grassroots programs and shelters serving battered women and their children in rural and urban areas throughout the United States. NCADV opposes the use of violence as a means of control over others and supports equality in relationships and strategies for helping women assume power over their own lives. NCADV also works to educate the public about domestic violence and supports state legislation that appropriately sanctions offenders.

National Network to End Domestic Violence (NNEDV)

The National Network to End Domestic Violence, founded in 1990, is a membership and advocacy organization of state domestic violence coalitions. NNEDV began as the Domestic Violence Coalition on Public Policy in 1990 and was instrumental in developing policy that became part of the landmark Violence Against Women Act of 1994. Its mission is to ensure that national public policy is responsive to the concerns and interests of battered women and their children; to strengthen the development of and relationships among domestic violence coalitions, which provide services, community education, and technical assistance to programs establishing shelter and related services to battered women and their children; and to educate the general public about issues concerning domestic violence.

National Coalition Against Sexual Assault (NCASA)

The National Coalition Against Sexual Assault, founded in 1978, is a membership organization committed to the prevention of sexual violence through intervention, education, advocacy, and public policy. NCASA promotes and advocates a national course of action based on the sexual assault victim/survivors perspective and works toward the empowerment of all victims and survivors: children and adults, women and men. Major NCASA initiatives include hosting an annual National Conference and Women of Color Institute as well as producing resources for National Sexual Assault Awareness Month in April.

Rape, Abuse & Incest National Network (RAINN)

The Rape, Abuse & Incest National Network, founded in 1994, is a nonprofit organization that operates the only national toll-free hotline for survivors of sexual assault. Founded in 1994 by singing artist Tori Amos, a survivor of sexual assault herself, RAINN provides hotline access to trained counselors 24 hours a day from anywhere in the country. Calls are automatically routed to local rape crisis centers, expanding the outreach and service of these centers. In just 3 years of operation, RAINN has helped more than 170,000 victims of sexual assault.

Parents of Murdered Children (POMC)

Parents of Murdered Children was founded in1978 by Charlotte and Bob Hullinger after the murder of their daughter Lisa. POMC has grown from a single self-help group in Cincinnati, Ohio, to a network of more than 200 local chapters serving 38,000 survivors each year. POMC's goal is to allow the grief of family members to be shared with others who have been through similar experiences, thereby breaking down the isolation that many families face.

Mothers Against Drunk Driving (MADD)

Mothers Against Drunk Driving, founded in 1980, was started by two mothers whose daughters were victimized by drunk driving. One was killed and the other became the country's youngest paraplegic. MADD's mission is to stop drunk driving and support victims of this violent crime. Each of the more than 500 MADD chapters across the country have at least one trained advocate who provides emotional support through one-on-one advocacy and support groups, guidance through the criminal justice system, and assistance with victim impact statements and compensation applications. MADD operates numerous education and prevention programs for children and adults of all ages and advocates for better public policy. The organization publishes a wide array of victim brochures and offers information and assistance through a 24-hour hotline.

National Center for Missing and Exploited Children (NCMEC)

The National Center for Missing and Exploited Children was established in 1984 with the passage by Congress of the Missing Children's Assistance Act. NCMEC serves as a clearinghouse and national resource center dedicated to helping exploited children. Since its creation, the center has handled more than one million calls to its 24-hour hotline, distributed millions of publications, and provided advice and technical assistance to thousands of parents, prosecutors, law enforcement officers, and child services professionals.

National Association of Crime Victim Compensation Boards (NACVCB)

The National Association of Crime Victim Compensation Boards, founded in 1977, represents State compensation programs on the national level.

NACVCB provides advocacy, training, and technical assistance, and fosters communication among state programs. NACVCB is a strong national voice on all matters affecting state compensation programs before Congress and the Office for Victims of Crime (OVC). In addition, it provides extensive training to its members on a wide range of issues facing programs today, from administration and funding matters to coverage of emerging areas of victimization.

Victims Assistance Legal Organization (VALOR)

The Victims Assistance Legal Organization was founded in 1979 by the late Frank Carrington. The organization is dedicated to promoting rights of crime victims in the civil and criminal justice systems. This is accomplished through public education, advancing public policy reforms, and professional training.

PUBLIC POLICY

Legal rights for victims were not enumerated in the United States Constitution. The rights and privileges exercised by crime victims have evolved through various local, state, and national efforts. A service or practice that benefits victims in one jurisdiction is soon discovered by victims in other areas, often through the assistance of advocacy groups. Policies that support these services and practices develop, thus formalizing their existence into rights. As more victims and organizations exercise and demand these rights, the social institutions become more accepting.

The demand for rights tends to be more evolutionary than revolutionary. As victims' rights become established through formal polices, victims and advocacy groups press for the next level of services and practices. But public policy is a process that is lethargic to change. It is also a process that often involves a compromise of competing interests or values.

Policy is developed by the three branches of government: legislative, judicial, and executive. The checks and balances accorded by the U.S. Constitution provide for the continual interactive and oversight roles of each branch of government.

PUBLIC POLICY: LEGISLATIVE BRANCH

Composed of two bodies, (on the national level it is the U.S. House of Representatives and the U.S. Senate) each body introduces bills, holds hearings, and conducts floor votes. Ultimately each body must agree on common language (via Conference Committee and final floor vote) for a bill to become an act of Congress/State. Only then can an act be approved by the Executive branch (signed by the President/Governor) in order to become law, or vetoed (not signed by the President/Governor). Similarly, local governments follow a process through city/county councils and Mayors/County Chairs.

The crime victims' field depends on two key types of legislative acts: Those that provide funding, and those that provide rights. Often, these laws are intertwined.

FUNDING

At the federal level, two key national laws provide the majority of funding for crime victim programs:

The Victims of Crime Act of 1984 (VOCA)

VOCA created the federal Crime Victims Fund, which has for the past 15 years provided a relatively stable source of funding for local victim assistance programs. Since the passage of VOCA, more than $2.5 billion has been distributed to local victim assistance programs and state compensation programs from fines and penalties assessed against federal offenders.

The Violence Against Women Act of 1994 (VAWA)

VAWA has made available $1.6 billion to support domestic violence and sexual assault programs and research. In addition, all states now provide funding for victim assistance programs, although the levels of funding and types of programs funded vary greatly by state. Today, at the state level, over 30 states provide funding for victim services, and all states support a crime victim compensation program. At the local level, communities are increasingly supporting victim service programs through voter tax assessments, budget line items, local levies (such as taxes on marriage and divorce decrees), and even community-budgeted victim assistance centers, such as those in Jacksonville, Florida.

VICTIMS' RIGHTS LEGISLATION

Considering the complicated and time consuming process of enacting legislation, it is remarkable that the legislative branch on the national and state levels have been responsible for the passage of over 30,000 victims' rights and related statutes in the past 20 years. Victims' rights laws were first enacted on the state level in the early 1980s. Today, every state has laws protecting victims' rights. Moreover, victims' rights have been strengthened in 32 states by constitutional mandate (New Directions, 1998). States have not established one standard set of rights for victims. Bills of Rights, the most common form of victims' rights laws, have been enacted in virtually every state. These Bills of Rights contain basic provisions for victims to be treated with dignity and compassion, to be informed of the status of their case, to be notified of hearings and trial dates, to be heard at sentencing and parole through victim impact statements, and to receive restitution from convicted offenders.

Each year, hundreds of new victims' rights laws and innovative practices are enacted and implemented across the country. For example, since 1990, after cases of stalking received national attention from the media and victim advocacy groups, all 50 states and the District of Columbia modified their laws to criminalize stalking (New Directions, 1998). Some state legislatures also reacted swiftly to the escalation of juvenile crime to record levels in the early 1990s by extending at least some rights to victims of juvenile offenders. In 1992, for example, only 5 states provided victims the right to be notified of a disposition hearing involving a juvenile. By 1995, 25 states provided this right.

Despite this record of success, however, victims are still being denied their right to participate in the justice system. Many victims rights laws are not being implemented, and most states still have not enacted fundamental reforms such as consultation by prosecutors with victims prior to plea agreements, victim input into important pretrial release decisions such as the granting of bail, protection of victims from intimidation and harm, and comprehensive rights for victims of juvenile offenders.

CONSTITUTIONAL RIGHTS FOR CRIME VICTIMS

Crime victim advocacy groups nationwide have worked to strengthen victims' rights in states through successfully advocating for the enactment of victims' rights constitutional amendments in over 30 states. In addition, a victims' rights constitutional amendment was first introduced on the national level in Congress in 1996. The idea of amending the U.S. Constitution to include rights for crime victims has received relatively strong bipartisan support. While hearings have been held in both the House and the Senate, there is still great debate on the scope of rights for crime victims' that a federal constitutional amendment should cover. What is agreed upon is that as long as the Constitution remains silent on rights for victims, while ensuring rights for those accused of crimes, that the scales of justice will remain unbalanced. Constitutional rights for crime victims will help ensure that fundamental rights are consistently accorded to crime victims throughout the nation.

CATEGORIES OF VICTIMS' RIGHTS

Victims' Rights Laws can be divided into the following six general categories:

Right to Information and Notification

Most states afford victims the right to notice of events and proceedings at various stages of the judicial process. Over 50 points of notification have been identified across the justice system. State law varies greatly on the type of victim notification required. For example:

- 25 states require notice of bail or pretrial release.
- 28 states notify victims of plea negotiations.
- 34 states provide notification of sentencing hearings.
- 37 states notify victims of parole hearings.
- 44 states inform victims of parole release (NCVC, 1996).

Right to be Heard

All states have passed laws allowing courts to consider victim impact information at sentencing, and at least 41 states allow victims to make oral statements during sentencing hearings (New Directions, 1998). Virtually every state requires victim impact information as part of the presentence report, and at least half of the states expressly require the court to consider that information in sentencing decisions. In addition, states provide victims the right to be heard at pretrial release hearings (National Center for Victims of Crime, 1996).

Right to Participate

Participatory rights have expanded greatly over the past decade. While victims were once kept out of trials and hearings, today most states allow victims to be present at many significant justice proceedings. For example,

- 35 states give victims the right to attend most criminal justice proceedings.
- 24 state constitutions address victims' rights to attend criminal justice proceedings.
- 21 states allow victims to attend bail hearings.
- 14 states allow victims to attend plea agreement hearings.
- 24 states give victims the right to attend the trial (New Directions, 1998).

Right to Protection from Intimidation and Harm

The rights to protection from intimidation and harm is an articulated right in all state bills of rights. However, extending actual protection to victims is a challenging task for criminal justice professionals. Specific statutes that address this right include anti-stalking statutes (as stated above, now enacted in all states) as well as the right for victims to receive orders of protection/restraining orders.

Right to Financial Redress

Three types of financial remedies are now extended to crime victims: crime victim compensation, restitution, and seeking redress through the civil justice system. Since 1965, all states have established compensation programs. The maximum award limits vary across states, generally ranging from 15,000 to 40,000 dollars.

Restitution laws also vary across states. For example,

- 26 states require mandatory restitution unless the judge offers compelling reasons for not ordering restitution.
- 24 states allow restitution to be discretionary.
- 29 states allow restitution orders to become civil judgements (NCVC, 1996).

The civil justice system offers an additional opportunity for victims to seek financial remedies. Over the past decade a new specialization of law has emerged, crime victims civil litigation, and crime victims are winning significant judgements against defendants, especially in cases involving sexual assault and crimes against children.

Victim-Oriented Criminal Justice Reform Measures

Legislation has been enacted over the past two decades aimed at improving the treatment of crime victims by the justice system. These laws range from requiring prompt property return and speedy trials for certain types of victims (children and the elderly) to specific rights and protections for different victim population groups, such as marital rape, rape shield, and name and address confidentiality laws. As a specific example, in 1992 Massachusetts passed landmark legislation that created a statewide computerized domestic violence registry and required judges to check the registry when handling such cases.

PUBLIC POLICY: EXECUTIVE BRANCH

The executive branch is headed by the President on the national level, Governor on the state level, and on the local level by mayor or county chair. The Executive branch must approve all legislative acts in order to become law/ordinance and oversees the workings of government. When a law is enacted, a federal/state agency is assigned to administer it. On the national level, while a multitude of federal agencies fall under the jurisdiction of the executive branch, crime victims rights and concerns are generally assigned to the U.S. Department of Justice or the Department of Health and Human Services.

U.S. Department of Justice, Office for Victims of Crime (OVC)

OVC was established by the Victims of Crime Act of 1984 (VOCA) to administer federal funds that support victim assistance and victim compensation programs around the country, and to advocate for the fair treatment of crime victims. To this end, OVC administers the Crime Victims Fund, which is derived not from tax dollars but from fines and penalties paid by federal criminal offenders. Over 90% of the fund is distributed to the states to help fund their victim assistance and victim compensation programs. OVC administers the remainder of the Fund to support services to federal crime victims, provide training designed to educate criminal justice and allied professionals regarding the rights and needs of crime victims, provide technical assistance to criminal justice and allied professionals, support training and victim assistance programs in Indian country, and initiate and support innovative projects with national impact. This office is one of five bureaus within the Office of Justice Programs, U.S. Department of Justice.

Violence Against Women Grants Office (VAWGO)

VAWGO was established in 1994; it administers the U.S. Department of Justices formula and discretionary grant programs authorized by the Violence Against Women Act of 1994. The program assists the nations criminal justice system in responding to the needs and concerns of women who have been, or potentially could be, victimized by violence. These grants are to provide enhanced delivery of services to women victimized by violence and to strengthen outreach efforts to minorities and disabled women. The program's grants also provide American Indian tribal governments with funds to develop and strengthen the tribal justice systems' response to violent crimes committed against Native American women. In addition, the Office provides technical assistance to state and tribal government officials in planning innovative and effective criminal justice responses to violent crimes committed against women. OVC works closely with the Violence Against Women Office, which is responsible for departmentwide coordination of this issue.

Local Government and Service Organizations

Regardless of the countless victims' rights laws that have been enacted, it is up to local government and service agencies to ultimately ensure the implementation of victims' rights. Law enforcement agencies, prosecutors' offices, the courts, community corrections, and social service and health agencies must implement these laws through the development of mandatory policy statements, protocols, and agency guidelines.

One of the earliest examples of implementation was in 1974, when the Federal Law Enforcement Administration funded the first victim-witness programs in local district attorneys' offices. The 1976 implantation of the first victim impact statements by Chief Probation Officer James Rowland is another example of executive implementation of policy.

PUBLIC POLICY: JUDICIAL BRANCH

The Judicial branch of government is charged with the duty of deciding whether the laws enacted by the legislative branch of government uphold the intent and purpose of individual protections granted by U.S. Constitution. This simple statement has resulted in literally millions of cases that have progressed through local, state, and federal courts over the past 200 plus years.

For crime victims' rights, key judicial decisions include

- State v. Ciskie (1988) is the first case to allow the use of expert testimony to explain the behavior and mental state of an adult rape victim. The testimony is used to show why a victim of repeated physical and sexual assaults by her intimate partner would not immediately call the police or take action. The jury convicts the defendant on four counts of rape.
- Simon & Schuster v. New York Crime Victims Board (1991). The U.S. Supreme Court ruled that New York's notoriety-for-profit statute was overly broad and, in the final analysis, unconstitutional. Notoriety-for-profit statutes had been passed by many states at this time to prevent convicted criminals from profiting from the proceeds of depictions of their crime in the media or publications. States must now review their existing statutes to come into compliance with the Supreme Court's decision.
- Payne v. Tennessee (1991). This was the U.S. Supreme Court's reversal of an earlier ruling that found victim impact statements unconstitutional.

IMPLICATIONS OF POLICY INITIATIVES ON RIGHTS AND PRACTICE

Karman (1996) identifies three areas where victims rights are gained at the expense of others.

OFFENDERS

There has been a public outcry against the perceived excessiveness of offenders rights; the public believes there is an imbalance between the rights of offenders versus the rights of the victim. The argument in favor of reform at the expense of offenders assumes that there is a fixed quantity of rights and that they should be evenly spread between offenders and victims—or, better yet, should tilt in favor of the victim.

Often it is the view that offender punishment is the same as victim rights. While many victims may favor enhanced retaliatory and punitive justice, these actions do not necessarily reflect the wants of all victims. They are less reflective of rights than they are of popular values.

CRIMINAL JUSTICE SYSTEM

The array of rights and organizational practices afforded to victims has created unintended consequences for the criminal justice system. To comply with the various victim rights requirements, agencies have had to assume additional responsibilities often without the benefit additional of personnel and financial resources. For many jurisdictions, compliance with victim rights compromises other important duties. "It is important to note that with the passage of legislation insuring more rights for the victim, there are consequences with regard to the loss of individuality (Frazier, 1998, p. 5).

EITHER OFFENDERS OR SYSTEM OR BOTH

There is an increased demand for full and active participation in the justice process. Proponents of this want victims to have an equal part in the justice process, having the same opportunity to be present and heard as offenders.

If the victim's view is consistent with the state, then the offender may view this participatory status as a further empowerment of the state to control and oppress offender rights. However, if the victim' view is counter to that of the state, then the victim may be viewed by justice officials as a meddler who does not have the broader social good in mind.

SUMMARY

There have been incredible gains over the past few decades. Through the initial efforts of a few, victims' rights and services have become a part of the public consciousness and, as a result, are reflected in public policy. As has been discussed previously in this book, though, it is easy for the public to forget, to ignore, or to blame. And it is easy for policies to not be funded or to not be enforced.

The value of national and even policies, such as a constitutional amendment of victims rights, cannot be overstated. However, most policy is not as grand as a constitutional amendment. Policies implemented at the local or organizational level often have greater impact on the lives of the crime victims that come through the doors of an agency. Advocacy is not a job just for national organizations. And legislators and agency directors cannot develop policy in a vacuum. Advocacy and public policy development is the responsibility of every person invested in rights and services for crime victims.

Issues for the Profession

13

Thomas L. Underwood

As a field that has its foundation in the grassroots movement started primarily by crime victims, victim assistance as an occupational area has seen tremendous growth both in terms of the numbers and types of services offered. It is also as a field that is in development. This maturation of an occupational area is often referred to as professionalization. This final chapter addresses the professionalization of victim assistance through discussion of roles, structural and individual characteristics, and program standards.

DEFINING VICTIM ASSISTANCE AS A PROFESSION

Victim assistance has been described as a "full-fledged advocacy and service field dedicated to meeting the physical, financial, and psychological needs of victims and their families" (New Directions, 1998, p. 153). This description provides a mission statement for victim assistance as a profession; a profession that is not restricted to one standard of practitioner, one type of organization, one type of crime victim, or one level of service. "The diversity of organizations and individuals who serve crime victims presents a challenge to the field's emergence as a profession" (NVAA, 2000d, p. 20.2).

Throughout this book various services have been described. While it is common to reference victim assistance as a field, it is a field that is ill-defined. How does one know whether they are a member of the field? It is typical, for example, to consider those working in domestic violence shelters or prosecutor office victim-witness programs as practitioners in the field of victim assistance. But what of persons employed in health care, mental health, or other allied areas? Can a person be a member of two professions? At what point is a person employed in an allied area

239

who works with crime victims considered a victim assistance professional? Is it an objective measurement, such as percentage of time spent, or is
it subjective based on the value placed by the individual and the employing organization?

Professionalization is multidimensional. It is both an individual and a
social construct. That is, it requires external as well as internal acceptance
of the status of profession. External acceptance refers to formal reinforcement by policy institutions and an awareness of the uniqueness of the
field's services by the general public. Internal acceptance refers to a
whole host of characteristics, such as the creation of a subculture and
guidelines for ethical practice (Houle, 1980). For the occupation of victim
services to achieve the external and internal acceptance necessary to
claim the status of profession, there must be definition and standards
regarding the field's practitioners and the service programs in which they
are employed.

FUNCTIONS OF PRACTICE

As these mutually dependent internal and external processes evolve, the
various roles and functions of victim assistance may be considered.
Referencing the continuum of victim services presented in the first chapter, specific activities are explored with reflection as to how applicable
these functions are, or should be, to the practice of victim assistance.

The first levels of services described in the continuum of victim assistance were primary and secondary prevention efforts. Yet prevention, by
definition, does not include victims. Can primary prevention efforts, such
as education, or secondary prevention efforts, such as skill building
efforts for at-risk families or community enhancement activities, be considered within the realm of victim assistance? Prevention is not an activity that receives financial support by the Office for Victims of Crime nor is
it mentioned as a part of the mission of most national victim organizations.
Yet "prevention is imperative. For a society to allow the human tragedy
of victims, survivors, and perpetrators is unconscionable" (Andrews,
1992, p. 141). Thus, prevention efforts must be within the purview of all
victim assistance practitioners.

Crisis was discussed as both a short-term and a long-term issue in
chapters 5 and 6 of this book. And while, as articulated in these chapters,
crisis response may be required throughout the process of recovery, it is
typically considered within the immediate context of the trauma. Yet
many victim assistance practitioners are not involved with the victim
until well after the criminal event and may not define themselves as crisis
intervenors. Crisis response skills are essential for any practitioner who
works with victims of crime, regardless of the length of time after the
victimization.

Another aspect of initial intervention is victim interviewing. Interviews that are investigative in nature are considered within the realm of law enforcement, but this is also a role of victim assistance if the interview, in addition to finding out important information for prosecution, is conducted to assess needs and provide an environment of comfort and support. The increased use of multidisciplinary teams, such as those used in sexual abuse cases, is an example of victim assistance role in not only the crisis intervention but the investigative interview process.

Recovery assistance involves the greatest range of activities, and possibly the greatest range of allied professions. Health, mental health, and legal services are but some of the allied areas that may employ practitioners who specialize in victim assistance. In addition to the tangible aspects of recovery, that is repair or compensation of property or person, two essential functions reflect the role of victim assistance at this level, regardless of the type of organization. One is victim preparation; as a witness, as a patient, as a parole hearing attendee, as a volunteer, and so forth. This requires practitioner broad-based knowledge of the activities and processes in which the victim may be involved. The other is assessment of victim needs at all levels. This involves not only relatively advanced assessment skills but also involves intervention skills that are victim-centered and problem-solving focused. It also involves awareness of professional and service resources available in the community for referral when appropriate.

Resource awareness is an essential aspect to the functions of collaboration. Some of the activities of collaboration include developing and maintaining a network of resources. At a broader level, the social advocacy is also a function of victim assistance practice that does not involve direct victim service but has been critical to the advancement of victim services through enhanced polices and resources. Collaboration and advocacy both involve practitioners from various types of organizations, including those of allied professions. Even though collaboration and advocacy do not involve direct service, they should be considered an essential function to ensure the delivery of services that are efficient and responsive to victim needs.

Considering these often inexact and broad-based functions, can victim assistance be considered a profession? An exploration of the structural and individual or attitudinal aspects of the profession are warranted to address this question.

PROFESSIONAL CHARACTERISTICS

The concept of profession can be considered as both two related but distinct social constructs: status and role. The social status of a profession refers to the structural attributes or the traits and features that indicate an occupation as a profession. The structural attributes of a profession include creation of a full time occupation, the establishment of formal education, formation of a professional association, the support of law, and formation of a code of ethics (Wilensky, 1964).

Role refers to the individual attitudes and behaviors associated with the professional status. The individual or attitudinal aspect involves the use of the professional organization as major referent, belief in service to the public, belief in self-regulation, a sense of calling to the field, autonomy (Hall, 1968), and belief in continuing competence (Schack & Hepler, 1979).

Status and role, and thereby structural attributes and attitudinal attributes, are intricately related though conceptually distinct. Each can be presented and studied separately. While it is assumed that both dimensions are present to a significant degree in highly professionalize fields, structures and individual attitudes do not necessarily vary together. A field such as medicine or law that is generally recognized as high on the structural dimensions may well have individuals in the profession who are low on the attitudinal dimensions. Conversely, emerging professions, such as victim assistance, may have high professional attitudes out of a sense of anticipatory socialization.

STRUCTURAL ASPECTS

Structural dimensions of a profession are tangible; they can be easily observed and measured. Following is a description of the five structural attributes of a profession with application to victim assistance.

Full-Time Occupation

A dynamic of victim assistance is the grass roots nature of the field. Historically, victim services were started and rendered by "predominantly lay people: volunteers and former victims (Davis & Henley, 1990, p. 163) who dedicated their time to victim supports and services, often in addition to their regular jobs. While volunteers continue to serve an essential service in the field, services are more often a function of full-time practitioners.

This does not mean that volunteers and part-time practitioners are not important to the field and the delivery of services to victims. Indeed, volunteers and part-time employees are the heart of many victim service organizations. Without them, many organizations, especially nonprofit community organizations, would not exist. Rather, it is a recognition that as a field there is an evolution from part-time, possibly sporadic, conviction to a cause to full-time commitment to a vocation.

Formal Education

As an occupation evolves toward a profession a formal process for the transmission of theory and skills is developed. Education, characteristically formal university-based programs of study, is seen as one of the key determinants of all other professional characteristics (Goode, 1966; Wilensky, 1964; Hughes, 1963). There are few university-based programs of study of victim assistance currently in existence in the United States, although recognition by academe of victim assistance as a distinct and recognizable field is increasing.

As academic institutions embrace victim assistance as a discipline of study, there will further evolve guidelines or standards for academic study. Informally, this has happened between California State University at Fresno, University of New Haven in Connecticut, and Washburn University in Kansas. These universities all have an undergraduate academic certificate programs that are very similar to one another and there have been efforts by these universities to develop academic standards.

Formation of a Professional Association

Associations serve to develop professional definition and tasks. While there are several national professional associations in the field, they do not serve as regulatory bodies that may impose standards in which practitioners must comply nor can they impose sanctions for practitioners who are incompetent or perform unethically. Further, in reflection of the diversity of areas previously discussed, no one national association fully represents or is endorsed by the entire field and there is some overlap between some of the organizations. While the existence of more than one national association in a field is not entirely unheard of, this competition of national associations lends itself to uncertainty in the field.

Support of Law

Legal support refers to the legislative, judicial, and administrative supports and rulings that protect the right of practice. To be recognized as such, professions vie for exclusivity (Cervero, 1989) by demonstrating the uniqueness of the occupational services. The multisystems nature of victim assistance makes it difficult to claim exclusivity; thus, legitimization as a profession may be resisted.

Credentialing, a formal means of identifying individuals in an occupational group, is often associated with this criteria. However, credentialing may take various forms and does not necessarily imply legal recognition.

One of the most important privileges of a profession that requires the support of law is that of privileged communication or confidentiality

(Greenwood, 1966). This right within victim assistance is inconsistent at best (Petersen and Martin, 1998). Arizona is the only state that provides for privileged communication between a crime victim and a victim advocate.

Code of Ethics

A professional code of ethics describes the relations with the client, other professions, and society (Greenwood, 1966; Harries-Jenkins, 1970). A code of ethics should provide broad guidelines for moral behavior that applies to every practitioner in the field; thus, it must be fluid and subject to reinterpretation (Houle, 1980). While there is not an accepted code of ethics for the field, the development of one has been recommended by the Office for Victims of Crime (New Directions, 1998). NOVA and MADD are two national organizations that have developed codes of ethics.

Review of these structural characteristics suggests that the field of victim assistance has made marginal progress and that the progress realized thus far has been turbulent. As the field continues to evolve in the development of these structural components, it is likely that the environment will continue to be difficult. Certain components may advance at rates different from the others and factions in the field may vie for dominance.

INDIVIDUAL ATTRIBUTES

Individual attributes refer to the attitudinal dimensions of practitioners toward professionalization. Research was conducted by the present author (2001) regarding these attitudinal aspects. Victim assistance practitioners were surveyed using a professionalization scale (Hall, 1968; Schack & Hepler, 1979) that measured six attitudinal dimensions. The scale utilizes a measurement of one to five, with one being a strong association and five being a weak association.

Information about certain individual and organizational characteristics was also collected. These included type of organization, gender, age, education level, role in agency, membership in a professional association, and participation in continuing education. The sample consisted of full-time paid victim assistance practitioners based in prosecutor offices and domestic violence shelters. The sample was drawn from the west north central region of the United States and were identified as having received VOCA funds in 1998.

The following is a description of the six attitudinal attributes of a profession with application to victim assistance. Research results are presented for each of the attitudinal dimensions.

Use of Professional Organization as a Major Referent

This refers to the extent in which the practitioner identifies with the occupational role-set, that is, the formal organization role-relationships and informal associations with colleagues. In other words, is the professional subculture that of victim assistance, or is it of an allied area?

The overall scale score for this dimension was 2.12, the second strongest attitudinal dimension for the sample. This suggests that victim assistance practitioners have a relatively strong identification with the occupation. It was found that participation in continuing education was statistically significant for this attitude. Those who participated in the most continuing education had stronger associations than those who participated in the least. However, the ranges in between were inconsistent.

Belief in Service to the Public

Professional service should be based on an ideal of public service over the self-interests of the practitioner (Goode, 1966) and that the work is essential to community interest (Barber, 1963). The public interest of victim assistance is evident. Victim assistance "is no longer focused on individual consumer of services but on the entire community itself. Advocacy is now viewed as a combination of counseling, community organizing, and justice making" (Nadolski, 1999).

The overall scale score for this dimension was 2.43. Although this was a strong association, it was surprising that this attitude, considering the passion of those in the field, was not higher. None of the factors were found to have any statistical significance on this attitude.

Belief in Self-Regulation

This belief presumes that it is the profession itself, with its unique body of knowledge, that is best suited to judge the work of others in the field. Considering the diversity of systems, education, and program services characteristic in victim assistance, this attitudinal dimension may be a challenge. Self-regulation can be a valued belief as the field continues to dialogue and searches for commonalities.

Surprisingly, the scale score for this dimension was the third highest; 2.37. It was found that role in the organization was a significant factor for this dimension, with those practitioners defined as direct care staff having a stronger association than those defined as administrative. This finding is contrary to theory and prior research.

Sense of Calling to the Field

This reflects the commitment to the profession and that the profession is viewed not as a means to an end but as an end in itself. In other words, practitioners are in the field of victim assistance because of the work, not because of the material rewards. Though with professionalization typically comes increased tangible benefits, commensurate compensation in victim assistance has been lacking.

The scale score for this dimension was 2.43, the same as belief in service to the public. Again, considering the "passion" of the field, it is surprising that this score, though still suggesting a strong identification, is not stronger. It was found that the level of education was a significant influence for this dimension though not in the way predicted by theory and prior research. The lower levels of education had greater association with this attitude. This may reflect the passion referred to earlier, though maybe it is more of a grass roots attitude. Also, possibly the lack of financial and social rewards expected with higher education has an eventual impact on those with higher levels of education.

Autonomy

Autonomy involves independent decision-making for the best interest of the client based on professional standards and that these decisions should not be influenced by other professions or the bureaucratic organizations. The extent that this value is embraced may depend on how the practitioner defines his or her role and whether autonomy is granted by the organization. For example, is the practitioner's client the victim or the prosecutor? Are there strict formulas of practice that must be followed or is discretion allowed?

Autonomy was the weakest of all the dimensions, with a score of 2.80. Education was found to significantly impact scores on this dimension with those with higher levels of education having a stronger association with this attitude. Possibly those with more education have a greater sense of ability to make independent decisions based on their educational accomplishments. Another possibility is that maybe those with higher levels of educational attainment hold positions that allow greater autonomy than those who have less education.

The research also found that membership in a professional association was significantly related to this dimension. Possibly this has to do with promotion of professional identity and support characteristic of many professional associations.

Belief in Continuing Competence

This refers to the personal commitment and responsibility to professional learning in order to maintain competence. "Every occupation that lays claim to the distinction conferred by the term profession seeks constantly to improve itself in certain distinctive ways (Houle, 1980, p. 10).

The scale score for this attitude was the strongest of all the scales: 2.01. Predictably, scale scores were stronger based on the extent of participation in continuing education. Further, the scores based on this variable were generally stronger than were the others. Statistical analysis, however, did not reveal that this participation in continuing education was a significant factor for this attitude. However, when all six scales were considered comprehensively, participation in continuing education was found to be significant.

Level of education was found to be significant with those with graduate degrees holding stronger attitudes than others. Scores were not significant based on other levels of education. Possibly those with graduate level education have a greater zest for learning, or maybe they just have more opportunity to attend continuing education programs.

Considering all six of the scale scores together, the sample of victim assistance practitioners scored 2.36 on the professionalization scale. This suggests that victim assistance practitioners hold at least moderately strong attitudes toward professionalization, even though the structural aspects of the field are relatively marginal.

PROFESSIONAL STANDARDS

The structural and individual attributes reflect the concept of profession. Internal and external recognition and acceptance of a field as a profession requires "consistency in the kind of services they offer and in the use of training of staff and volunteers to deliver these services" (New Directions, 1998). Standards that reflect the field of practice enhances overall recognition of the field as well as accountability of services. While much of the literature on standards for the victim assistance field has focused on services delivered by the criminal justice system, standards are commonly applied to services provided within social service, health care, mental health settings.

Standards should measurably define a range from the minimum to the optimum for the various activities of victim assistance (Jerin & Moriarity, 1998; Young, 1993; Tomz & McGillis, 1997). Guidelines of service delivery should be developed with definition as to the types of victims served, when services should be available, the types of services provided, and practitioner qualifications (Young, 1993). Along with the human resources required to perform the functions, materials and location resources should also be identified.

The National Victim Assistance Standards Consortium, an Office for Victims of Crime funded initiative, has proposed standards for programs, practitioner competencies, and ethics. Program standards are guidelines that reflect those things that are commonly associated with the organizational delivery of services. These include such things as definition of geographic service area, clientele, accessibility, range of services, fees, safety, confidentiality, and administration. Practitioner competency standards describe the basic knowledge, skills, and abilities necessary for the delivery of service. These include such things as awareness of services and systems, communication skills, assessment and referral, and individual advocacy skills. Ethical standards reflect the core values of the field and reflect one's personal obligation to things such as understanding legal responsibility, maintaining professional competence, conducting positive collegial relationships, preserving confidentiality, and assuring professional interactions with victims.

While the development and acceptance of national standards may, like the structural aspects discussed, face turbulence in the process, it will settle and stabilize as the field continues its growth as a profession. National standards should eventually become institutionalized and will not be unduly influenced by local interpretations and supports—at least not to the extent that currently exists.

SUMMARY

Victim assistance is a most eclectic field. Services are provided by a diversity of individuals with varying personal, employment, and educational backgrounds. Services are offered by a diversity of organizations, ranging from community-based to systems-based, from large to small, from international to local. Services are provided to a diversity of victims, ranging from all types of crimes to specific types of crimes, from all groups to special needs groups. It is little wonder that this is a field that lacks clear definition.

In spite of this diversity and lack of definition, it is a field that has made tremendous strides toward professionalization. Though structurally marginal, attitudes of practitioners are strong. The process of professionalization of victim assistance has been described as turbulent. As a relatively young field, though, turbulence is to be expected; this is something akin to the angst of adolescence. As the field of victim assistance continues its evolution, its growth, the angst will lessen. Though the field must guard against the complacency of maturity, with maturity comes wisdom of the profession.

The challenge to practitioners, then, is to serve crime victims, in whatever function that may be, in a manner that reflects the professional attitudes as supported by the structures of that profession. In so doing, the professional critically reflects on individual practice, organizational policy, and societal responses, thereby enhancing the potential for service at all levels.

References

Abbot, J., Johnson, R., Kosial-McClain, J., & Lowenstein, S. (1995). Domestic violence against women: Incidence and prevalence in an emergency room population. *Journal of the American Medical Association (JAMA)*, (273), 1763–1767.

Abrams, K. M., & Robinson, G. E. (1998). Stalking. Part I: An overview of the problem. *Canadian Journal of Psychiatry, 43*(5), 473–476.

Abrams, K. M., & Robinson, G. E. (1998). Stalking. Part II: Victims' problems with the legal system and therapeutic considerations. *Canadian Journal of Psychiatry, 43*(5), 477.

Aguilera, D. C. (1990). *Crisis intervention: Theory and methodology* (6th ed.). St Louis, MO: V. V. Mosby.

Alba, R. A. (Ed.). (1985). *Ethnicity and race in the U.S.A.* New York: Routledge.

Albanese, J. S. (1999). *Criminal justice.* Needham Heights, MA: Allyn and Bacon.

Allen, H. A., & Simonsen, C. E. (1998). *Corrections in America: An introduction* (8th ed.). Upper Saddle River, NJ: Prentice Hall.

Allen, J. (1995). *Coping and trauma: A guide to self-understanding.* Washington, DC: APA.

Allen, J. (1995). Perspectives: The spectrum of accuracy in memories of childhood trauma. *Harvard Review Psychiatry, July-Aug.*, 84–95.

Alport, G. (1979). *Nature of prejudice.* Cambridge, MA: Addison-Wesley.

Amick-McMullen, A., et al. (1989). Family survivors of homicide victims: Theoretical perspective and exploratory study. *Journal of Traumatic Stress, 2*(1).

American Psychiatric Association. (1994). *Diagnostic and Statistical Manual of Mental Disorders* (4th ed.). Washington, DC: American Psychiatric Association.

Ammeman, R. T., & Herson, M. (Eds.). (1990). *Treatment of family violence: A sourcebook.* New York: John Wiley.

Amsel, R., & Fichten, C. S. (1988). Effects of contact on thoughts about interaction with students who have a physical disability. *Journal of Rehabilitation, 54*, 61–65.

Anderson, R. (2001). Deaths: Leading causes for 1999. *Center for Disease Control National Vital Statistics Report, 49*(11). Available: www. cdc. gov/nchs/releases/01facts/99mortality. htm

Andrews, A. B. (1992). *Victimization and survivor services: A guide to victim assistance.* New York: Springer Publishing Co.

Arntz, A. (1994). Treatment of borderline personality disorder: A challenge for cognitive-behavioural therapy. *Behaviour Research and Therapy, 32,* 419–430.

Austin, L. S., & Godleski, L. S. (1999). Therapeutic approaches for survivors of disaster. *The Psychiatric Clinics of North America, 22,* 4, 897.

Bard, M., & Sangrey, D. (1986). *The crime victims book.* New York, Brunner/Mazel.

Basemore, G., & Umbreit, M. S. (1994). Balanced and restorative justice project. Florida Atlantic University.

Bayley, J. (1991). The concept of victimhood. In D. Sank & D. Caplan (Eds.), *To be a victim: Encounters with crime and justice.* New York: Plenum Press.

Beck, A. J. (2000). *Prisoners in 1999.* Washington, DC: Bureau of Justice Statistics (NCJ 183476)

Becker, G. (1997). *The gift of fear: Survival signals that protect us from violence.* New York: Little Brown.

Benton, D. M. (1999). African Americans and elder mistreatment: Targeting information for a high-risk population. In T. Tatara (Ed.), *Understanding elder abuse in minority populations* (pp. 49–64). Philadelphia, PA: Brunner/Mazel.

Berkman, C., & Zinberg, G. (1997). Homophobia and heterosexism in social workers. *Social Work, 42*(4), 319–332.

Billings, A. G., & Moos, R. H. (1981). The role of coping responses and social resources in attenuating the stress of life events. *Journal of Behavioral Medicine, 4*(2), 139–157.

Bordow, S., & Porritt, D. (1979). An experimental evaluation of crisis intervention. *Social Science and Medicine, 34,* 251–256.

Boscarino, J. A. (1997). Diseases among men 20 years after exposure to severe stress: Implications for clinical research and medical care. *Psychosomatic Medicine, 59,* 605–614.

Bower, B. (1997). Physical ills follow trauma response. *Science News, 152*(24), 372.

Brady, K. (1979). *Father's days.* New York: Dell Publishing.

Brady, J. L., Guy, J. D., & Poelstra, P. L. (1999). Vicarious traumatization, spirituality, and the treatment of sexual abuse survivors: A national survey of women psychotherapists. *Professional Psychological Resource Press, 30*(4), 386–393.

Bremner, J. D., Randall, P., Scott, T. M., Bronen, R. A., Seibyl, J. P., Southwick, S. M., Delaney, R. C., McCarthy, G., Charney, D. S., &

Innis, R. B. (1995). MRI-based measurement of hippocampal volume in patients with combat-related posttraumatic stress disorder. *American Journal of Psychiatry, 152*(7), 973–981.

Breslau, N., Chilcoat, H. D., & Kessler, R. C. (1999). Previous exposure to trauma and PTSD effects of subsequent trauma: Results from the Detroit Area Survey of Trauma. *American Journal of Psychiatry, 156*(6), 902–907.

Brett, D. (1992). *More Annie stories: Therapeutic storytelling techniques.* New York: Imagination Press.

Bromfield, R. (1993). *Playing for real: A child therapist explores the world of play therapy and the inner worlds of children.* New York: Penquin Books.

Brookoff, D. (1997). *Drugs, alcohol, and domestic violence in Memphis.* Washington, DC: U. S. Department of Justice.

Brown, D., Scheflin, D., & Hammond, D. (1998). *Memory, trauma treatment and the law.* New York: W. W. Norton & Co.

Brunner, E. (1997). Stress and biology of inequality. *British Medical Journal, 314,* 1472–1475.

Bureau of Justice Assistance. (2000). *Hate crime series: Promising practices against hate crimes.* Washington, DC: U. S. Department of Justice.

Bureau of Justice Statistics. (2000). *Sourcebook of Criminal Justice Statistics* [On-line]. Available: www. albany. edu/sourcebook/index. html.

Bureau of Justice Statistics (2001). *Criminal victimization in United States, 1999 statistical tables* (NCJ 184938) [On-line]. Available: www. ojp. usdoj. gov/bjs/abstract/cvusst. htm

Burt, M. S., & Burt, R. B. (1996). *Stepfamilies: The step by step model of brief therapy.* New York: Brunner/Mazel.

Buster, J. E. (1993). Oral dehydroepiandrosterone in physiologic doses modulates immune function in postmenopausal women. *American Journal of Obstetric Gynecology, 169,* 1536–1539.

California Youth Authority. (2001). *Death notification procedures.* CYA Office of Prevention and Victim Services [On-line]. Available: www. cya. ca. gov/organization/opvs/death. html

Caplan, G. (1964). *Principles of preventive.* New York: Basic Books.

Carlson, E. (1997). *Trauma assessments: A clinician's guide.* New York: The Guilford Press.

Carlson, E. B., & Rosser-Hogan, R. (1991). Trauma experiences, posttraumatic stress, dissociation, and depression in Cambodian refugees. *American Journal of Psychiatry, 144,* 1567–1572.

Carlson, C. R., & Hoyle, R. H. (1993). Efficacy of abbreviated progressive muscle relaxation training: A quantitative review of behavioral medicine research. *Journal of Consulting and Clinical Psychology, 61,* 1059–1067.

Cervero, R. (1989). Continuing education for the professions. In S. Merriam & P. Cunningham (Eds.), *Handbook for adult and continuing education.* San Francisco, CA: Jossey-Bass.

Champion, J. (1999). Effects of abuse on self-perception of rural Mexican-American and non-Hispanic white adolescents. *Archives of Psychiatric Nursing, 13*(1), 12–18.

Cohen, J. A. (1998). Summary of the practice parameters for the assessment and treatment of children and adolescents with posttraumatic stress disorder. *Journal of the American Academy of Child and Adolescent Psychiatry, 37*(9), 997.

Cohen, S., Mermelstein, R. J., Kamarck, T., & Hoberman, H. M. (1985). Measuring the functional components of social support. In I. G. Sarason & B. Sarason (Eds.), *Social support: Theory, research and application.* The Hague, Holland: Martinus Niijhoff.

Cohen, S., & Williamson, G. M. (1991). Stress and infectious disease in humans. *Psychological Bulletin, 109*, 5–25.

Cohen, L., & Felson, M. (1979). Social change and crime rate trends: A routine activities approach. *American Sociological Review, 44*, 588–608.

Cohen, L., Kluegal, J., & Land, K. (1981). Social inequality and predatory criminal victimization: An exposition and test of a formal theory. *American Sociological Review, 46*, 505–524.

Cook County State's Attorney's Office (1994). *Prosecutor's guide to disabilities.* Chicago, IL: Author.

Corneil, W., & Kirwan, S. (1997, April 6). *Cost effectiveness of a comprehansive CISM program.* Presentation at the Fourth World Congress on Stress, Trauma and Coping in the Emergency Services, Baltimore, MD.

Courtois, C. (1999). *Recollections of sexual abuse: Treatment principles and guidelines.* New York: W. W. Norton & Co.

Cruz, J., & Firestone, J. (1998). Exploring violence and abuse in gay male relationships. *Violence and Victims, 13*(2), 159–173.

Cummock, V. (1996). Journey of a young widow. In K. Doka (Ed.), *Living with grief after sudden loss.* Hospice Foundation.

Curtis, J. M. (1995). Elements of critical incident debriefing. *Psychological Reports, 77*, 91–96.

Dansky, B. S., Brady, K. T., Saladin, M. E., Killeen, T., Becker, S., & Roitzsch, J. (1996). Victimization and PTSD in individuals with substance use disorders: Gender and racial differences. *American Journal of Drug/Alcohol Abuse, 22*(1), 75–93.

Dansky, B. S., Brewerton, T. D., Kilpatrick, D. G., & O'Neil, P. M. (1997). The National Women's Study: Relationship of victimization and posttraumatic stress disorder to bulimia nervosa. *International Journal of Eating Disorders, 21*(3), 213–228.

Darves-Bornoz, J. M., Lepine, J. P., & Degiovanni, A. (1998). Predictive factors of chronic Post-traumatic Stress Disorder in rape victims. *European Psychiatry, 33*, 71–79.

Davis, L. (1990). *The courage to heal workbook: For women and men survivors of child sexual abuse.* New York: Harper Publications.

Davis, R., & Henley, M. (1990). Victim service programs. In A. Lurigio, W. Skogan, & R. Davis (Eds.), *Victims of crime*. Newbury Park, NJ: Sage.

Davis, R. C., & Smith, B. (1994). Victim impact statements and victim satisfaction with justice: An unfulfilled promise? *Journal of Criminal Justice, 22*(1), 1–12.

Davies, J. M., & Frawley, M. G. (1994). *Treating the adult survivor of childhood sexual abuse: A psychoanalytic perspective*. New York: Basic Books.

Deakin, J. F., & Graeff, F. G. (1991). 5-HT and mechanisms of defense. *Journal of Psychopharmacology, 5*, 305–315.

De Becker, G. (1997). *The gift of fear: Survival signals that protect us from violence*. New York: Little Brown Co.

Deinzer, R., & Schuller, N. (1998). Dynamics of stress-related decrease of salivary immunoglobulin A (sIgA): Relationship to symptoms of the common cold and studying behavior. *Behavioral Medicine, 23*(4), 161–169.

Derogatis, L. R., Abeloff, M. D., & Melisaratos, N. (1979). Psychological coping mechanisms and survival time in metastatic breast cancer. *Journal of the American Medical Association, 242*(14), 1504–1508.

Des Pres, T. (1976). *The survivor: An anatomy of life in the death camps*. New York: Pocket Books.

Devilly, G. J., & Spence, S. H. (1999). The relative efficacy and treatment distress of EMDR and a cognitive behavioral trauma treatment protocol in the amelioration of post traumatic stress disorder. *Journal of Anxiety Disorders, 13*, 131–157.

Devilly, G. J. (1996). EMDR and PTSD: The score at half time. *Psychotherapy in Australia, 3*, 26–31.

DeVore, W., & Schlesinger, E. (1999). *Ethnic sensitive social work practice*. Boston: Allyn and Bacon

Ditton, P. (2000). *Jails in Indian country, 1998 and 1999*. Washington, DC: Bureau of Justice Statistics (NCJ 173410).

DiLeo (1970). *Young children and their drawings*. New York: Brunner Mazel, Inc.

Doerner, W. G., & Lab, S. P. (1998). *Victimology* (2nd Ed). Cincinnati, OH: Anderson Publ.

Doka, K. (Ed.). (1995). *Children mourning: Mourning children*. Hospice Foundation.

Doka, K., & Grodon, J. (1996). *Living with grief after sudden loss*. Hospice Foundation.

Dyregrov, A. (1996, March 17–20). *Presentation on the history and status of CISD*. First European Congress on Stress in Emergency Personnel and Peace Keeping Forces. Sheffield, United Kingdom.

Epstein, J., & Langenbahn, S. (1994). *The criminal justice community response to rape*. Washington, DC: S Dept of Justice.

Epstein, J. N., Saunders, B. E., Kilpatrick, D. G., & Resnick, H. S. (1998). PTSD as a mediator between childhood rape and alcohol use in adult women. *Child Abuse and Neglect, 22*(3), 223–234.

Erez, E., & Tontodonato, P. (1990). The effect of victim participation in sentencing on sentencing outcomes. *Criminology, 28,* 451–474.

Eths & Pynoos, R. (Eds.). (1985). *Post-traumatic stress disorder in children.* Washington, DC: APA.

Everly, G. S. (1989). *A clinical guide to the treatment of the human stress response.* New York: Plenum Press.

Everly, G. S. (1995). The role of the CISD process in disaster counseling. *Journal of Mental Health Counseling, 17,* 278–290.

Everstein, D. (1993). *The trauma response: Treatment for emotional injury.* New York: W. W. Norton.

Falsetti, S. A., & Resnick, H. S. (1997). Frequency and severity of panic attack symptoms in a treatment seeking sample of trauma victims. *Journal of Trauma and Stress, 10*(4), 683–689.

Fattah, E. A. (1997). Toward a victim policy aimed at healing, not suffering. In R. C. Davis, A. J. Lurigo, & W. G. Skogan (Eds.), *Victims of crime* (2nd ed.). Thousand Oaks, CA: Sage

Fawzey, F. I., Fawzey, F. I., Hyn, C. S., Elashoff, R., Guthrie, D., Fahey, J. L., & Morton, D. L. (1993). Malignant melanoma: Effects of an early structured psychiatric intervention, coping, and affective state on recurrence and survival six years later. *Archives of General Psychiatry, 338*(25), 1851–1852.

Federal Bureau of Investigation Uniform Crime Report—Hate crime statistics 1998 [On-line]. Available: http://www. fbi. gov/publish/hatecrime. htm.

Federal Bureau of Investigation Uniform Crime Report—Hate crime statistics 1999 [On-line]. Available: http://www. fbi. gov/publish/hatecrime. htm

Ferraro, K. (1995). *Fear of crime: Interpreting victimization risk.* Albany, NY: State University of New York Press.

Figley, C. R. (1985). *Trauma and its wake.* New York: Bruner/Mazel Publications.

Fine, L. J. (1996). Editorial: the psychosocial work environment and heart disease. *American Journal of Public Health, 86,* 301–303.

Finkelhor, D. (1986). *A sourcebook on child sexual abuse.* Beverly Hills, CA: Sage.

Fischer J. E., Calame A., Dettling A. C., Zeier H., & Fanconi S. (2000). Experience and endocrine stress responses in neonatal and pediatric critical care nurses and physicians. *Critical Care Medicine, 28*(9), 3281–3288.

Foa, E. B. (1997). Trauma and women: course, predictors, and treatment. *Journal of Clinical Psychiatry, 58,* 25–28.

Folkman, S., & Lazarus, R. S. (1988). *Manual for the ways of coping questionnaire.* Consulting Psychologists Press.

Follette, V., Ruzek, J., & Abueg, F. (Eds.). (1998). *Cognitive-behavioral therapies for trauma.* New York: The Guilford Press.

Fonagy, P., Steele, M., Steele, H., Higgitt, A., & Target, M. (1994). The Emanual Miller Memorial Lecture 1992: The theory and practice of resilience. *Journal of Child Psychology and Psychiatry and Allied Disciplines, 35,* 231–257

Fontana, A., & McLaughlin, M. (1998). Coping and appraisal of daily stressor predict heart rate and blood pressure levels in young women. *Behavioral Medicine, 24*(1), 5–12.

Forbes, E. J., & Pekala, R. J. (1993). Psychophysiological effects of several stress management techniques. *Psychological Reports, 72,* 19–27.

Ford, J. D., Racusin, R., & Daviss, W. B. (1999). Trauma exposure among children with oppositional defiant disorder and attention deficit-hyperactivity disorder. *Journal of Consulting and Clinical Psychology, 67*(5), 786–789.

Fox, J. A., & Zawitz, M. W. (2000). Homicide trends in the United States. Washington, DC: Bureau of Justice Statistics [On-line]. Available: www. ojp. usdoj. gov/bjs/homicide.

Frazier, J. (1998). *Oklahoma victim rights—coming full circle: From the perspective of a prosecutor-based victim advocate.* Unpublished professional paper. Center on Violence and Victim Studies, Washburn University, Topeka, KS.

Freedy, J. R., Kilpatrick, D. G., & Resnick, H. S. (1993). Natural disasters and mental health: Theory, assessment, and intervention. *Journal of Social Behavior and Personality, 8*(5), 49–103.

Freedy, J. R., & Kilpatrick, D. G. (1994). Everything you ever wanted to know about natural disasters and mental health (well, almost). *NCP Clinical Quarterly, 4*(2).

Freedy, J. R., Resnick, H. S., & Kilpatrick, D. G. (1994). The psychological adjustment of recent crime victims in the criminal justice system. *Journal of Interpersonal Violence, 9,* 450–468.

Frey, R. J. (1999). *Stress.* Gale Encyclopedia of Medicine, Ed. 1. Gale Research, Inc., 2736.

Fried, S., & Fried, P. C. (1996). *Bullies & victims: Helping your child through the schoolyard battlefield.* New York: M. Evans & Co.

Frueh, B. C., Turner, S. M., & Beidel, D. C. (1996). Trauma management therapy: A preliminary evaluation of a multicomponent behavioral treatment for chronic combat-related PTSD. *Behaviour Research and Therapy, 34,* 533–543.

Fuller, M. G., Diamond, D. L., & Jordan, M. L. (1995). The role of a substance abuse consultation team in a trauma center. *Journal of Studies on Alcohol, 56,* 267–271.

Gaarder, E. (2000). Gender politics: The focus on women in the memory debates. *Journal of Child Sexual Abuse, 9*(1), 91–97.

Garvin, C. D., & Seabury, B. A. (1997). *Interpersonal practice in social work: Promoting competence and social justice.* Boston: Allyn and Bacon.

Gelles, R., & Straus, M. (1988). *Intimate violence.* New York: Simon and Schuster.

Gil, E. (1996). *Treating abused adolescents.* New York: Guilford Press.

Gil, M., & Tuffy, L. (1997). Sexual identity issues for male survivors of child sexual abuse: A qualitative study. *Journal of Child Sexual Abuse, 6*(3), 31–47.

Gillespie, M. (1999). Public opinion supports death penalty. Gallup News Service. http//www. gallup. com.

Glaser, R., Keicolt-Glaser, J. K., Speicher, C. E., & Holliday, J. E. (1985). Stress, loneliness, and changes in herpesvirus latency. *Journal of Behavioral Medicine, 8,* 249–260.

Glaser, R., Pearson, G. R., & Jones, I. F. (1991). Stress-related activation of Epstein-Barr virus. *Brain, Behavior and Immunology, 5,* 219–232.

Glaser, R. (1999). Stress related changes in proinflammatory cytosine production in wounds. *Journal of General Psychiatry, 56,* 450–456.

Glaser, R., Kiecolt-Glaser, J. K., Marucha, P. T., MacCallum, R. C., Laskowski, B. F., & Malarkey, W. B. (1999). Stress-related changes in proinflammatory cytosine production in wounds. *Archives of General Psychiatry, 56*(5), 450–456.

Goldenbert, I., & Goldenberg, H. (2000). *Family therapy: An overview.* Brooks Cole.

Goldensen, R. M. (Ed.). (1984). *Longman dictionary of psychology and psychiatry.* New York: Longman.

Goode, W. (1966). Professions and non-professions. In H. Vollmer & D. Mills (Eds.), *Professionalization.* Englewood Cliffs, NJ: Prentice-Hall.

Gordon, N., Faskerow, N., & Maida, C. (1999 April). *Children and disasters.* Philadelphia: Brunner/Mazel.

Green, J. (1982). *Cultural Awareness in the Human Services.* New York: Prentice Hall.

Green, B. L., Grace, M. C., Lindy, J. D., Gleser, G. C., Leonard, A. C., & Kramer, T. L. (1990). Buffalo Creek survivors in the second decade: Comparison with exposed and nonlitigant groups. *Journal of Applied Social Psychology, 20,* 1033–1050.

Green, B. L., Grace, M. C., Vary, M. G., Kramer, T. L., Gleser, G. C., & Leonard, A. C. (1994). Children of disaster in the second decade: A 17 year follow-up of the Buffalo Creek survivors. *Journal of Applied Social Psychology, 20,* 1033–1050.

Greene, G. J., Lee, M., Trask, R., & Rheinscheld, J. (2000). How to work with clients strengths in crisis intervention. In A. R. Roberts (Ed.), *Crisis Intervention Handbook: Assessment, treatment and research* (2nd ed.). London: Oxford University Press.

Greenachre, P. (1969). *Trauma growth & personality.* New York: International Universities.

Greenfield, L. A., & Smith, S. K. (1999). *American Indians and crime.* Washington, DC: Bureau of Justice Statistics (NCJ 173386).

Greenwood, E. (1966). The elements of professionalization. In H. Vollmer & D. Mills (Eds.), *Professionalization.* Englewood Cliffs, NJ: Prentice-Hall, Inc.

Greer, S., Morris, T., & Pettingale, K. W. (1979). Psychological response to breast cancer: effect on outcome. *Lancet, 2*(8146), 785–787.

Gries, L., Goh, D., Andrews, M. B., Gilbert, J., Praver, F., & Stilzer, D. (2000). Positive reaction to disclosure and recovery from childhood sexual abuse. *Journal of Child Sexual Abuse, 9*(1), 29–51.

Grossman, A. B. (1991). Regulation of human pituitary responses to stress. In M. B. Brown, G. F. Koob, & C. Rivier (Eds.), *Stress: Neurobiology and neuroendocrinology* (pp. 151–171). New York: Marcel Dekker.

Groth, N., & Birnbaum. (1978). Adult sexual orientation and attraction to underage persons. *Archives of Sexual Behavior, 7*(3), 175–181.

Gunnar, M. R., & Nelson, C. A. (1994). Event-related potentials in year-old infants: Relations with emotionality and cortisol. *Child Development, 65,* 80–94.

Gurley, D. N. (1990). *The context of well-being after significant life stress: Measuring social support and obstruction.* Lexington, KY: University of Kentucky.

Hall, R. H. (1968). Professionalization and bureaucratization. *American Sociological Review, 33,* 92–104.

Hanson, R. F., Kilpatrick, D. G., Falsetti, S. A., Resnick, H. S., & Wewaver, T. (in press). Violent crime and psychosocial adjustment. In J. R. Freedy & S. E. Hobfoll (Eds.), *Traumatic stress: Theory and practice.* New York: Plenum Press.

Harries-Jenkins, G. (1970). Professionals in organizations. In L. Curry, J. Wergin, & Associates (Eds.), *Professions and professionalization.* London: Cambridge University Press.

Harrison, C. A., & Kinner, S. A. (1998). Correlates of psychological distress following armed robbery. *Journal of Trauma and Stress, 11*(4), 787–789.

Hawkins, D. (1995). Controlling crime before it happens: Risk-focused prevention. *National Institute of Justice Journal,* August, 10–18.

Hawkins, D., Catalano, R., & Brewer, D. (1995). Preventing serious, violent and chronic juvenile offending. In J. Howell & S. Bilchik (Eds.), *Comprehensive Strategy for Serious, Violent, and Chronic Juvenile Offenders.* Washington, DC: U. S. Department of Justice.

Heath, L., & Gilbert, K. (1996). Mass media and fear of crime. *American Behavioral Scientist, 39*(4), 379–386.

Heinsbroek, R. P. W., van Haaren, F., Feenstra, M. P. G., Boon, P., & van de Poll, N. E. (1991). Controllable and uncontrollable footshock and monoaminergic activity in the frontal cortex of male and female rats. *Brain Research, 551*, 247–255.

Helzer, J., Robins, L., & McEvoy, L. (1987). Post-traumatic stress disorder in the general population. *New England Journal of Medicine, 317*, 1630–1634.

Herman, J. (1997 Rev.). *Trauma and recovery: The aftermath of violence from domestic abuse to political terror.* New York: Basic Books.

Henggeler, S. W., Schoenwald, S. K., Borduin, C. M., Rowland, M. D., & Cunningham, P. B. (1998). *Multisystemic treatment of antisocial behavior in children and adolescents: Treatment manuals for practitioners.* New York: The Guilford Press.

Henry, J. P., Stephens, P. M., & Ely, D. L. (1986). Psychosocial hypertension and the defense and defeat reactions. *Journal of Hypertension, 4*, 687–697.

Herbert, J. (1995). The age of dehydroepiandrosterone. *Lancet, 345*, 1193–1194.

Herbert, J. (1997). Stress, the brain, and mental illness. *British Medical Journal, 315*, 530–536.

Herman, J. (1994). *Trauma and recovery: The aftermath of violence from domestic abuse to political terror.* New York: Basic Books.

Herman, J. (1996). Presuming to know the truth. *Nieman Report, 48*(1), 43–45.

Hicks, R. (1993). *Failure to scream.* Tennessee: Thomas Nelson.

Hindelang, M. J., Gottfredson, M. R., & Garofalo, J. (1978). *Victims of personal crime: An empirical foundation for a theory of personal crime.* Cambridge, MA: Ballinger.

Holmes, M. C., French, K. L., & Seckl, J. R. (1995). *Molecular Brain Research, 28*, 186–192.

Hopps, J., Pinderhughes, E., & Shankar. (1995). *The power to care: Clinical practice effectiveness with overwhelmed clients.* New York: The Free Press.

Horn, B. J. (Ed). (1996). *Victim empowerment: Bridging the systems—mental health and victim service providers.* Washington, DC: U. S. Dept of Justice.

Horton, A., & Williamson, J. (Eds.). (1988). *Abuse and religion: When praying isn't enough.* New York: Lexington Books.

Houle, C. (1980). *Continuing learning in the professions.* San Francisco, CA: Jossey-Bass.

Holyroyd, K. A., & Gorkin, L. (1983). Young adults at risk for hypertension: Effects of family history and anger management in determining responses to interpersonal conflict. *Journal of Psychosomatic Research, 27*, 1311–1318.

Hubler, R. E. (1969). *On death and dying.* New York: McMillan Publ.

Hughes, E. (1963). Professions. *Daedalus, 92*, 655–668.

Hunt, L., Marshall, M., & Rowlings, C. (Eds.). (1997). *Past trauma in late life: European perspective on therapeutic work with older people.* London and Bristoe: Jessica Kingsley Publishers

Hunter, M. C. (1990). *Abused boys: Healing for the man molested as a child.* Massachusetts: Lexington Books.

Hytten, K., & Hasle, A. (1989). Firefighters: A study of stress and coping. *Acta Psychiatrica Scandinavia, 80*(suppl. 355), 50–55.

Jabaaij, L., Groheide, P. M., Heijtink, R. A., Duivenvoorden, H. J., Ballieus, R. E., & Vingerhoets, AJJM. (1993). Influence of perceived psychological stress and distress on antibody response to low doses of rDNA hepatitis B vaccine. *Journal of Psychosomatic Research, 37,* 361–369.

Jacobs, S. (1999 March). *Traumatic grief: Diagnosis and treatment.* Philadelphia: Burnner/Mazel.

James, S. A., & Kleinbaum, D. G. (1976). Socioecologic stress and hypertension related mortality in North Carolina. *American Journal of Public Health, 66,* 354–359.

Janoff-Bulman, R. (1992). *Shattered assumptions: Towards a new psychology of trauma.* New York: The Free Press.

Janosick, E. H. (1986). *Crisis counseling: A contemporary approach.* Monterey, CA: Jones and Bartlett.

Jerin, R. A., & Moriarity, L. J. (1998). *Victims of crime.* Chicago: Nelson-Hall, Inc

Jenkins, M. A., Langlais, P. J., Delis, D., & Cohen, R. (1998). Learning and memory in rape victims with posttraumatic stress disorder. *American Journal of Psychiatry, 155*(2), 278–282.

Joseph, R. (1999). The neurology of traumatic "dissociative" amnesia: Commentary and literature review. *Child Abuse and Neglect, 23*(8), 715–727.

Kanel, K. (1999). *A guide to crisis intervention.* Pacific Grove, CA: Brooks/Cole Publishing.

Karmen, A (1996). *Crime victims: An introduction to victimology* (3rd ed.). Belmont, CA: Brooks/Cole Publishing.

Katakami, Y. (1998). Earthquake-induced stress: Relationships and trends noticed in health examination data from survivors of the great Hanshin-Awaji earthquake. *Rinsho Byori, 46*(6), 599–604.

Kelly, R. (1993). *Bias crimes.* Chicago, IL: University of Chicago.

Kelly, D. P., & Erez, E. (1997). Victim participation in the criminal justice system. In R. C. Davis, A. J. Lurigo, & W. G. Skogan (Eds.), *Victims of crime* (2nd ed.). Thousand Oaks, CA: Sage.

Kennedy, L., & Sacco, V. (1998). *Crime victims in context.* Los Angeles, CA: Roxbury Publishing.

Kenardy, J. A., Webster, R. A., Lewin, T. J., Carr, V. J., Hazell, P. L., & Carter, G. L. (1996). Stress debriefing and patterns of recovery following a natural disaster. *Journal of Traumatic Stress, 9,* (1), 37–49.

Kiecolt-Glaser, J. K., Glaser, R., Gravenstein, S., Malarkey, W. B., & Sheridan, J. (1996). Chronic stress alters the immune response to influenza virus vaccine in older adults. *Proceedings of National Academy of Science, USA, 93,* 3043–3047.

Kilpatrick, D., Edmunds, C., & Seymour, A (1992). Rape in America. Washington, DC: National Center for Victims of Crime.

Kilpatrick, D., Amick, A., & Resnick, H. (1990). *The impact of homicide on surviving family members.* Charleston, SC: Crime Victims Research and Treatment Center.

Kilpatrick, D., & Saunders, B. (1997). The prevalence and consequences of child victimization. *NIJ Research Preview.* Washington, DC: U. S. Dept of Justice.

Kimmerling, R., Armistead, L., & Forehand, R. (1999). Victimization experiences and HIV infection in women: Associations with serostatus, psychological symptoms, and health status. *Journal of Trauma and Stress, 12*(1), 41–58.

Kirschbaum, C., Pirke, K. M., & Hellhammer, D. H. (1995). Preliminary evidence for reduced cortisol responsivity to psychological stress in women using oral contraceptive medication. *Psychoneuroendocrinology, 20*(5), 509–514.

Kirschbaum, C., Wust, S., & Hellhammer, D. (1992). Consistent sex differences in cortisol responses to psychological stress. *Psychosomatic Medicine, 54,* 648–657.

Klein, C. (1975). *How it feels to be a child.* New York: Harper & Row

Knox, S. S. (1993). *Perception of social support and blood pressure in young men. Perceptual and Motor Skills, 77,* 132–134.

Knox, S., Svennson, J., Waller, D., & Theorell, T. (1988). Emotional coping and the psychophysiological substrates of elevated blood pressure. *Journal of Behavior Medicine, 52*–58.

Kolk, B. A., & Hart, O. (1989). Pierre Janet and the breakdown of adaptation in psychological trauma. *American Journal of Psychiatry, 146*(12), 1530–1538.

Koss, M. (1991). *The rape victim.* Thousand Oaks, CA: Sage Publications.

Krug, E. G., Kresnow, M., Peddicord, J. P., Dahlberg, L. L., Powell, K. E., Crosby, A. E., & Annest, J. L. (1998). Suicide after natural disasters. *New England Journal of Medicine, 338*(6), 373–378.

Kuhn, J., Arellano, C., & Chavez, E. (1998). Correlates of sexual assault in Mexican American and white non-Hispanic adolescent males. *Violence and Victims, 13*(1), 11–20.

LaManna, M. A., & Riedman, (1997). *Marriages and families.* Wadsworth Thompson Learning.

Lasenza, S. (1989). Some challenges of integrating sexual orientation into counselor training and research. *Journal of Counseling and Development, 68*(1), 73–76.

Laub, J. H. (1997). Patterns of criminal victimization in the United States. In R. C. Davis, A. J. Lurigio, & W. G. Skogan (Eds.), *Victims of crime.* Thousand Oaks: California: Sage Publications.

Lazarus, R. S., & Folkman, S. (1984). *Stress, appraisal, and coping.* New York: Springer.

Leakey, R. (1994). *The origins of humankind.* New York: Basic Books.

Lee, J. (1994). *The empowerment approach to social work practice.* New York: Columbia University Press

Left, D. A., & Smith, R. E. (1983). Steroid-induced psychiatric syndromes. *Journal of Affective Disorders, 5*, 319–332.

Leibenluft, E. (1998). Why are so many women depressed? Scientific America, 9(2) [On-line]. Available: www. sciam. com/1998/ 0698womens/0698leibenluft. html

Leor, J., Poole, W. K., & Kloner, R. A. (1996). Sudden cardiac death triggered by an earthquake. *The New England Journal of Medicine, 334*(7), 413–417.

Lerner, H. E. (1983). Female dependency in context: Some theoretical and technical considerations. *American Journal of Orthopsychiatry, 53*(4), 697–705.

Leserman, J., Jackson, E. D., Petitto, J. M., Golden, R. N., Silva, S. G., Perkins, D. O., Cai J., Folds, J. D., & Evans, D. L., (1999). Progression to AIDS: The effects of stress, depressive symptoms, and social support. *Psychosomatic Medicine, 61*(3), 397–406.

Lev-Wiesel, R. (2000). Quality of life in adult survivors of childhood sexual abuse who have undergone therapy. *Journal of Child Sexual Abuse, 9*(1), 1–13.

Levinson, D. (1989). *Family violence in cross-cultural perspective.* Newbury Park, CA: Sage Publications.

Lew, M. (1988). *Victims no longer: Men recovering from incest and other sexual child abuse.* New York: Nevraumont Publishing Company.

Linares, L. O., Groves, B. M., Greenberg, J., Bronfman, E., Augustyn, M., & Zuckerman, B. (1999). Restraining orders: A frequent marker of adverse maternal health. *Pediatrics, 104*, 249–257.

Lintz, D., Schommer, N., & Hellhammer, D. H. (1995). Persistent high cortisol responses to repeated psychological stress in a subpopulation of healthy men. *Psychosomatic Medicine, 57*, 468–474.

Lobel, K. (1986). *Naming the violence: Speaking out about lesbian battering.* The Seal Press.

Lord, J. H. (1987). Survivor grief following a drunk-driving crash. *Death Studies, 11*(6), 413–435.

Lown B., DeSilva R. A., Reich P., & Murawski B. J. (1980). Psychophysiological factors in sudden cardiac death. *American Journal of Psychiatry, 137*, 1325–1335.

Luckenbill, D. (1977). Criminal homicide as a situated transaction. *Social Problems, 25,* 176–186.

Lurigio, A. J., Skogan, W. G., & Davis, R. C. (Eds.). (1990). *Victims of crime: Problems, policies, and programs.* Newbury Park, CA: Sage.

Luster, A. D. (1998). Chemokines: Chemotactic cytokines that mediate inanimation. *New England Journal of Medicine, 338,* 436–445.

Lystad, M (1988). *Mental health response to mass emergencies: Theory and practice.* New York: Brunner/Mazel.

Malchiodi, C. (1998). *Understanding children's drawings.* New York: The Guilford Press.

Marcus, E. (1993). *Is it a choice: Answers to 300 of the most frequently asked questions about gays and lesbians.* San Francisco: Harper.

Marmot, M. G., Rose, G., Shipley, M., & Hamilton, P. J. S. (1978). Employment grade and coronary heart disease in British civil servants. *Journal of Epidemiology Community Health, 32,* 244–249.

Marmot, M. G., Shipley, M. J., & Rose, G. (1984). Inequalities in death-specific explanations of a general pattern. *Lancet, 1,* 1003–1006.

Masters, et al (1988). Helping families of homicide victims: A multi-dimensional approach. *Journal of Traumatic Stress, 1*(1), 109–125.

Matsakis, A. (1994). *Post-traumatic stress disorder: A complete treatment guide.* New Harbinger Publishers.

Mauer, M. (1995). The International Use of Incarceration. *The Prison Journal 75*(1), 113–123.

McCann, I. L., & Pearlman, L. A. (1990). *Psychological trauma and the adult survivor: Theory, therapy, and transformation.* New York: Brunner/Mazel.

McFarlane, A. C. (1998). Epidemiological evidence about the relationship between PTSD and alcohol abuse: The nature of the association. *Addictive Behavior, 23*(6), 813–825.

McEwen, B. S. (1997). Stress, adaptation and disease: Allostasis and allostatic load. *Academy of Science, 57,* 275–283.

McLaughlin, K. A., Brilliant, K., & Lang, C (1995). *National bias crime training for law enforcement and victim assistance professionals.* Washington, DC: U. S. Dept of Justice.

Melody, J. (1997). *Violent attachments.* Northvale, NJ: Northvale Jason Aronson, Inc.

Mezey, G., King, M., & MacClintock, T. (1998). Victims of violence and the general practitioner. *British Journal of General Practice, 48*(426), 906–908.

Micale, M. (1989). Hysteria and its historiography: A review of past and present writings. *History of Science, 27.*

Miczek, K. A., Thompson, M. L., & Tornatzky, W. (1990). Subordinate animals: Behavioral and physiological adaptations and opioid tolerance. In M. R. Brown, G. F. Koob, & C. Rivier (Eds.), *Stress: Neurobiology and neuroendocrinology.* New York: Marcel Dekker.

Miley, K., O'Melia, M., & DuBois, B. (1998). (New Edition released 2001). *Generalist social work practice: An empowering approach* (3rd ed.). Boston: Allyn Bacon.

Miller, A. (1983). *For your own good: Hidden cruelty in child rearing and the roots of violence.* New York: Farrar Straus Giroux.

Miller, T. A., Cohen, M. A., & Wiersema, B. (1996). *Victim costs and consequences: A new look.* Washington, DC: U. S. Department of Justice and U. S. Department of Health and Human Services (NCJ 155282).

Minino, A. M., & Smith, B. L. (2001). Deaths: Preliminary data for 2000. *Center for Disease Control National Vital Statistics Report 49*(12). [Online]. Available: http//www.cdc.gov/nchs/products/pubs/pubd/nvsr/49/49-12. htm#49#12

Mohr, D. C., Goodkin, D. E., Bacchetti, P., Boudewyn, A. C., Huang, L., Marietta, P., et al., (2000). Psychological stress and the subsequent appearance of new brain MRI lesions in MS. *Neurology, 55,* 55–61.

Moi San, P., & Sanders-Phillips, K. (1997). Ethnic differences in circumstances of abuse symptoms of depression and anger among sexually abused black and Latino boys. *Child Abuse and Neglect, 21*(5), 473–488.

Mollica, R. F., Poole, C., & Tor, S. (1998). Symptoms, functioning and health problems in a massively traumatized population. In B. P Dohrenwend (Ed.), *Adversity, Stress and Psychopathology* (pp. 34–51). New York: Oxford University Press.

Mollica, R. F., McInnes, K., Sarajlic, N., Lavelle, J., Sarajlic, I., & Massgli, M. P. (1999). Disability associated with psychiatric comorbidity and health status in Bosnian refugees living in Croatia. *The Journal of the American Medical Association, 282*(5), 433–436.

Montagu, A. (1971). *Touching: The human significance of the skin.* New York: Columbia University Press.

Moore, D. (1998). *As confidence in police rises, Americans' fear of crime diminishes.* The Gallup Organization.

Moore, M., & Toney, M. (1999). *Youth violence in America.* NIJ News.

Morrison, R. L., Bellack, A. S., & Manuck, S. B. (1985). Role of social competence in borderline essential hypertension. *Journal of Consulting Clinical Psychology, 53,* 248–255.

Muldray, T. (1982). Contemporary attitudes towards violence. In C. G. Warner & G. R. Braen (Eds.), *Management of the physically and emotionally abused: Emergency assessment, intervention and counseling.* Long Beach, CA: Capistrano Press.

Murberg, M. M., McFall, M. E., & Veith, R. C. (1990). Catecholamines, stress and posttraumatic stress disorder. In E. L. Giller (Ed.), *Biological assessment and treatment of post-traumatic stress disorder.* Washington, DC: American Psychiatric Press.

Myers. D. (1996). *Social psychology.* New York: McGraw-Hill.

Myers, M., & Hagan, J. (1979). Private and public trouble: Prosecutors and the allocation of court resources. *Social Problems, 26*(4), 439–451.

Nadolski, S. (1999). *Pay equity within the victim service provider field.* Unpublished professional paper, Center on Violence and Victim Studies. Topeka, KS: Washburn University.

National Elder Abuse Incidence Study. (1998). Washington, DC: U. S. Department of Health and Human Services.

National Burglar and Fire Alarm Association. (2001). *Quick facts and stats about the electronic systems industry* [On-line]. Available: ww. alarm. org/Industry/Statistics/Quick_Facts/quick_facts

National Center for Health Statistics. (2001). *Fast stats* [On-line]. Available: www. cdc. gov/nchs/fastats.

National Center for Victims of Crime. (1996). 1996 victims' rights sourcebook: A compilation and comparison of victims' rights laws [On-line]. Available: www. ncvc. org/Infolink.

National Center for Victims of Crime. (1997). Overview of the criminal justice system [On-line]. Available: www. ncvc. org/Infolink.

National Center for Victims of Crime. (1997). Homicide survivors [On-line]. Available: www. ncvc. org/Infolink

National Center for Victims of Crime. (1997). Male rape [On-line]. Available: www. ncvc. org/Infolink

National Center for Victims of Crime. (1998). Sexual assault [On-line]. Available: www. ncvc. org/Infolink

National Highway Traffic Safety Administration. (2000). 2000 Traffic Safety Fact Sheets [On-line]. Available: www. nhtsa. dot. gov/people/ncsa/factshet. html.

National Victim Assistance Academy. (1999a). *Respecting diversity: Responding to underserved victims of crime.* Washington, DC: U. S. Department of Justice.

National Victim Assistance Academy. (1999b). *Rural victims.* Washington, DC: U. S. Department of Justice.

National Victim Assistance Academy. (2000a). *Military justice.* Washington, DC: U. S. Department of Justice.

National Victim Assistance Academy. (2000b). *Tribal justice.* Washington, DC: U. S. Department of Justice.

National Victim Assistance Academy. (2000c). *Sexual assault.* Washington, DC: U. S. Department of Justice.

National Victim Assistance Academy. (2000d). *Professionalizing the discipline of victim services.* Washington, DC: U. S. Department of Justice, Office for Victims of Crime.

National Victim Assistance Academy. (2000d). *Drunk driving.* Washington, DC: U. S. Department of Justice, Office for Victims of Crime.

Nerenberg, L. (1996, January). *Older battered women: Integrating aging and domestic violence services.* San Francisco, CA: San Francisco Consortium for Elder Abuse Prevention.

Nerenberg, L. (1999a). Culturally specific outreach in elder abuse. In T. Tatara (Ed.), *Understanding elder abuse in minority populations* (pp. 205–220). Philadelphia, PA:Brunner/Mazel.

Nerenberg, L. (1999b, February). *Victims' rights and services: Assisting elderly crime victims.* San Francisco, CA: San Francisco Consortium for Elder Abuse Prevention.

Newport, F. (1998). *No single problem dominates Americans' concerns today.* The Gallup Organization.

Newton, P. (Spring, 1978). Homosexual behavior and child molestation: Review of the evidence. *Adolescence, XIII*(49), 29–43.

Norris, F. H. (1992). Epidemiology of trauma: Frequency and impact of different demographic groups. *Journal of Consulting and Clinical Psychology, 60,* 409–418.

North, C. S., Nixon, S. J., Shariat, S., Mallonee, S., McMillen, J. C., Spitznagel, et al., (1999). Psychiatric disorders amoung survivors of the Oklahoma Bombing. *The Journal of the American Medical Association, 282*(8), 755–764.

Nosek, M. A., & Howland, C. A. (1998, February). *Abuse and women with disabilities.* Pennsylvania: National Resource Center on Domestic Violence, VAWnet [On-line]. Available: http://www. vaw. umn. edu/Vawnet/disab. htm

Office for Victims of Crime (1998). *New directions from the field: Victims' rights and services for the 21st century.* Washington, DC: U. S. Department of Justice.

Olsheluski, J., Katz, A. Knight, B. (May 1999). *Stress reduction for caregivers.* Philadelphia: Brunner/Mazel.

Orwin, R., Maranda, M., & Brady, T. (2001). *Impact of prior physical and sexual victimization on substance abuse treatment outcomes.* Fairfax, VA: Caliber Associates, Center for Substance Abuse Treatment Contract No. 270-97-7016

Ouimette, P. C., Wolfe, J., & Chrestman, K. R. (1996). Characteristics of posttraumatic stress disorder-alcohol abuse comorbidity in women. *Journal of Substance Abuse, 8*(3), 335–346.

Palmer, N. (1991). Feminist practice with survivors of sexual trauma. In N. Bricker-Jenkins, Hoeyman, & N. Gottlieb (Eds.), *Feminist social work practice in clinicals settings.* Thousand Oaks, CA: Sage.

Palmer, N. (1994 & 1996). *Rape/sexual assault: Risk reduction and recovery.* (Guide for college students). Topeka, KS: Washburn University.

Palmer, N. (1997). Resilience in adult children of alcoholics: A nonpathological approach to social work practice. *Health and Social Work, 22*(3), 201–209.

Parad, H. J., & Parad, L. G. (1990). *Crisis intervention, book 2: The practitioner's sourcebook for brief therapy.* Milwaukee, WI: Family Service America.

Parnell, L., & Bridgeman, B. (1999). Transforming trauma-EMDR. *The American Journal of Psychology, 112*(3), 465–469.

Parsons, E. R. (1985). Ethnicity and traumatic stress: The intersecting point in psychotherapy. In C. R. Figley (Ed.), *Trauma and its wake*. New York: Brunner/Mazel.

Pearlman, L., & Saakvitne, K. (1995). *Trauma and the therapist: Countertransference and vicarious traumatization in psychotherapy with incest survivors*. New York: W. W. Norton & Co.

Pedersen, P. (1990). The constructs of complexity and balance in multicultural counseling theory and practice. *Journal of Counseling and Development, 68*(5), 550–554.

Perlik, A. (2001). Crime concern buyer link. *SDM, 31*(1) [On-line]. Available: Doc. No. 03032776.

Perry, B. D., Pollard, R., Blakely, T., Baker, W., & Vigilante, D. (1995). Childhood trauma, the neurobiology of adaptation and "use dependent" development of the brain: how "states" become "traits. " *Infant Mental Health Journal, 16*(4), 271–291.

Peterson, S. R. (1991). Victimology and blaming the victim: The case of rape. In D. Sank & G. Caplan (Eds.), *To be a victim: Encounters with crime and injustice*. New York: Plenum Press.

Peterson, L., & Hardin, M. (1997). *Children in distress: A guide for screening children's art*. New York: W. W. Norton & Company.

Pierard, L. A., Lancellotti, P., & Kulbertus, H. E. (1999). ST-segment elevation during dobutamine stress testing predicts functional recovery after acute myocardial infarction. *American Heart Journal, 137*, 500–512.

Power, C., & Hertzman, C. (1997). Social and biological pathways linking early life and adult disease. *British Medical Bulletin, 53*, 210–221.

Putman, F. (1997). *Dissociation in children and adolescents: A developmental perspective*. New York: The Guilford Press

Read, J. P., Stern, A. L., Wolfe, J., & Ouimette, P. C. (1997). Use of screening instrument in women's health care: detecting relationships among victimization history, psychological distress, and medical complaints. *Women's Health, 25*(3), 1–17.

Reaves, B. A. (2001). *Felony defendants in large urban counties, 1998*. Washington, DC: U. S. Department of Justice.

Reaves, B. A., & Goldberg, A. L. (1999). *Law enforcement management and administrative statistics, 1997*. Washington, DC: U. S. Department of Justice (NCJ 171681).

Rennison, C. M. (2000). *Criminal victimization 1999: Changes 1998-99 with trends 1993-99*. Washington, DC: U. S. Department of Justice (NCJ 182734).

Rennison, R. M., & Welchans, S. (2000). *Intimate partner violence*. Washington, DC: Department of Justice (NCJ 178247).

Rennison, C. M. (2001). *Intimate partner violence and age of victim, 1993-99.* Washington, DC: U. S. Department of Justice (NCJ 187635).

Renzetti, C., & Miley, C. (Eds.). (1996). *Violence in gay and lesbian domestic partnerships.* New York: The Haworth Press.

Reviere, S. (1996). *Memory of childhood trauma: A clinician's guide to the literature.* New York: The Guliford Press.

Roberts, A. L. (1990). *Helping crime victims: Research, policy, and practice.* Newbury Park, CA: Sage Publications.

Roberts, A. L. (1990). *Crisis intervention handbook: Assessment, treatment, research.* Belmont, CA: Wadsworth.

Roberts, A. R., & Dziegielewski, S. F. (1995). Foundation skills in applications of crisis intervention and cognitive therapy. In A. R. Roberts (Ed.), *Crisis intervention and time-limited cognitive treatment.* Thousand Oaks, CA: Sage Publications.

Roberts, A. R. (Ed). (1996). *Crisis management and brief treatment: Theory, technique, and applications.* Chicago, IL: Nelson-Hall Publ.

Roberts, A. R. (2000). An overview of crisis theory and crisis intervention. In A. R. Roberts (Ed.), *Crisis Intervention Handbook: Assessment, treatment and research* (2nd Ed.). New York: Oxford University Press.

Roberts, J. (1998). Therapeutic treatment for physically abused children. *Child Abuse and Neglect, 22*(1), 69.

Robinson, R. C., & Mitchell, J. T., (1993). Evaluation of psychological debriefings. Journal of Traumatic Stress, 6(3), 367–382.

Rodriguez, M., Bauer, H., McLoughlin, E., & Grumbach, K. (1999). Screening and intervention for intimate partner abuse: Practices and attitudes of primary care physicians. *Journal of the American Medical Assocation, 282*(5).

Rotter, J. B. (1966). Generalized expectancies for internal versus external control of reinforcement. *Psychological Monographs: General and Applied,* 80 (1, Whole No. 609).

Rountree, P. W. (1998). A reexamination of the crime-fear linkage. *Journal of Research in Crime and Delinquency, 35*(3), 341–372.

Rubenson, K. (1989). The sociology of adult education. In S. Merriam & P. Cunnigham (Eds.), *Handbook of adult and continuing education.* San Francisco, CA: Jossey-Bass.

Ruiz, A. S. (1990). Ethnic identity: Crisis and resolution. *Journal of Multicultural Counseling and Development, 18*(1), 29–40.

Ryckman, R. (1989). *Theories of personality.* Pacific Grove, CA: Brooks/ Cole Publications.

Saad, L. (2000). Most important problem facing America. Gallup News Service [On-line]. Available: http//www. gallup. com.

Saakvitne, K., & Pearlman, L. (1996). *Transforming the pain: A workbook on vicarious traumatization.* New York: W. W. Norton & Co.

Sakheim, D., & Devine, S. (1992). *Out of darkness: Exploring satanism & ritual abuse.* Lexington MA: Lexington Books.

Sampson, R. J., & Bartusch, D. J. (1998). Legal cynicism and (subcultural?) tolerance of deviance: The neighborhood context of racial differences. *Law and Society Review, 32*(4), 777–804.

Sanders, B., & Moore, D. L. (1999). Childhood maltreatment and date rape. *Journal of Interpersonal Violence, 14*(2), 115–124.

Sank, D., & Sank Firschein (1991). Why the concern for victims? In D. Sank & G. Caplan (Eds.), *To be a victim: Encounters with crime and injustice.* New York: Plenum Press.

Sapolsky, R. M. (1996). Why stress is bad for your brain. *Science, 273,* 749–750.

Sapolsky, R. M., Krey, L. C., & McEwen, B. S. (1986). The neuroendocrinology of stress and agin: The glucorticoid cascade hypothesis. *Endrocronology Review, 7,* 284–301.

Sattler, J. C. (1998). *Clinical and forensic interviewing of children and families: Guidelines for the mental health, education, pediatric and child maltreatment fields.* San Diego: Jerome Sattler Publishers.

Schack, D., & Hepler, C. (1979). Modification of Hall's professionalism scale for use with pharmacists. *American Journal of Pharmaceutical Education, 43,* 98–104.

Schnall P. L., Landsbergis P. A., & Baker, D. (1994). Job strain and cardiovascular disease. *Annual Review of Public Health, 15,* 381–411.

Schreuder, J. N. (1997). Post-traumatic re-experiencing in old age: Working through or covering up. In L. Hunt, M. Marshall, & C. Rowlings (Eds.), *Past trauma in late life: European perspective on therapeutic work with older people.* London and Bristoe: Jessica Kinglsey Publishers.

Schulman, E. D. (1986). *Intervention in human services: A guide to skills and knowledge.* New York: Macmillan.

Schumacher, E. F. (1973). *Small is beautiful: A study of economics as if people mattered* (2nd ed.). New York: Hartley & Marks.

Schwartz, M. W., & Seeley, R. J. (1977). Neuroendocrine responses to starvation and stress. *The New England Journal of Medicine, 336*(25), 1801–1811.

Seligman. M. E. P. (1975). *Helplessness: On depression, development, and death.* San Francisco, CA: W. H. Freeman.

Seligman, M. E. P. (1995). The effectiveness of psychotherapy. *American Psychologist, 29*(12), 965–974.

Selye, H. (1936). A syndrome produced by diverse nocuous agents. *Nature, 138,* 32–39.

Selye, H. (1956). *Stress of life.* New York: McGraw-Hill.

Shirar, L. (1996). *Dissociative children: Bridging the inner and outer worlds.* New York: W. W. Norton.

Shriner, S. (1992). *Victim programs to serve Native Americans.* Washington, DC: US Dept of Justice.

Sims, A.,& Sims, D. (1998). The phenomenology of post-traumatic stress disorder: A symptomatic study of 70 victims of psychological trauma. *Psychopathology, 31*(2), 96–112.

Slaikeu, K. A. (1990). *Crisis intervention: A handbook for practice and research* (2nd ed.). Boston: Allyn and Bacon.

Smith, B. E., & Hillenbrand, S. W. (1997). Making victims whole again: Victim-offender reconciliation programs, and compensation. In R. C. Davis, A. J. Lurigo, & W. G. Skogan (Eds.), *Victims of crime* (2nd ed.). Thousand Oaks, CA: Sage Publications.

Smith, S. K., Steadman, G. W., & Minton, T. D. (1999). *Criminal victimization and perception of community safety in twelve cities, 1998.* Washington, DC: U. S. Dept of Justice (NCJ 173940).

Snyder, H., & Sickmund, M. (1999). *Juvenile offenders and victims: 1999 national report.* Washington, DC: Office of Juvenile Justice and Delinquency Prevention.

Solomon, S. D., & Davidson, J. R. (1997). Trauma: prevalence, impairment, service use and cost. *Journal of Clinical Psychiatry, 58*(9), 5–11.

Sonkin, D. J., Martin, D., & Walker, L. E. (1985). *Male batterer.* New York: Springer Publications.

Sonnenberg, S., Blank, A., & Talbott, J. (Eds.). (1985). *The trauma of war: Stress and recovery in Viet Nam veterans.* Washington, DC: AP

Sprang, G. (1997). The Traumatic Experiences Inventory: A test of psychometric properties. *Journal of Psychopathology and Behavioral Assessment, 19*(3), 257–271.

Stamm, B. H. (1966). Contextualizing death and trauma: A preliminary attempts. In C. F. Figley (Ed.), *Death and Trauma.* New York: Brunner/Mazel.

Stamm, H. (Ed.). (1995). *Secondary traumatic stress: Self-care issues for clinicians, researchers, & educators.* Maryland: Sidran Press.

Stein, H., Fonagy P., Ferguson, K., & Wisman, M. (2000). Lives through time: An ideographic approach to the study of resilience. *Bulletin of the Menninger Clinic,* 281–305.

Stephens, C. (1996). PTSD in the New Zealand Police. *The Australian Journal of Disaster and Trauma Studies* [On-line]. Available: www.massey.ac.nz/~trauma/issues/1997-1/cvs. html.

Stewart, S. H. (1996). Alcohol abuse in individuals exposed to trauma: Critical review. *Psychological Bulletin, 120*(1), 83–112.

Stewart, S. H., Pihl, R. O., & Conrod, P. J. (1998). Functional associations among trauma, PTSD, and substance-related disorders. *Addictive Behaviors, 23*(6), 797–812.

Straus, M. (1994). *Beating the Devil out of them.* Lexington, MA: Lexington Books.

Straus, M, Gelles, R., & Steinmetz, S. (Eds.). (1980). *Behind closed doors. Violence in the American family.* New York: Doubleday/Anchor.

Summit, R., & Miller, T. (1998, Monograph 8). The child sexual abuse accommodation syndrome: Clinical issues and forensic implications. In P. Miller (Ed.), *Children of traum: stressful life events and their effects on children and adolescents.* Madison, WI: International Universities Press.

Sue, D. W., & Sue, D. (1990). *Counseling the culturally different: Theory and practice.* New York: Wiley Publications.

Talbot, A., Manton, M., & Dunn, P. J. (1992). Debriefing the debriefers: An intevention strategy to assist psychologists after a crisis. *Journal of Traumatic Stress, 5*(1), 45–62.

Taylor, S. E. (1991). Stress and coping: An anthology. The Science and The Field, 3, 62–80.

Taylor, S. E., Peplau, L. A., & Sears, D. O. (1997). *Social psychology* (9th ed.). Upper-Saddle River, NJ: Prentice-Hall.

Terr, L. C. (1994). *Too scared to cry: Psychic trauma in childhood: How unexpected unknowledgable and uncontrollable happenings affect children and ultimately us all.* New York: Harper & Row.

Terr, L. C. (1994). *Unchained memories: True stories of traumatic memories, lost and found.* New York: Basic Books.

Thoits, P. A. (1982). Conceptual, methodological, and theoretical problems in studying social support as a buffer against life stress. *Journal of Health and Social Behavior, 23,* 145–159.

Thompson, M. P., Norris, F. H., & Ruback, R. B. (1998). Comparative distress levels of inner-city family members of homicide victims. *Journal of Trauma and Stress, 11*(2), 223–242.

Tjaden, P., & Thoennes, N. (2000). *Extent, nature, and consequences of intimate partner violence: Findings from the national violence against women survey.* Washington, DC: U. S. Department of Justice and Centers for Disease Control and Prevention (NCJ 181867).

Tomz, J. E., & McGillis, D. (1997). *Serving crime victims and witnesses* (2nd ed.). Washington, DC: U. S. Department of Justice.

Townsend, P., Davidson, N., & Whitehead, M. (1990). *Inequalities in health: The Black report: the health divide.* London: Penguin.

Tucker-Ladd, C. E. (1999a). Disliking others without valid reasons: Prejudice. In C. E. Tucker-Ladd, *Psychological self-help.* N/A: Mental Health Net [On-line]. Available: http://mentalhelp. net/psyhelp/chap7/chap7l. htm

Tucker-Ladd, C. E. (1999b). Prejudice: How prejudice is learned and unlearned. In C. E. Tucker-Ladd, *Psychological self-help.* N/A: Mental Health Net [On-line]. Available: http://mentalhelp.net/psyhelp/chap7/chap7m. htm

Tyiska, C. G. (1998). Working with victims with disabilities. *Office for Victims of Crime Bulletin.* Washington, DC: U. S. Department of Justice, Office for Victims of Crime.

Uchino, B. N., Cacioppo, J. T., Malarkey, W., Glaser, R., & Keicolt-Glaser,

J. K. (1995). Appraisal support predicts age-related differences in cardiovascular function in women. *Health Psychology, 14,* 556–562.

Uchino, B. N., & Garvey, T. G. (1997). The availability of social support reduces cardiovascular reactivity to acute psychological stress. *Journal of Behavioral Medicine, 20,* 15–27.

Uchino, B. N., Cacioppo, J. T., & Keicolt-Glaser, J. K. (1996). The relationship between social support and psychological processes: A review with emphasis on underlying mechanisms and implications for health. *Psychological Bulletin, 119,* 488–531.

Umbreit, M. S., & Bradshaw, W. (1995). *Victim-sensitive offender dialogue model.* St. Paul, MN: Center for Restorative Justice and Mediation, University of Minnesota.

Underwood, T. (2001). *The professionalization of victim assistance: Implications for victim assistance and adult education.* Unpublished doctoral dissertation. Kansas State University, Manhattan, KS.

U. S. Department of Justice. (2000). *Attorney general guidelines for victim and witness assistance, 2000.* Washington, DC: Office of the Attorney General (NCJ 178249).

U. S. Department of Labor (n. d.). *Disability initiative* [On-line]. Available: www. doleta. gov/access/chklst. htm

Van Derkolk, B., Weisaeth, L., & Van DerHart, O. (1996), History of trauma in psychiatry. In B. Van DerKolk, A. McFarlane, & L. Weisaeth (Eds.), *Traumatic stress: The effects of overwhelming experience on mind, body and society.* New York: The Guilford Press

Van Ness, D., & Heetderks Strong, K. (1997). *Restoring justice.* Cincinnati, OH: Anderson.

Vergano, D. (1996). Stress may weaken the blood-brain barrier. *Science News, 150*(24), 375–381.

Violanti, J. M. (1995). Survivors' trauma and departmental response following deaths of police officers. *Psychological Reports, 77*(2), 611.

Walker, L. (Eds.). (1984). *The battered woman syndrome.* New York: Springer Publishing.

Walker, L. (1987). *Terrifying love: Why battered women kill and how society responds.* New York: Harper Perennial.

Walker, L. (2000). *The battered women syndrome* (2nd ed.). New York: Springer Publishing.

Wallace, H. (1998). *Victimology: Legal, psychological, and social perspectives.* Needham Heights, MA: Allyn and Bacon.

Wallace, H. (2002). *Family violence: Legal, medical, and social perspectives* (3rd ed). Boston: Allyn and Bacon.

Webb-Boyd, N. (Ed.). (1991). *Helping bereaved children.* New York: The Guilford Press.

Webb-Boyd, N. (Ed.). (1991). *Play therapy with children in crisis: A casebook for practitioners.* New York: The Guilford Press.

Wertheimer, R. (1991). Preferring punishment of criminals over providing for victims. In D. Sank & G. Caplan (Eds.), *To be a victim: Encounters with crime and injustice.* New York: Plenum Press.

Widom, C. S. (1999). *Posttraumatic stress disorder in abused and neglected children grown up.* American Journal of Psychiatry, 156(8), 1223–1229.

Wilcox Rountree, P. (1998). A reexamination of the crime-fear linkage. *Journal of Research in Crime and Delinquency 35*(3), 341–363.

Wilensky, H. (1964). The professionalization of everyone? *American Journal of Sociology, 70,* 137–158.

Williams, K. (1976). The effects of victim characteristics on the disposition of violent crimes. In W. McDonald (Ed.), *Criminal justice and the victim.* Beverly Hills, CA: Sage Publications.

Williams, C. (1995). *Invisible victims: Crime and abuse against people with learning disabilities.* London: Jessica Kingsley Publishers.

Williams, F., & McShane, M. (1998). *Criminology theory: Selected classic readings* (2nd ed.). Cincinnati, OH: Anderson Publishing.

Windmeyer, S. L., & Freeman, P. W. (1998). *Out in fraternity row: Personal accounts of being gay in a college fraternity.* Los Angelos, CA: Alyson Publications.

Winnicott, D. W. (1971). *Therapeutic consultations in child psychiatry.* New York: Basic Books.

Wise, T. N. (1986). *Handbook of stress, reactivity, and cardiovascular disease.* New York: Wiley.

Wohl, A., & Kaufman, B. (1985). *Silent screams and hidden cries: An interpretation of art work by children from violent homes.* New York: Brunner/Mazel.

Wolf, S. (1976). Protective social forces that counterbalance stress. *Journal of the South Carolina Medical Association,* suppl., 57–59.

Wolf, S., Grace, K., Bruhn, J., & Stout, C. (1973). Roseta revisited: Further data on the incidence of myocardial infarction in Roseta and neighboring Pennsylvania communities. *Transactions of the American Clinical and Climatological Association, 85,* 100–108.

Wolfgang, M. E. (1958). *Patterns in criminal homicide.* Philadelphia: University of Pennsylvania Press.

Wolfgang, M. E. (1978), Family violence and criminal behavior. In R. L. Sadoff (Ed.), *Violence and responsibility.* Jamaica, NY: Spectrum Publications.

Wolkowitz, O. M. (1994). Prospective controlled-studies of the behavioral and biological effects of exogenous corticosteroid. *Psychoneuroendorinology, 19,* 233–255.

Yehuda, R., Kahana, B., Binder-Brynes, K., Southwick, S. M., Matson, J. W., & Giller, E. L. (1995). Low urinary cortisol excretion in holocaust survivors with posttraumatic stress disorder. *American Journal of Psychiatry, 152*(7), 982–986.

Yllo, K., & Straus, M. (1981). Interpersonal violence among married and cohabiting couples. *Family Relations, 30,* 339–347.

Young, A. H. (1994). Glucocorticoids, serotonin and mood. *British Journal of Psychiatry, 165,* 271–272.

Young, M. (1991). Survivors of crime. In D. Sank & D. Caplan (Eds.), *To be a victim.* New York: Plenum Press.

Young, M. A. / NOVA (1993). *Victim assistance: Frontiers and fundamentals.* Dubuque, Iowa: Kendall/Hunt Publications.

Zlotnick, C., Warshaw, M., Shea, M. T., Allsworth, J., Pearlstein, T., & Keller, M. B. (1999). Chronicity in posttraumatic stress disorder (PTSD) and predictors of course of comorbid PTSD in patients with anxiety disorders. *Journal of Trauma and Stress, 12*(1), 89–100.

Index

Springer Publishing Company

Stalking

Perspectives on Victims and Perpetrators

Keith E. Davis, PhD, Irene Hanson Frieze, PhD, and Roland D. Maiuro, PhD, Editors

"...contains cutting-edge research by the foremost scholars in the area of stalking. The editors have successfully brought together a must-read collection of articles that researchers and practitioners will find professionally invaluable. There is no doubt in my mind that these articles will be highly cited as they address fundamental stalking issues. Collectively, the authors have helped to set the stalking research agenda in several disciplines for the next several years."

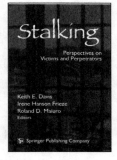

—**Bonnie Fisher,** PhD
Department of Criminal Justice, University of Cincinnati

At what point does following a person, or trying to intimidate him or her into accepting one's advances, become "stalking"? How is stalking related to gender? Who is the stalker? What are the long-term effects of stalking?

These are among the many issues explored in this groundbreaking empirical investigation. This book presents in-depth findings on both victim and perpetrator, and includes a new understanding of the categories of stalking behavior: simple obsession-love obsessional, and erotomanic.

Partial Contents:
Victimization Issues
• Comparing Stalking Victimization From Legal and Victim Perspectives, *P. Tjaden, et al.*
• Clinical Implications for Assessment and Intervention, *M.B. Mechanic*
• An Empirical Study of Stalking Victimization, *B. Bjerregaard*
• Perpetrator Issues
• An Integrative Contextual Developmental Model of Male Stalking, *J. White, et al.*
• Stalking as a Variant of Intimate Violence, *T.K. Logan, C. Leukefeld, and B. Walker*
• Stalking by Former Intimates, *M.P. Brewster*
• Overview
• Research on Stalking: What Do We Know and Where Do We Go?
K.E. Davis and I. Hanson Frieze

2002   400pp   0-8261-1535-7   hard

536 Broadway, New York, NY 10012 • Telephone: 212-431-4370
Fax: 212-941-7842 • Order Toll-Free: 877-687-7476
Order On-line: www.springerpub.com

Springer Publishing Company

Counseling Female Offenders and Victims

A Strengths-Restorative Approach

Katherine van Wormer, PhD

"... a real contribution to existing feminist social work literature. The use of motivational interviewing within a cognitive behavioral model in work with incarcerated women is certainly timely and of value."
—**Elaine P. Congress,** ACSW, DSW
Professor and Director of the Doctoral Program
Graduate School of Social Services, Fordham University

Counseling Female Offenders and Victims
A Strengths-Restorative Approach

Katherine van Wormer

Springer Series on Family Violence

In this volume van Wormer establishes a link between the crimes of female offenders and environmental factors such as substance abuse and sexual abuse. Combining strategies from the fields of criminal justice and social work, she shows how to empower female offenders and how to rehabilitate them to society by building on their personal strengths. From her unique "strengths-restorative" approach the author presents strategies for anger management, substance abuse treatment, and domestic violence counseling.

Partial Contents:
Part I. From Victimization to Empowerment
- Women and the Justice System
- Skills of Empowerment Counseling
- Partner Abuse, Rape, and Incest
- Victim Empowerment Counseling and Prevention

Part II. The Woman as Offender
- The Nature of Female Crime
- Women in Prison
- Counseling the Female Offender

Springer Series on Family Violence
2001   0-8261-1395-8   392pp   hard

536 Broadway, New York, NY 10012 • **Telephone: 212-431-4370**
Fax: 212-941-7842 • **Order Toll-Free: 877-687-7476**
Order On-line: www.springerpub.com